Woodrow Wilson and the Paris Peace Conference

PROBLEMS IN AMERICAN CIVILIZATION

Under the editorial direction of
Edwin C. Rozwenc
Amherst College

Woodrow Wilson and the Paris Peace Conference

Second Edition

Edited and with an introduction by

N. Gordon Levin, Jr.
Amherst College

D. C. HEATH AND COMPANY
Lexington, Massachusetts Toronto London

CONTENTS

IV WILSON AND BOLSHEVISM AT PARIS

V WILSON'S CONCEPTIONS OF A LIBERAL WORLD ORDER ASSESSED

INTRODUCTION

When the Paris Peace Conference convened early in 1919, in the immediate aftermath of the defeat of the Central Powers, the Allied leaders confronted a world in considerable political disarray. The German imperial position in Africa and Asia was gone, as was the Ottoman Empire in the Near East. The victorious Allies would have to determine, therefore, to what extent these power vacuums were to be filled by indigenous peoples or by some alternative form of empire. In Europe itself, the Conference was faced both with the task of settling defeated Germany's borders and reparations obligations as well as with the problem of establishing viable successor states out of the ruins of what had been the Austro-Hungarian Empire. In addition, the Allied statesmen who gathered at Paris in 1919 were concerned with the possibility that Bolshevism might spread westward from Russia to engulf those sections of central and eastern Europe most overcome by economic collapse, sociopolitical chaos, and the disorientations of military defeat. In short, the Allied leaders needed to fashion a peace settlement which would consolidate their victory, maintain their unity, and protect postwar Europe from the interrelated dangers of war, socioeconomic dislocation, and revolutionary socialism.

Did the men who made decisions at Paris in 1919 successfully meet the challenges they faced? Did the Treaty of Versailles and the League of Nations combine to form a foundation upon which a lasting world peace might have been constructed? One might choose simply to answer such questions in the negative on the basis of the fact that the international order established at Paris in 1919 collapsed twenty years later with the outbreak of World War II. In defending this negative judgement historians have tended to see the Treaty of Ver-

sailles either as too harsh and the source of German ravanchism, or
as too lenient in the controls it established over the defeated Germans.
Historians have also criticized the Paris Peace Conference for bringing about the alienation of Soviet Russia from the world community
and for establishing too many weak and contentious nation states in
the heart of Europe. Yet it might be possible to argue conversely that
the Versailles settlement was not foredoomed to failure. Hitler's rise
to power in Germany was not inevitable, and European statesmen
made a number of crucial decisions after 1919 which helped to determine the course of events. Above all, contrary to the expectations of
the Allied leaders at Paris, the Versailles order was denied the potentially stabilizing presence of the United States in the League of Nations because the Senate rejected the League in the aftermath of the
Paris Peace Conference.

To mention the League of Nations controversy in the United States
is immediately to call to mind the figure of Woodrow Wilson. Despite
some tentative beginnings under presidents William McKinley and
Theodore Roosevelt, it was really President Wilson who first brought
American power and influence fully to bear on the determination of
world political issues beyond the Western Hemisphere. America's intervention in World War I was a decisive act, crucial to the defeat
of the Central Powers, and it earned Wilson a pivotal role at the Paris
Peace Conference. Moreover, Wilson's influence at Paris was enhanced by America's economic preeminence and by the desire of the
Allied leaders to ensure a continuing role for the United States in the
maintenance of postwar order.

Wilson's great influence rested, however, not only upon American
power. It rested, paradoxically perhaps, even more on the President's
denial of the legitimacy of power-politics; on the assumption by Wilson of the leadership for liberal reform of the world political system.
To millions around the world Wilson offered the hope of a New Diplomacy designed to banish the Old Diplomacy of alliances, power balances and traditional imperialism. It was just because he represented
a fusion of seeming opposites—emergent American power and the
New Diplomacy—that Wilson's postwar influence was so vast. However, contemporaries and historians both, to the extent that they have
seen Wilson in almost mythical terms, have tended to overemphasize
Wilson's responsibility for the successes and failures of Paris. The

point is not to deny Wilson's due share of responsibility, but simply to note that other strong forces and personalities were at work at the Peace Conference.

In addition, while it is partially legitimate to see Wilson at Paris as the spokesman for a liberal New Diplomacy against the evils of Europe's Old Diplomacy, such a perspective is too one-dimensional. It makes of the Paris Peace Conference too much of a personal morality play in which every decision is weighed against some absolute Wilsonian norm. It can produce contradictory criticisms in which Wilson is accused of excessive idealism or of too little idealism. It ignores the extent to which Lloyd George sided with Wilson and even occasionally went beyond the President in defense of the New Diplomacy. It leads, finally, to an underestimate of the degree to which Woodrow Wilson practiced a successful pragmatic statesmanship at Paris. Wilson's own tendency to moralize should not be allowed to obscure the extent to which Wilson, throughout his career, permitted liberalism to be tempered by political reality. What follows, then, before a brief description of the readings in this collection, is a sketch of the most essential aspects of Wilson's policies at the Paris Peace Conference so that the reader will recognize the issues around which this volume has been organized.

During the autumn of 1918 Germany collapsed militarily and politically, and as the Paris Peace Conference approached, President Wilson hoped to combine peacemaking with reform in the construction of a liberal international order—based on the League of Nations. In such an American-inspired system of global reform Wilson envisaged moral and economic preeminence for the United States. From the Right this Wilsonian vision of progress was threatened, however, by the plans of some Allied conservatives who had won crucial postwar elections, and who hoped to use the Peace Conference to reaffirm the terms of the secret treaties negotiated during the war. On the Left, the President's reformist but nonrevolutionary hopes were challenged by revolutionary socialist elements in the defeated countries who sought to activate the potential for revolution latent in situations of sociopolitical dislocation and national humiliation. Thus, as the Paris Peace Conference opened in early 1919 Wilson faced a Europe where pro-Wilsonian liberal and moderate socialist elements were on the defensive, and where political forces of the Left and Right projected programs hostile to Wilson's vision of liberal world order under a League of Nations.

More specifically, there was great concern in the Wilson Administration, early in 1919, over the possibility that Germany might go Bolshevik, and a concern as well that Allied extremism would exacerbate the danger of revolutionary socialism in Germany. The German settlement had to be moderate enough, therefore, to buttress those German social democrats and liberals who sought to win Wilson's support against extreme Allied demands in return for checking German Bolshevism and promising a peaceful Germany in the European diplomatic arena. Toward this end, Wilsonians sought at Paris to get food relief into Germany, to lessen the severity of the Allied blockade, to arrange a rational reparations settlement, and generally to urge a peace which would make possible the economic and political reintegration of Germany into a non-Bolshevik community of European states. In this connection, Wilson's weight at the Peace Conference was thrown, often with British support, against French efforts to detach the Rhineland and the Saar irrevocably from Germany.

Yet Wilson's reintegrationist tendency toward Germany at Paris was counterbalanced by his desire to punish and to control the defeated Germans. Wilson, in other words, was more moderate toward Germany than Clemenceau and, on some issues, Lloyd George, but Wilson's greater moderation was often a matter of degree and was never enough to please those German political elements who had hoped for his support. Indeed, on the issues concerning the Polish border the President took an even more anti-German position than Lloyd George. Moreover, while Wilson feared that the German Revolution might extend all the way to Bolshevism, he was also concerned that the German Right still retained to much influence even after the Kaiser's fall. The President was not entirely averse, then, to punishing and controlling Germany from outside, as he could not completely trust the Germans within.

Wilson's lingering distrust of Germany combined with his fear of revolution and inhibited whatever desire he may have had more publicly to champion the New Diplomacy during the negotiations. Fearful of disrupting Allied unity, and unwilling or unable fully to coordinate his opposition to French extremism either with his own staff or with the often sympathetic Lloyd George, the President tended rather to obtain concessions from the French on the Rhineland, and other issues, by trading American guarantees of European security for greater French moderation. Moreover, due in part to such Wilsonian tactics, the League of Nations which emerged at Paris had not only the character of the nucleus for a new liberal world order, but it possessed as well the character of a continuing alliance of the victorious powers designed to enforce the terms of the settlement on Germany. In other words, the League of Nations contained within itself the basic Wilsonian contradiction established at Paris between a reintegrationist and a punitive orientation toward Germany.

In a still broader sense, the colonial-mandate framework of the League represented an uneasy compromise between a pragmatic Wilsonian acquiescence in the division of colonial spoils by the secret treaties, and an idealistic American attempt to reform—but not to revolutionize—the poliitcal and economic relations between the developed and the underdeveloped nations. The President's grudging acceptance of Japan's position on the Chinese province of Shantung at Paris, after the Japanese had threatened to boycott the League, reflected this Wilsonian tendency to compromise temporarily with traditional imperialism in the hope of reforming the Old Diplomacy further, in and through the League of Nations, at a later date.

In relation to eastern European and Russian affairs during the Peace Conference, American policy tended to seek a containment of Bolshevism without at the same time encouraging either large-scale Allied intervention or political reaction. In eastern Europe Wilsonians favored the creation of orderly liberal-nationalist successor states to the Austro-Hungarian Empire, and the Americans were concerned with the mutually reinforcing challenges posed to peaceful liberalism in that area by French-supported militarism among the victors and by revolutionary socialism among the defeated, especially the Hungarians. The Wilsonian answer stressed free trade, food relief administered by Herbert Hoover, and diplomatic pressures designed to help maintain peace in eastern Europe and to contain and then oust the Hungarian Bolshevik regime of Béla Kun in the summer of 1919.

In regard to Russia, the Wilson Administration pursued, with some hesitancy, an essentially anti-Bolshevik policy along two lines during 1919. At Paris the President opposed plans for massive Allied intervention and sought unsuccessfully to negotiate the Bolsheviks out of

League as Wilson's force

power by means of an all-Russian peace conference sponsored by the Allies. Wilson had intended that such a conference involve acceptance by all Russian political factions, including the Bolsheviks, of a new unified liberal-nationalist Russian polity in which each political faction could play its legal role. The President, however, despite the hopes of Lenin and the urgings of such left-liberals as William C. Bullitt, never intended to recognize a purely Bolshevik regime in all or part of Russia. It was this basic anti-Bolshevik orientation on Wilson's part which helps to explain the failure of Bullitt's famous peace mission from Paris to Russia in the late winter of 1919.

Not only did Wilson refuse to recognize the Bolsheviks but he continued, albeit ambivalently, to permit the continuance throughout 1919 of a joint American-Japanese military intervention in Siberia engaged in maintaining the Trans-Siberian railroad supply line for Admiral Kolchak's White Russian forces. As the Paris Peace Conference drew to a close for Wilson in the spring of 1919, and Kolchak's military fortunes appeared to be on the rise, the President sought to establish Kolchak's liberal credentials and finally joined with the other Allied leaders in expressing the willingness to seek a return to Russian liberal nationalism through Kolchak.

The readings which make up this volume are designed to permit further exploration of the issues introduced above. The selection from Daniel M. Smith's *The Great Departure* provides a concise and thorough narrative treatment of Wilson's role at the Peace Conference. Smith follows Wilson step-by-step through his negotiations on the League, and the German, Russian, Italian and Far Eastern questions at Paris. Smith also includes a balanced judgment of Wilson's postwar policies in his overview.

The second set of readings examines the conflict between Wilson's New Diplomacy and the Old Diplomacy of Europe. The documents convey Wilson's hope that the League of Nations will provide the basis for a new liberal world order beyond power politics, and they also evidence instances in which the President directly challenged the values of the Old Diplomacy with his vision of liberal reform. The section concludes with conflicting conceptions of Wilson's role at Paris by two of his European contemporaries. In a selection from *The Economic Consequences of the Peace,* John Maynard Keynes attacks Wilson from the perspective of British liberalism. Keynes argues that Wilson hopelessly compromised his New Diplomacy at Paris, and then permitted the New Diplomacy to befoul the Old Diplomacy by trying self-righteously to make a virtue out of the necessity of compromise. In contrast to Keynes, André Tardieu, writing from an official French perspective, defends the Paris deliberations in his *The Truth about the Treaty.* Rather than accept Keynes' concept of Wilson as compromiser, Tardieu emphasizes the President's constructive statesmanship at Paris.

The third group of readings is designed to explore the German question at Paris in greater depth. Seth P. Tillman's book, *Anglo-American Relations at the Paris Peace Conference of 1919,* provides a healthy corrective to the notion of a unified Old World front against Wilson's New Diplomacy. In the selections reprinted concerning German borders and reparations, Tillman shows that Wilson and Lloyd George often found themselves substantially in agreement, if not always effective partners, against Clemenceau. In the section reprinted from his *Woodrow Wilson and World Politics,* this writer argues that Wilson attempted to use the League of Nations to reconcile the tension between his reintegrationist and punitive approaches to Germany. The documents are meant to supply primary evidence of the complexity of Wilson's approach to the German question at Paris.

The fourth section of readings is focused on the problem of Bolshevism at the Paris Peace Conference. In his *Russia and the West under Lenin and Stalin,* George F. Kennan surveys with a jaundiced eye the record of Allied efforts to deal with the Russian Civil War from Paris. In the section reprinted from his *Politics and Diplomacy of Peacemaking,* Arno J. Mayer carries further the theme of Wilson and Bolshevism at Paris. Mayer believes that Wilson's role at the Paris Peace Conference is best understood in the larger context of the relationship between reform, revolution and counterrevolution in postwar European politics. The documents presented in this section contain evidence of the evolution of Wilson's Russian policy at the Peace Conference where he found himself torn between his distaste for Bolshevik revolutionary authoritarianism and his equal distaste for continued Allied intervention in Russia.

Consideration of the German and Russian questions at Paris sug-

German question (margin annotation)

Bolshevik question (margin annotation)

gests immediately the obvious historical connection between Wilson's policies at the Peace Conference and the diplomatic problems of the interwar years and the Cold War which followed. With such considerations in mind, the final set of readings has been designed to explore the place of Wilson's New Diplomacy in the broader tradition of twentieth-century American foreign policy.

The first three selections present various forms of the criticism of Wilsonian diplomacy developed by the realist school of foreign affairs analysts in the aftermath of World War II. The realists stress power realities in world affairs and the desirability of a national sense of limits. They criticize what they see as American tendencies towards excessive legalism, moralism, and idealistic crusading in international politics, and believe Woodrow Wilson to have exhibited the faults of uncontrolled idealism in his diplomacy. Walter Lippmann in his *U.S. Foreign Policy* criticizes Wilson for not possessing a more realistic appreciation of alliance politics, and George F. Kennan in his *American Diplomacy, 1900–1950* sees Wilsonian idealism as partly responsible for the destruction of the European power balance in World War I.

In the selection from his *Wilson the Diplomatist* Arthur S. Link, Wilson's leading biographer, defends the President's statesmanship at Paris and insists that Wilson did successfully combine realism with idealism and point the way to the collective-security orientation which triumphed in the American sponsorship of the United Nations after World War II. Yet, while seeing the United Nations as the vindication of Wilsonian collective security, Link doubts that America's Cold War alliances such as NATO are consonant with the earlier Wilsonian effort to establish a universal security system through the League to transcend alliances and power politics.

The final selection from William Appleman Williams' influential book *The Tragedy of American Diplomacy* takes a different tack entirely. As dean of the radical revisionist school of recent American historiography, Williams tends to be critical of Wilson's hostility to the Bolshevik Revolution. In Williams' radical view, Wilson's liberal internationalism was not really idealistic *enough,* since Wilson sought to spread a peculiarly American concept of capitalist political economy throughout the world. With the views of Williams, then, we have come historically full circle and find the problem of Wilson at Paris linked to many of the issues which confront us today as American citizens in a post-Vietnam era—full of questions as to the nature and legitimacy of a continued global role for the United States in world power politics.

I WILSON AT PARIS: AN OVERVIEW

Daniel M. Smith

THE STRUGGLE FOR AN ENDURING PEACE

Daniel M. Smith is professor of history at the University of Colorado. He is the author of several studies dealing with the foreign policies of the Wilson Administration. The present selection provides a concise narrative and a balanced assessment of Wilson's role at the Paris Peace Conference. What judgement can you form as to Wilson's negotiating capacities after reading Smith's description?

On the morning of December 4 [1918] the president boarded the *S. S. George Washington* for the voyage to Europe, accompanied by members of the peace commission and experts from the Inquiry,[1] with numerous studies and maps. The great ship departed a few hours later, to the accompaniment of circling planes and salutes from other ships in the harbor; the great adventure was under way. The crossing was uneventful, although already some of Wilson's fellow commissioners began to complain of the president's vagueness and uncommunicativeness about plans for the settlement. In one very revealing statement, however, Wilson told the assembled experts that at Paris the Americans would be the only disinterested group and would be confronting Allied spokesmen who did not truly represent the desires of their own people. A league of nations was mandatory, he asserted, as the indispensable means to guarantee the peace and independence of all states and to correct any inequities which might be embodied in other parts of the treaty. Thus the league would provide both security and elasticity, the very antithesis of archaic balances of power. He closed the interview with an appeal to the assembled scholars to tell him what was right at Paris and he would fight for it with all his energy.

Wilson's remarks indicated not only that he was convinced of the central importance of a league of nations but that he was laboring under several serious delusions as he approached the conference.

From Daniel M. Smith, *The Great Departure, The United States and World War I, 1914–1920* (New York, 1965), pp. 117–135, 149–157, 160–165, 170–176. Copyright © 1965 by John Wiley & Sons, Inc. Reprinted by permission.

[1] The Inquiry was a group of scholars convened by Wilson before the Paris Peace Conference to advise him on problems likely to arise at Versailles.—Ed.

The Allied leaders were not unprincipled, even if they did speak for more materialistic national interests than did Wilson. Britain and France particularly had paid a great price for survival in the war and necessarily their leaders, especially the French, were concerned with safeguards for the future. Furthermore, the great majority of their people did in fact endorse their plans for achieving security and retribution from the defeated enemy. Wilson represented a country which had paid a very small price comparatively for national security and therefore had few concrete demands to make at Paris. The Allied leaders regarded the noble American goals as a luxury possible only because the Allies had borne the brunt of the war and had served as a protective shield for the United States. Wilson was to discover painfully that these leaders, and not himself, represented only too well the desires of their people for a vindictive peace.

The peace conference did not begin its deliberations until nearly a month after the Americans arrived. The delay no doubt was tragic, in view of the general chaos in central Europe and the need for a quick peace to raise the blockade and restore normal conditions. Germany was seething with revolt; the Austro-Hungarian empire had disintegrated and new turbulent states were emerging; Russia was in civil war, and the virus of Bolshevism seemed daily to flourish on the widespread hunger and despair. It took time, however, to assemble the delegates of the thirty-two great and small powers at Paris, to secure quarters, and to organize the conference physically. In addition there was an understandable lethargy after long years of war, as western Europe prepared to enjoy its first postwar Christmas holiday.

President Wilson utilized the interval to visit England and Italy where his receptions generally were enthusiastic and often tumultuous. Paris welcomed him first with a parade and crowds unequaled in the memory of observers; the English reception was perhaps a little less demonstrative but nonetheless flattering and amply satisfying; and Rome's greeting was a delirium of shouting, weeping, and cheering crowds hailing the messiah from the west. Wilson could hardly avoid the conviction that he was the voice of world opinion, that he represented the instincts of the masses for an equitable peace. Perhaps reflection should have suggested to him that there probably was a very wide discrepancy between the popular concept of a just peace and his own ideas. The president also managed to anger some by his

FIGURE 1. Wilson the Judge! From *L'Asino*, Rome, October 1918. (Historical Pictures Service, Chicago)

reluctance to praise publicly the gallantry of the British and Allied soldiers in the war or to visit battlefields and cemeteries. His refusal, based on the desire to remain dispassionate for the task ahead, was most creditable but impolitic.

The conference, which finally began work on January 12, has been described as a kind of order within chaos. The atmosphere was frenzied and feverish, with milling delegates, anxious representatives of small powers requesting favors, spokesmen of minority and ethnic groups seeking special treatment, and the ubiquitous and usually frustrated members of the press. Officially the assembly was known as the Preliminary Peace Conference, for the German delegates did not participate until May 7 when the formal peace conference briefly came into being. The preliminary conference theoretically was controlled by the plenary sessions of all the participating powers. In practice, it was dominated by the great powers—France, Great Britain, the United States, Italy, and, to a limited degree, Japan. The Big Four of Wilson, Clemenceau, Lloyd George, and Vittorio Orlando (of Italy) carried on the most important work of the conference, at first through the Council of Ten (chiefs of state and premiers with their foreign ministers), and subsequently in the Council of Four. Under the Council of Ten were sixty commissions, established to deal with the specific problems of territorial, economic, and military settlements. Contrary to their expectations, the numerous reporters discovered that "open covenants openly arrived at" did not mean full freedom to cover the deliberations but only the receipt of prepared short news releases and the coverage of the rare and usually arid formal plenary sessions of the conference. President Wilson wanted a more generous policy but was overruled by the other leaders. Many Americans promptly came to the erroneous conclusion that one of the Fourteen Points had been violated at the outset of the peace conference.

Wilson was preeminent among the leaders of the great powers at Paris in terms of detailed knowledge and his great efforts to comprehend and solve intelligently the various problems which arose. He was courteous and usually patient in relations with the other leaders and seldom displayed annoyance at their delays and endless maneuvering. Wilson listened closely to the discussions in the councils and commissions and expended much energy in an effort to master the complexities of every problem. He thereby placed a great strain on his already frail physique. Lloyd George, however, impressed observers with his rather imperturbable ignorance and erratic behavior. He was an able and magnetic politician who apparently operated without a plan. His opportunism probably has been exaggerated—on the whole he advocated a reasonable settlement at Paris and agreed with Wilson on most basic issues—but he was able to reverse course with amazing equanimity. Lansing aptly depicted Lloyd George as notable rather for the alertness than for the profundity of his mind. Without the aid of his able foreign secretary, Arthur J. Balfour, it was generally agreed that the British premier would have been decidedly outclassed in the council chambers at Paris. In general, Lloyd George sought to meliorate the treatment of Germany lest future war-breeding Alsace-Lorraines be created and valuable British markets in Germany lost. Undoubtedly he also hoped to avoid an undue enhancement of French dominance on the Continent. Only in regard to the issues of reparations and disposal of the German colonies did he depart noticeably from a moderate course. Clemenceau, the French premier, was nearly eighty years of age and often dozed during conference discussions of little importance to France. Stooped, white haired, with a jutting jaw and drooping moustaches, Clemenceau was popularly nicknamed "The Tiger." A realist and a cynic, his central aim at the conference was revenge on Germany and security for a war-weakened France. Lansing described him as nearly Oriental in appearance: "He was a striking type, indicative of intellectual force, of self-mastery, and of cold, merciless will power. . . . [H]e watched the course of events with Oriental stoicism and calculated with . . . unerring instinct . . . the interests of France. . . ."[2] Clemenceau was often puzzled by Wilson's idealism and apparently viewed him with an ironic condescension. The last of the Big Four, Italian Premier Orlando, impressed Lansing and other observers as an able, realistic, and usually moderate political leader. He alone among the Big Four leaders could not speak English and his role was largely restricted to aspects of the treaty directly affecting Italy.

The criticism so often raised during and after the conference that

---

[2] Robert Lansing, *The Big Four and Others of the Peace Conference* (Boston, 1921), p. 33.

Wilson lacked preparation at Paris and failed to consult others was only partly valid. The Inquiry, as noted before, had labored diligently to prepare materials on the principal questions to be considered at the conference. At Paris, Wilson apparently utilized extensively both these reports and the service of the experts he had brought to Europe. He was seldom, if ever, deceived or confused by the Allied leaders and usually had the firmest grasp of the problems under consideration.

Unfortunately, however, Wilson generally neglected his fellow commissioners, with the exception of Colonel House. Lansing, Bliss, and White were rarely consulted or informed by the president and were often reduced to gleaning information from the British delegation about the progress of the Big Four. Lansing, a lawyer by training, had wanted to prepare a skeleton treaty for the guidance of the American delegation but Wilson brushed him aside with the curt and insulting remark that "he did not intend to have lawyers drafting the treaty of peace."[3] As a result there was a certain lack of central direction and coordination among the American representatives, and to a degree the initiative and the machinery of the conference consequently were left in French hands. Adoption of a detailed treaty plan would have made possible a greater consistency of effort in framing the terms of the various settlements. It was only in this limited way, however, that Wilson can correctly be accused of lack of a program at Paris. The relative neglect of the commissioners (they were of course active in some of the work of the conference) was doubly unfortunate, for they were men of talent whose fuller utilization could have relieved Wilson of some of his burdens and probably would have contributed to some improvement in the completed treaty. Apparently the president was absorbed by his plans for the League and in any case he preferred to work in solitary concentration without trying to persuade his fellow commissioners. In addition he was annoyed at Lansing's efforts to organize the delegation, had less and less confidence in his abilities, and received with ill-concealed hostility the secretary's suggestions for a different kind of league.

Colonel House at first basked in Wilson's confidence and played

---

[3] Robert Lansing, *The Peace Negotiations, A Personal Narrative* (Boston, 1921), p. 107.

an important part in the conference. He took an obviously condescending attitude toward his less fortunate fellow plenipotentiaries. As he confided to his diary, "I feel embarrassed every day when I am with them."[4] He did urge the president, without notable success, to hold more conferences with the other three commissioners. Wilson rarely appeared at the regular meetings of the American delegation and House attended infrequently. Instead, Wilson often bypassed the rooms of Lansing, Bliss, and White in the Hotel Crillon enroute to House's suite, and the representatives of the Allies also frequented the colonel's apartment on affairs of high state. As a result of these snubs, and dissatisfaction with aspects of the settlements incorporated into the treaty, Lansing particularly became increasingly disgruntled and even considered not signing the treaty. Wilson was sufficiently concerned to have intermediaries approach the secretary to ensure that he would sign.

Lansing's wrath was especially aroused when, during Wilson's brief illness in April, House represented the president on the Council of Four. House at first continued his well-established techniques for managing the president and preserving his tenuous influence and power. No doubt with a note of bitterness, Lansing, after a conference between the president and the other commissioners, recorded the secret of the colonel's success: "How well Col. House understands the President's character! He does not openly oppose him but endeavors to change him by putting his own interpretation on the President's words. The method seems to work, but I could not follow it. I cannot give the President the idea that I agree with him when I do not."[5] Yet slowly the Wilson-House relationship also cooled. House apparently was less flattering and subservient to the president than he had been in the past, and in his official position he often felt compelled to give Wilson criticism and painful advice. In addition it seems that Mrs. Wilson, long jealous of the role of the colonel, was affronted by the favorable publicity that House received as the "American prime minister," and that Wilson himself came to look sceptically on his intimate friend. The denouement was not a dramatic break but a gradual withdrawal by Wilson of his confidence in

4 January 8, 1919, House Diary.
5 January 1, 1919, Appendix, Lansing Desk Diary.

House. By June, as the German treaty was completed, House too was complaining bitterly to his fellow commissioners that he was unable to confer with the president privately and was uninformed about the activities of the Council of Four.

Despite lack of formal agreement or coordination, an Anglo-American community of interest generally prevailed at the Paris conference. A study by Seth P. Tillman of relations between the two states at Paris reveals that British and American goals were generally similar and that both governments usually supported adjustments that were moderate and that accorded with practical and idealistic considerations. At the highest level, President Wilson and Prime Minister Lloyd George did not establish an intimate rapport, because of strikingly different temperaments and Wilson's self-imposed isolation, but close if informal communication and cooperation existed between the other members of the two delegations. The consequent agreement on the essentials of the peace contributed greatly to the more reasonable and progressive aspects of the final treaty with Germany.

One of the most important manifestations of Anglo-American harmony was the drafting of the Covenant of the League of Nations. Collective security through an international concert of power reflected the Anglo-American legalistic and constitutional tradition of government as one of laws and not of men and brute force. Since each country in the past had felt relatively secure and detached from the continental struggles for power, it had been comparatively easy to avoid the development of a militaristic tradition and to advocate the settlement of all serious international disputes by processes of conciliation and arbitration. Peace groups in both countries had been stimulated by World War I to develop the concept of an international organization which would encourage peaceful adjustments and prevent aggression. When British and American political figures became interested in the idea, French leaders conversely were less attracted and more sceptical unless somehow the idealistic proposal could be converted into an alliance of the victorious powers to preserve a new status quo favorable to French security and power. The charter achieved at Paris was the fruition of this movement and if the British were mainly responsible for the drafting of the concrete provisions of the League of Nations, Wilson preeminently was its sponsor and godfather.

After the American involvement in the war, Wilson resisted suggestions for an Anglo-American committee to draft a detailed plan for a league. The specifics of the league, he explained, should emerge more spontaneously and should evolve from democratic discussions and consultation. He envisioned the league as an organic growth and not as an artificial graft. A deeper reason for his refusal probably was his aversion to translating general principles into detailed arrangements, and perhaps a desire to control the process personally. Action was compelled, however, when the British war cabinet endorsed a plan in early 1918 known as the Phillimore Report. House warned Wilson that American and British opinion probably would crystallize around some unofficial or foreign scheme unless the president himself acted. As the colonel persuasively commented, such a result would be unfortunate, for the future league ought to be identified with the president's name as its chief architect. After Wilson received a copy of the Phillimore Report, therefore, he directed the colonel to revise it in accordance with the ideas he and House had previously discussed. The Phillimore Report had suggested an alliance against nations which went to war in violation of procedures for the peaceful settlement of disputes. A subsequent draft, by Lord Robert Cecil, provided for a permanent council of the major powers to invoke sanctions. France also had a committee, headed by Léon Bourgeois, which devised a scheme for the use of economic and military sanctions against an aggressor, to be imposed by an international council commanding an international force. Both Britain and the United States were to oppose the French proposal as merely an alliance of the victors to preserve a new balance of power. House revised the Phillimore Plan and then Wilson altered it to include economic as well as military retaliations against transgressor states. He also deleted House's provision for an international court and for a council solely of the great powers, while emphasizing the need for disarmament. This was the plan that Wilson took to Paris for further development.

On arrival in Europe, Wilson had received a copy of the Smuts proposal for a league, Jan Christian Smuts, one of the Dominion of

South Africa's representatives to the peace conference, had outlined a detailed plan for an organization with a general assembly composed of all members and a council comprising the principal powers as permanent members plus several representatives of the lesser states chosen on a rotational basis. A secretariat and a court of arbitration were also included. In essence, Smuts had broadened the British concept to a global organization concerned not merely with deterring aggression but in other ways to promote world progress and peaceful evolution. Wilson was particularly impressed with Smuts' emphasis on the creation of a league as the most important task of the peace conference and his description of the proposed organization as the heir or successor to the disintegrating empires of Europe. The president incorporated a number of ideas from the Smuts plan in his first Paris draft of the Covenant.

Wilson had not required Smuts' encouragement to insist that the League must constitute the heart of the peace treaty. He was determined to combine the charter of the new organization with the territorial and economic settlement; liberal opinion would probably have been disappointed at anything less, and he had long conceived of a league as the vital center of the postwar edifice. He also was to conclude that embodying the League in the peace treaty was the best means of checkmating his opponents in Congress. Perhaps it would have been wiser, as some critics and scholars have suggested, to have incorporated only a general provision for the League in the peace treaty while postponing the details for more leisurely consideration. Although the drafting of the Covenant took place in late afternoon and evening sessions when the main conference was inactive and therefore did not delay the conclusion of the peace treaty, its postponement except for a general reference would have prevented critics from charging that Wilson's obsession with the League had cruelly retarded the restoration of a peace so desperately needed by the world. On the other hand, Wilson feared that if the League were not fully established by the treaty, its creation might be long postponed or avoided altogether by the other great powers. Its existence was needed immediately, he believed, to mitigate some of the inequities which almost inevitably would be incorporated in the general settlement. Finally the historian must note that what was to happen to the Covenant subsequently at the Senate's hands did not indicate that separate negotiations on the League would have led to happier results in that body.

On January 22 President Wilson obtained approval from the Council of Ten of a resolution to make the charter of the League of Nations an integral part of the peace treaty. A special commission was created to draft the document which included the representatives of the great powers and some of the lesser states. A few days later Wilson explained the reasons to a plenary session of the conference: "It is a solemn obligation on our part, therefore, to make permanent arrangements that justice shall be rendered and peace maintained. . . . Settlements may be temporary, but the action of the nations in the interest of peace and justice must be permanent."[6]

The work of writing the League's birth certificate was dominated by Wilson, Smuts, House, and Cecil. Wilson regarded these duties as the most pleasant and rewarding of the conference, and he labored diligently and ably at the task. Lloyd George and Clemenceau, conversely, declined to sit as delegates on the League Commission, preferring to concentrate on political and territorial aspects of the settlement. The commission met in almost daily afternoon or evening sessions and used as its working text a joint Anglo-American draft. France made an effort to incorporate clauses promoting its security against a possible German revival by establishing an international army and general staff under the League. The most that its delegates could obtain, however, was the deletion of a general denunciation of military conscription and the acceptance of a rather innocuous provision for a military advisory committee on possible military sanctions. The major provisions of the Covenant created an assembly of all members for discussion purposes; a council charged with the primary responsibility for preserving peace and deterring aggression, to be composed of the five major powers as permanent members with elected representatives of the smaller states; and a secretariat entrusted with administrative duties. Unanimity was required for council action on substantive matters. Article X of the Covenant embodied Wilson's concept of a mutual guarantee of the territorial integrity and independence of member states as an obligation on all members,

League provisions

---

[6] U. S. State Department, *Papers Relating to the Foreign Relations of the United States: the Paris Peace Conference,* 13 vols. (Washington, 1943), III, pp. 178–181.

and the council was authorized to recommend means to implement the pledge. Sanctions which could be invoked by the council ranged from economic pressure and boycotts of communications to the use of armed force against transgressors. The British Dominions were admitted to the assembly as sovereign states. In general the Anglo-American concept of a more democratic world organization dependent primarily upon public opinion and machinery of conciliation to preserve peace had emerged triumphant over the desires of France for a military grand alliance.

Except for House, who sat with Wilson on the League Commission, the other American commissioners were largely ignored in the drafting of the Covenant. This was probably unfortunate for, apart from the unnecessary humiliation of three able men, their talents could have been used to advantage in the framing of a more tightly written document. Furthermore, some of the objections to the charter held by the three were also current in America and alteration of the League to meet their views might well have enhanced its chances for approval in the Senate.

Lansing had long been sceptical of what he knew of Wilson's thoughts about a collective security organization. He was not an isolationist or even an intense nationalist like Theodore Roosevelt. He did object, however, to a supranational government and wanted to retain American diplomatic freedom. Within that context, he enthusiastically supported codification of international law and the creation of a world court to adjudicate otherwise insoluble issues. Firmly convinced of the inherent peacefulness of democracies, any world organization in his view should restrict membership to democratic states. As he learned more of the plans of Wilson and House, his distress increased. On the trip over on the *George Washington,* he pointed out to the president that the contemplated mutual territorial guarantee, backed by economic and military sanctions, was a dangerous provision if it could be invoked by a simple majority of League members and unworkable if it depended on unanimity. The guarantee, he predicted, would arouse great opposition in the United States: "It is simply loaded with dynamite and he must not go on with it."[7] White and subsequently Bliss concurred that the presidential plan was too

---

[7] December 11, 1918, Appendix, Lansing Desk Diary.

vague and contained unwise provisions. Lansing wanted to substitute for the positive mutual guarantee a negative guarantee or a disclaimer by each member that it would do nothing to impair the integrity and independence of other states. He strongly recommended this substitution for Article X as necessary to avoid possible Senate rejection of the Covenant on the grounds of an unconstitutional invasion of the war-making powers of Congress. In addition, the positive guarantee would place the burden of enforcement on the great powers and thereby turn the League into a new alliance, whereas a self-denying ordinance would preserve its universal and equalitarian character.

Despite some gestures of assent, apparently designed to soothe the irritated secretary of state, House remained committed to the positive guarantee. David Hunter Miller, a law partner of House's son-in-law and one of the experts utilized by Wilson to draft the Covenant, agreed that Lansing's negative guarantee was preferable, especially since it would preclude possible European interventions in Latin America and consequent infringements of the Monroe Doctrine. Wilson apparently never gave the secretary's plan any serious consideration and brushed it aside as a legalistic quibble typical of Lansing's narrow vision. Events were to suggest that it might have been wiser to have adopted a provision similar to Lansing's suggestion. Opposition to the League in the United States was to center on Article X and the mutual guarantee as a dangerous commitment contrary to the Constitution. Not only would a lesser obligation have facilitated Senate approval but it might have improved the image of the League itself in the 1930s. The positive guarantee in practice turned out to be unworkable, or at least it was not successfully utilized. The major defect of Wilson's collective security guarantee proved to be that it depended in fact on great-power unanimity to enforce, and yet the significant challenges to world peace could only come from the great powers themselves. A League which promised less initially at least would have had the virtue of being unpretentious and to that extent perhaps would have avoided subsequent disillusionment.

The supreme moment for Wilson at Paris undoubtedly came on February 14 when he presented the hastily drafted Covenant to a plenary session of the conference. After he had read the provisions to the assembled delegates, a note of intensity and hope entered Wilson's speech as he emphasized the importance of the Covenant:

> *this document . . . is not a straitjacket, but a vehicle of life. A living thing is born . . . it is at one and the same time a practical document and a humane document. . . . I think it is an occasion, therefore, for the most profound satisfaction that this humane decision should have been reached in a matter for which the world has long been waiting. . . .*[8]

One of the Fourteen Points had advocated the impartial adjustment of colonial claims with regard to the interests of the inhabitants involved. That principle evolved into the concept of mandates exercised under the jurisdiction of the League of Nations. On the *George Washington,* Wilson had indicated that the most desirable solution for the captured enemy colonies would be to incorporate them into trusteeships held by smaller states and administered for the welfare of the people therein. His idea apparently was derived from the American system for the orderly transition of territories into statehood and from the nation's role of stewardship in the Philippine Islands. Smuts' plan advocated the creation of three classes of mandates under the League to apply to former Russian, Austrian, and Turkish dependencies. Wilson incorporated this proposal into his draft Covenant and enlarged it to include German possessions in Africa and the Pacific area. Liberal sentiment was insistent that the peace should not sanction imperialistic conquests and transfers of dependent people, but Wilson's solution especially ran athwart the aspirations of the British Dominions and Japan.

Lloyd George was willing to accept the mandate system insofar as British claims were involved, but the Dominions of South Africa, Australia, and New Zealand insisted that the German colonies they had seized must be under their control and formally incorporated within their territories. Japan, under the special arrangements with the Allies in 1917, also sought title to the German islands in the Pacific north of the equator. Very sharp exchanges ensued in the Council of Ten between Wilson and Prime Minister William M. Hughes of Australia. Dominion spokesmen justified outright annexation as necessitated by strategic and administrative requirements. Although the debate became sufficiently warm to endanger the continuation of the conference, a compromise was achieved between Wilson's initial idea of small states administering trusteeships and Smuts' exclusion of the German colonies from the proposed mandates. The Turkish territories and the German colonies were to be classified as class A, B, or C mandates and administered under League supervision by the powers which had conquered them. Class A mandates, such as the former Turkish possessions in Asia, by definition required only minimum tutelage prior to achieving complete independence. The German colonies in Southwest Africa and the Pacific islands, allegedly because of sparse and scattered populations or primitive conditions, were classified as C mandates to be administered as integral parts of the mandatary's territory, with military fortifications prohibited. The solution was denounced by many disappointed liberals as hypocrisy, a fraud to conceal an imperialistic division of the spoils. Although Wilson was by no means entirely satisfied, he regarded it as the best solution obtainable. The Allies and Japan were in physical occupation of the areas and could not be pried loose by diplomatic means, but the mandate system at least placed some restrictions on their rule of the colonial peoples and promised eventual self-government for the more advanced. Although it could not then be clearly foreseen, the mandate solution presaged the passing of the age of colonialism. The concept of stewardship under international supervision may not always have worked out well in practice, but morally it implied that exploitation of one people by another was wrong and advocated the ideal goal of independence for all peoples. It must be viewed as in fact a significant if incomplete victory for Wilsonian principles.

With the drafting of the Covenant completed, President Wilson left the conference on February 14 for a hurried return to the United States to handle urgent legislative problems. In addition he hoped to explain the Covenant to the people and to dispel the fears and false rumors already voiced by the opposition. When the details of the new charter were published in America, Republican critics had at first hesitated about whether to attack the League as too weak to be of value in preserving world peace or so strong as to diminish American sovereignty and to constitute a world superstate. Apparently it was decided that more political mileage could be found in the second approach and before Wilson could return to the United States, critics had begun the assault. House had urged the president to utilize courtesy and tact by reserving a defense of the Covenant for the congressional foreign relations committees. Instead, after landing to a tumultuous reception in Boston, Senator Lodge's own domain, Wilson made a fighting speech in defense of his handiwork. He challenged the senatorial opposition:

> *We set this Nation up to make men free . . . and now we will make men free. If we did not do that all the fame of America would be gone and all her power would be dissipated. She would then have to keep her power for those narrow, selfish, provincial purposes which seem so dear to some minds that have no sweep beyond the nearest horizon. I should welcome no sweeter challenge than that. I have fighting blood in me. . . .*[9]

The effort at presidential conciliation of the Senate was obviously reluctant and too belated to have much chance for success. At Wilson's request, the members of the House and Senate foreign affairs committees were his guests at a White House dinner. After the dinner, Wilson spoke for over two hours, attempting to explain and defend the Covenant. Although he maintained a reasonable and persuasive tone, he failed to assuage the hostility of many Republican opponents. Senator Lodge had viewed Wilson's Boston address as a characteristic violation of his own request that public debate on the League be avoided until he could explain it to Congress. Lodge reacted coldly to Wilson's after-dinner defense and recorded afterward that the group had learned nothing really new about the Covenant from the president: "He did not seem to know it very thoroughly and was not able to answer questions."[10] Wilson's supporters left the White House convinced that he had been effective in explaining the charter, while critics were thus unimpressed and unpersuaded. Wilson was highly irritated by the affair and more than ever was disinclined to a conciliatory approach. It would be necessary, he was soon convinced, to appeal over the heads of his narrow-minded and par-

---

[9] *Congressional Record,* 65th Congress, 3rd Session, Vol. 57, 4201–4203.
[10] Henry Cabot Lodge, *The Senate and the League of Nations* (New York, 1925), p. 100.

tisan opponents directly to the people and to educate them to the great opportunity and the solemn duty awaiting America.

The Republican opposition quickly manifested its hostility. Several speeches critical of the League Covenant were made in the Senate as the session of Congress drew to an end. Lodge spoke two days after the White House dinner and urged that peace be speedily restored by separating the main treaty from the Covenant, which he asserted could then be taken up more leisurely. After warning his audience on the dangers of entangling alliances and the abandonment of isolationism, he indicated in some detail his criticisms of the draft Covenant and recommended that the framers would be wise to give them serious consideration. The Covenant was imprecisely phrased; it must be amended to prevent League intrusion into such domestic questions as immigration restriction; and Article X as it then was phrased endangered the sacred Monroe Doctrine and threatened to involve the United States in wars through the votes of other nations. Other objections or questions were also indicated and Lodge emphasized the need for amendments on these points before the United States should adhere to the League of Nations. The senator concluded his remarks with a slur on the intelligence of some of the framers—clearly intended, it would seem, to infuriate the sensitive president.

Wilson's mood was further darkened when the Republicans compelled the calling of a special session of Congress by using a filibuster to block passage of a needed appropriations bill. The object obviously was to obtain an official platform from which to mount a continuous attack on Wilson's labors at Paris. Finally, as the president prepared to return to Europe, Lodge read to the Senate a pronouncement signed by thirty-nine senators or senators-elect (six more than would be needed to prevent the necessary two-thirds majority to approve the treaty), that the Covenant as presently drafted was unacceptable. This Republican "Round-Robin" not only gave Wilson notice of the existence of a determined opposition but clearly informed his Paris conferees that the president probably would not be able to control the new Congress. His diplomatic position was weakened and his subsequent labors at Paris for a reasonable settlement were greatly compounded. Unfortunately, although understandably, Wilson retaliated by telling an audience in New York

Senate vs. Wilson

City that regardless of the amazing ignorance and selfish vision of some American critics, when the completed treaty was laid before the Senate the Covenant would be so tied to the general settlement as to defy separation without destroying the whole.

Despite his defiant reaction in America, Wilson at Paris reluctantly reconvened the League of Nations Commission. He feared that appeasing the Senate would only encourage his opponents at home and that other countries would exploit reopening the subject to force the incorporation of enfeebling changes of their own. On the other hand, friends of the League, such as former-President Taft, strongly recommended certain amendments as necessary to prevent serious opposition to the Covenant. In several exhausting evening sessions of the committee, Wilson and House secured adoption of the desired amendments and fended off efforts of other powers to include further alterations. Provisions that a member could decline a proffered mandate and the exemption from League jurisdiction of questions affecting the domestic affairs of a state met little opposition. Greater difficulty was experienced with the proposals that the Monroe Doctrine should be specifically safeguarded from League control or abrogation and that a member could renounce membership in the League after two years notification and the faithful performance of all obligations.

Great Britain and France objected that these changes would seriously impair the ability of the League to preserve peace and to guarantee the security of its members. Lloyd George declined to approve a clause recognizing the Monroe Doctrine with the reasonable argument that it was an improper recognition of a purely regional arrangement. The actual motive behind the British objection, however, was to bargain with the concession in order to persuade the United States to curtail its naval construction. Wartime programs if completed would create an American navy at least equal to the British fleet or would compel a costly naval construction race by England to retain its traditional supremacy. Committed to a policy of security through naval superiority and unable to perceive any practical American need for parity, Lloyd George was determined to obtain an agreement supporting the naval status quo. It seems that he also still feared that Wilson would launch a vigorous effort in behalf of freedom of the seas. Americans, however, recalled only too well the numerous Allied violations of neutral rights in the early years of the war, and some citizens also were convinced that naval equality was required because of potential danger from the Anglo-Japanese alliance. President Wilson had directed continuation of naval expansion even after the Armistice, apparently in part to strengthen his diplomatic position at the peace conference. The French motive in raising objections to the proposed amendments allegedly weakening the security of France, seems to have been to try to obtain additional safeguards against Germany. Compromises were finally arranged and the amendments were approved. The United States agreed to suspend naval construction planned beyond the existing program and to consult with Great Britain regularly on naval problems; France, the evidence suggests, was mollified by the provisions for military occupation of the Rhineland area. The League Commission then completed its work and the revised Covenant was approved by the plenary session of the Peace Conference on April 28.

President Wilson was unwilling to go beyond these changes in the Covenant to assuage critics in America. He viewed the subject as closed thereafter; the Senate would have to accept the Covenant as it was or do the unbelievable and reject it. Later during the conference, when Lansing relayed additional criticism from America and suggestions for changes relating to Article X, Wilson replied that it was too late and that the only answer to troublemakers in the United States was to meet them in a direct counterattack. The Senate could either accept the existing Covenant or reject the entire treaty, and he promised to adopt a militant and aggressive course upon his return to America. His attitude augered ill for the conciliation and compromise necessary to secure senatorial approval of the treaty. . . .

The conclusion of the Armistice with Germany in November 1918 removed the military justification behind the interventions. President Wilson was convinced that Communism reflected Russian economic and social distress and that on both moral and practical grounds military intervention was an inadequate antidote. He was not opposed to socialistic governments per se, as long as they were democratic in nature. As he wrote Lansing, in an oversimplified analysis: "The real thing with which to stop Bolshevism is food."[11] At the Paris

---

[11] Wilson to Lansing, January 10, 1919, Wilson Papers.

Peace Conference, therefore, he joined Prime Minister Lloyd George in opposition to schemes for direct military action against the Bolshevik government. Lloyd George concurred that Communism indicated grave underlying social ills in Russia and that in any case the principles of self-determination precluded further intervention. Clemenceau, however, still hoped to strangle Bolshevism by economic blockade and he was attracted by the proposals of Winston Churchill, the British minister of war, for the sending of volunteer troops and large quantities of military supplies to support the anti-Bolshevik forces. Lloyd George and Wilson vetoed such plans and the American president made it clear to the Council of Ten that in his view the Allied forces already in Russia had achieved nothing positive and should be withdrawn as quickly as possible. Further action would harm the Russian people, outrage public sentiment in America and Great Britain, and strengthen the hold of the Bolsheviks within Russia.

An effort was made to end the civil war by inviting representatives of all Russian factions to a conference planned for Prinkipo Island in the Sea of Marmara. The Bolsheviks signified acceptance but the White groups[12] refused to attend with the Communists and the plan was stillborn. An unofficial fact-finding mission to Moscow by William C. Bullitt, a young and idealistic member of the American delegation, also failed despite his report that the Bolsheviks were firmly in control and were willing to accept an armistice as the prelude to peace negotiations among the factions and to the withdrawal of Allied troops. Apparently because when he made his report prospects seemed unusually promising for a sweeping victory by Admiral Kolchak's armies, driving westward from Omsk, Bullitt's proposal with its promise of peace and probable diplomatic recognition of the Bolsheviks received no official attention. Perhaps also Wilson decided that the pledges of Lenin and Trotsky were totally unreliable. Public opinion in America and England in any event was adverse to recognition of the Communist regime. The Council of Four, therefore, agreed to promise Kolchak further aid and support, though not yet diplomatic recognition, in return for assurances about eventual free elections, social reforms, and democratic government in Russia.

---

[12] The "White groups" referred to here are the Russian forces fighting the Reds (Bolsheviks) in the Russian Civil War.—Ed.

Wilson reluctantly agreed, although he told his colleagues that he had long thought it desirable to withdraw and to let the Russians fight to a decision themselves on the future of their country. Kolchak proved to be incapable of surviving without the transfusion of additional Allied manpower; by June 1919 his drive on Moscow had collapsed and by the end of the year his capital at Omsk had fallen to Trotsky's Red armies. Shortly thereafter his regime completely disintegrated. To avoid direct clashes with the Bolshevik forces, and because of dissatisfaction with Japan's course in Siberia, American troops were therefore withdrawn from Vladivostok by April 1920. The units in north Russia had been removed earlier, in June 1919.

The fruits of the limited interventions were bitter. The Bolshevik government accused the United States of hostility and a deliberate effort, along with the Allies, to strangle Communism in its cradle. There seems little doubt but that the effects of the interventions were to worsen the Russian civil war and paradoxically at the same time to increase the popular appeal and strength of the Bolshevik party and regime. Within America many liberals came to deplore the interventions and to attribute subsequent Communist noncooperative actions and attitudes of enmity and suspicion primarily to that cause.

In recent years some scholars have ceased castigating the intervention as unwise in itself and have begun to criticize Wilson for not acting decisively enough. More extensive aid to the anti-Bolshevik regimes, it has been argued, perhaps would have toppled the Communists, while support of the separatist movements would have circumscribed Soviet power. Yet a more extensive American involvement would not have been assured of success. A genuine revolution was underway in Russia which was beyond the power of the United States and the Allies to suppress. Efforts to do so would merely have led to even more turmoil and chaos in Russia and to increased bitterness in subsequent relations with the Communist state.

Wilson undoubtedly was too visionary in his faith that the Russian people if left alone would find their way toward a democratic form of society and government, and his acquiescence in limited interventions in northern Russia and Siberia was, in view of Allied purposes and Russian conditions, highly impractical and unworkable. Yet he avoided full-scale military intervention, with all its probable consequences, and thereby saved both Russia and the West from an even

costlier entanglement. He clung tenaciously to his belief that principle and reason required nonintervention in the Russian Revolution.
In picking his path through a jungle of conflicting pressures and interests, he displayed much wisdom and commendable restraint. A
half-century later, it is hard to perceive how he could have achieved
more.

*   *   *

Upon President Wilson's return to the peace conference, on March
14, he immediately revealed discontent with House's management of
affairs during his absence. From the first days of the conference
there had been much discussion of the need to conclude a preliminary treaty embodying the essential military and naval terms. With
the lifting of wartime restrictions and the return to at least a sem-
blance of peace, it was hoped that the conference could approach
the framing of the definitive peace treaty at a more leisurely pace.
Wilson approved of the idea of peace in two installments, but
evidently he insisted that the Covenant of the League must be incorporated in the first treaty. Apparently he conceived of the preliminary
convention as an executive agreement or a kind of exalted armistice,
rather than a formal treaty, which would allow him to bypass the
American Senate and get the League of Nations into immediate operation; then when the definitive treaty came before the Senate, that
body would presumably find it more difficult to change or reject a
functioning League in which the United States was already a partici-
pant. During his absence, however, the Allied leaders persuaded
House to accept the inclusion of nonmilitary terms in the projected
preliminary arrangement. The French government feared that if the
territorial and economic provisions were separated from the military
terms and were imposed later, Germany might be encouraged to resist. It would be safer, Clemenceau and his advisers believed, to present all the basic terms at the same time and while the Allied armies
were still at full strength. The enlarged project obviously could be
put into effect only if it were submitted to the Senate as a treaty, and
so Wilson, greatly irritated at House's compromising, decided to
abandon the scheme. The subsequent cooling of Wilson's relations
with Colonel House probably had its beginning in the president's keen
disappointment at this development.

House-Wilson split

The overriding problem complicating almost every phase of peace-making with Germany was the determination of France to obtain lasting security against a revival of German power. As a consequence, the major clauses were interlocking compromises which tried to achieve a workable balance between security requirements and the dictates of justice. When discussions began on the military clauses, France proposed a German army to be composed of a maximum of 200,000 men conscripted for one year of service. French officials were unwilling to have conscription prohibited, in apprehension that the ban might be made universal in application and thus affect the French conscript system; if Germany were limited to a small and short-term conscripted army, it was believed that no high levels of military efficiency and skills could be attained. The Anglo-Americans, who would have preferred a general abolition of conscription, advocated instead a German army of 200,000 men who would voluntarily enlist for minimum terms of twelve years each. Clemenceau reluctantly accepted the plan but insisted that the number be reduced to a maximum of 100,000 men, as the longer term of service would otherwise permit Germany to build a large trained cadre of commissioned and non-commissioned officers able to lead the nation-in-arms whenever opportune. Most of these provisions had been tentatively hammered out during Wilson's trip to America. Upon his return he accepted them with reluctance, though with minor modifications. The clauses embodied in the Treaty set a limitation of 100,000 men for the German army and prohibited use of tanks, poison gas, and military aircraft; and the general staff, the central planning agency, was to be disbanded. The navy was also to be severely restricted in manpower and the number and tonnage of surface warships sharply curtailed; possession of submarines was entirely prohibited. These terms were theoretically related to the provision of the Covenant for universal arms reduction to the level consistent with internal security. Wilson hoped that German disarmament would in fact serve as the vestibule to that goal. Subsequent events were to disappoint that hope and an embittered Germany alone was to remain partially disarmed.

The French government made a major effort to dismember Germany and to establish the Rhineland area as an autonomous state under the control of France. A similar desire was expressed for an-

German Army

Rhine

nexation of the Saar Valley. With the return to France of Alsace and Lorraine, Germany thereby would be deprived of a very large slice of territory and the French frontier in effect solidly based on the Rhine River. These proposals were defended on the grounds of defense against possible future German invasions, France's historic frontiers before 1814, and the need for compensation for war damages. Detachment of the Rhineland would deprive Germany of nearly six million people and extensive industry, and loss of the Saar would strip Germany of a number of factories and coal mines. Wilson opposed both of these demands as contrary to the principle of self-determination, an affront to German nationalism which would disturb the peace of Europe indefinitely if consummated. He was also cognizant of the serious economic consequences for Germany and for all Europe. Finally, he did not desire the permanent elimination of German power and influence. Lloyd George joined him in opposition to the French schemes, out of principle but even more from fear that an explosive *irredenta* issue would be created threatening the future peace of Europe. On these issues, the British and American leaders stood firm; principle and practical considerations forbade what they regarded as unrealistic and excessive French desires for security and revenge.

Clemenceau fought vigorously for the Rhineland and the Saar. At one conference the French premier angrily accused Wilson of being pro-German; when the president replied that it seemed that Clemenceau wanted him to leave the conference and return home, the furious premier retorted no, but that he himself would and he stalked from the room. Lloyd George finally suggested a compromise proposal that the Rhineland be demilitarized and left within the German republic, with French security to be pledged by Great Britain and the United States. As for the Saar, all admitted that France was entitled to compensation for the coal mines in northern France which had been flooded by the retreating German armies. Wilson, however, remained adamant against annexation. Lloyd George concurred, but under pressure he shifted to a position establishing the Saar as an autonomous area, presumably under French control.

In early April the deadlock reached dangerous proportions. All the unresolved issues seemed to reach the crisis stage simultaneously. In the League Commission, Britain and France were resisting the proposed changes in the Covenant recognizing the Monroe Doctrine and the right to withdraw from membership; the reparations question was the center of sharp disagreement between the Americans and the Allies; and the French were adamant in their demands for security through detachment of the Rhineland and the Saar Valley. On April 3 Wilson suddenly became violently ill. His temperature rose alarmingly and he was wracked with spasms of coughing and labored breathing. His doctor diagnosed it as influenza, but medical experts now believe that the president was the victim of arteriosclerosis, worsened by the tensions and conflicts at Paris, and that he possibly had suffered a mild cerebral thrombosis or stroke. For three days he lay ill in bed; as he began to recover, the other members of the Big Four met in the adjoining room, with House sitting in as Wilson's representative. Grimly the sick president vetoed proposal after proposal which he felt fell far short of an equitable solution to the Saar and the Rhineland. On April 7 he even threatened to bolt the conference, letting it be known that he had ordered the waiting *George Washington* prepared for an immediate return to America. Although some sneers circulated that Wilson was behaving like a small boy who runs home to mother when thwarted, the threat had beneficial effects—Clemenceau accepted a compromise. France received the right to occupy bridgeheads along the Rhine River, for fifteen years and the Rhineland was to be demilitarized to a distance of fifty kilometers east of the river. As for the Saar, France obtained use of the valuable coal mines and a customs union for fifteen years. The area would be administered by a League commission, and a plebiscite would be held after fifteen years to determine whether the Saar should return to Germany or be incorporated into France. In compensation for receiving less than France had sought, bilateral security treaties were concluded among the three powers. Clemenceau, undoubtedly aware that the American Senate might reject the security pact, protected France through a clause in the general peace treaty which permitted a prolonged occupation of the Rhenish bridgeheads beyond the specified fifteen years under certain conditions. He was thereby enabled to defend to the French parliament the acceptance of less than had been desired in regard to the Rhine frontier.

The treaties signed between Britain and France and the United States and France promised assistance if Germany should endanger French security by launching an aggressive attack on France. The

Final assistance + territorial terms

two treaties would go into effect only if ratified by both Great Britain and the United States. Although the pacts were speedily approved by the British and French legislative bodies, the American Senate's failure to ratify the Franco-American treaty in effect negated British approval. Lansing, Bliss, White, and other members of the American commission were opposed to the assistance treaty because it appeared to be contrary to the collective security principles of the League Covenant. The security treaties granted France a favored status in protection against aggression and seemed to create a new triple alliance to dominate Europe and control the League. Secretary Lansing also predicted that the pact would arouse a torrent of isolationist criticism in America and would be rejected. Wilson, however, viewed the unprecedented treaty as merely a temporary expedient to reassure and protect France until the League could begin to function. The treaty with France specifically provided that it could be terminated by the League Council when that body believed that the League could assure security to France. Wilson therefore did not envision it as a permanent military alliance or as an Anglo-American-French directorate to control the postwar world.

The treaty of guarantee was a reasonable effort to assuage French fears and to achieve a better peace. Perhaps the president should have been more apprehensive about the reaction in the Senate, but he very reasonably assumed that if the American people accepted the League they would not balk at temporary security arrangements. In fact several important Republicans, including Senator Lodge, were favorably inclined toward such pacts and apparently would have preferred them as a substitute for the League, to preserve the new status quo without a diminution of American sovereignty. Editorial opinion in America seemed to be evenly divided on the advisability of the assistance treaty. It never was fully debated, however, and certainly not on its merits, because of the inflamed passions characterizing the greater struggle over the Versailles Treaty. Senate rejection of the latter, consequently, doomed the security treaty as well.

The reparations settlement is generally conceded to have been one of Wilson's major defeats at Paris. The American delegation was committed to limiting assessments against Germany to civilian damages and to the determination of a fixed sum based on estimated capacity to pay over a limited and reasonable period of time. If payments could be restricted to a period of not more than thirty years, it was believed that reparations could be held to a feasible and fair amount. France was determined to squeeze the maximum sum from the prostrate foe, not only to secure revenge but to render Germany powerless in the future. In addition, France needed far more capital than it could raise easily for a speedy reconstruction of the areas devastated by the German invasion. Unfortunately, Anglo-American harmony broke down on this issue. The British public, as those in the other Allied countries, had visions of a rich golden harvest to be garnered from the defeated enemy. In the 1918 elections, members of Lloyd George's coalition ministry had felt it necessary to exploit the general mood of hate and greed, and had made extravagant promises of the sums to be secured. At the conference, therefore, the British and other Allied delegations were under great popular pressures to extract as much of the total costs of the war as possible from Germany.

The American delegates won the first round of the reparations battle but they lost the campaign. In the discussions in the Reparations Commission, the Allies sought to include general war costs within the civilian damages specified by the Pre-Armistice Agreement and spoke of amounts to be extracted in excess of 100 billion dollars. The Americans insisted that such astronomical figures were wholly unrealistic and ruled out general war costs as contrary to the promises made to Germany. A formula was offered and accepted whereby Article 231 of the final treaty held Germany and her allies theoretically and morally responsible for the entire costs of the war—the war-guilt clause—but Article 232 limited actual reparations to civilian damages. Other provisions also authorized trial of Kaiser Wilhelm for alleged war crimes, although he was to escape prosecution.

Most of the other concessions, however, were made by the United States. Wilson was persuaded by British arguments, effectively presented by General Smuts whom he admired and trusted, to include military pensions and separation allowances as allowable civilian damages. Britain feared that otherwise it would receive little from Germany while the bulk of the indemnities would go to war-ravaged France and Belgium. When some of his experts reproached him for this departure from the logic of the Pre-Armistice Agreement, the harried president exclaimed, "I don't give a damn for logic. I am going to include pensions!"[13] Apparently he then expected the treaty to set a definite sum to be charged Germany and he did not care how it was divided among the claimants. Unfortunately, subsequent concessions, which Colonel House made during Wilson's brief illness, abandoned the effort to fix a specific amount in the treaty and to set a time limit for payments. Instead, a Reparations Commission was to be created to determine the total charges based on claims rather than on Germany's capacity to pay. The addition of pensions more than doubled the indemnities assessed against Germany, which the commission in 1921 computed at thirty-three billion dollars.

Wilson's retreat probably would have been less serious if the United States had ratified the Treaty and had played its expected role on the Reparations Commission. Germans bitterly resented being saddled with sole accountability for the war under Article 231. Subsequently, many historians in England and America agreed with them that it was preposterous to attribute all responsibility to Germany and Austria for initiating the conflict. The reparations settlement was also denounced as a violation of the Pre-Armistice Agreement and as impossible to pay. Whatever the actual capacity of Germany to meet the obligations imposed by the commission, in fact it was to remit only a small part of the total.

In redrawing the map of postwar Europe, the American and British delegations were generally in agreement and worked for boundaries based primarily upon ethnic considerations. Conversely, France supported the creation of a big Poland, Czechoslovakia, and Roumania as potential allies with which to check German power in eastern and central Europe. Wilson and Lloyd George had to recognize economic and strategic factors, of course, but they did make a great effort to adhere to principles of nationality, on the grounds of justice and of a lasting settlement. The Americans were more sympathetic to Polish aspirations than were the British and supported the claims of the new state for a corridor to the Baltic Sea through German territory and the annexation of the German-inhibited port of Danzig. When Lloyd George strongly condemned the proposed line as a violation of German nationality, Wilson and the American experts defended it as eco-

Europe remapped

---

[13] T. W. Lamont, "Reparations," in E. M. House and C. Seymour, eds., *What Really Happened at Paris* (New York, 1921), p. 272.

nomically and strategically necessary. A compromise was achieved through the designation of Danzig as a free city under League super-vision but linked economically with Poland. The eastern frontiers of Poland were not settled at the same time because of the absence of Russia from the conference, one more indication of the unfortunate results of the failure at Paris to achieve a solution to the Russian problem. Insofar as seemed feasible, the boundaries of Roumania and Greece were drawn along ethnic lines, whereas Czechoslovakia was allocated the heavily German-inhabited areas on the borders of Bohemia in order to give the new state a natural defensive frontier against Germany. Fully aware that the settlement did not and could not entirely conform to the principle of self-determination, Wilson and Lloyd George cooperated in a successful effort to impose treaties for the protection of minorities upon the new states. When the minority treaties were protested as a violation of sovereignty, Wilson reason-ably replied that since the primary responsibility for the preservation of peace rested upon the major powers, they must insist upon the elimination of potential dangers to that peace.

Under the terms of the secret Treaty of London, Italy laid claim to the Trentino and Austrian-inhabited South Tyrol. President Wilson was persuaded that Italy needed the South Tyrol for strategic reasons and readily consented, despite the principle of self-determination. He also conceded the acquisition of Trieste and most of Istria on the Adriatic Sea. But when Italy made a determined bid for the port city of Fiume and the Dalmation coast south of the Istrian peninsula, the American president balked. The Allies in the Treaty of London in effect had reserved Fiume for Serbia, the nucleus of the new state of Yugoslavia. Wilson's Fourteen Points had also promised the South Slavs an adequate outlet on the Adriatic Sea. With Trieste already conceded to Italy, acquisition of Fiume would have left Yugoslavia without a major port. In addition, although the core of the city was in-habited by Italians, the suburbs and surrounding areas were over-whelmingly Slavic in population. This was also true of Dalmatia. For these reasons, Wilson was determined in his rejection of the Italian claims.

The inevitable deadlock ensued. Anxious to avoid alienating Italy, Colonel House suggested a very complicated arrangement which would have given Italy eastern Istria and established a League trusteeship over Fiume and northern Dalmatia. With a few exceptions, the American commissioners and advisers were unanimous in condemnation of the proposed compromise. Lansing expressed the opinion of many when he exclaimed to House's emissary that the plan "would never work, that I was utterly sick of these impossible compromises, that there had been far too much of it, and that we were simply sowing future wars by not standing rigidly by principle."[14] Orlando rejected such plans in any case as inadequate in terms of the defense needs of Italy.

The president needed little encouragement to remain firm in his opposition. Perhaps he regretted the earlier concessions to Italy and now sought to make amends. He could not perceive any valid economic or strategic reasons why Italy should receive Fiume and Dalmatia. To force Premier Orlando and his government to retreat, Wilson resorted to a technique he had often used successfully at home. He would appeal over the heads of Orlando and his ministers to the Italian people who had recently cheered him with abandon and whose innate sense of justice he hoped to arouse. Unfortunately, he neither understood the nationalistic mood of the Italians nor could he manipulate the situation as he desired. His public statement, therefore, despite its well-reasoned arguments, was a serious blunder. Orlando did not permit its publication in Italy until his own defense was ready for release. In the interval he left the conference and returned home to appeal to the inflamed nationalism of his people. He of course received an overwhelming endorsement of his position. How Wilson could have expected a different outcome has long puzzled students of the conference. The episode revealed once again his rather inflexible attitude of moral rectitude and his messianic sense of mission.

The repercussions of the Fiume clash further weakened Wilson's position at the conference. Since Lloyd George and Clemenceau had agreed with him on this issue, the president had hoped that they would give him public support and face Italy with a united front. Those two statesmen, however, chose to remain in the background while Wilson bore the onus of refusing Italy's demands. Perhaps the way thus was eased for Italy's subsequent return to the conference, for Orlando came back after an absence of ten days; meanwhile Wil-

---

[14] April 17, 1919, Lansing Desk Diary.

son received the anger of the Italian people. In addition, Wilson's firm stand alienated large numbers of Italian-American voters in the United States and provided additional maneuvering room for his domestic critics. Finally, it turned out to have been a largely futile defense of principle in any case, for Italy subsequently (1920 and 1924) imposed its own solution on the weaker Yugoslav state.

*   *   *

Japan presented a strong legal case to the Council of Ten in Paris, claiming Shantung on the basis of conquest and treaties made with China in 1915 and 1918. Furthermore, Great Britain and France were constrained by previous agreements to support the Japanese contentions. The principle of self-determination, though invoked, did not really apply to the issue. There never was any suggestion that China did not possess theoretical sovereignty over the area. The Americans did have good reason to believe, however, that in practice Chinese control had been seriously impaired by the expanded political and military operations of Japan beyond the confines of the former German leasehold. Consequently, the Chinese delegation was given much American aid and sympathy in presenting its case that China's entry into the war had canceled the German concessions which then had reverted to the Chinese nation. The treaties with Japan, relating to the transfer of the holdings, were denounced by the Chinese delegates as the product of coercion and hence invalid.

President Wilson initially requested that Japan, in accordance with the Chinese claims, simply restore the area to China. When that failed, he proposed a face-saving solution whereby Germany would cede its former possessions to the Allied and Associated powers, who would act as trustees until final disposition. Japan rejected these proposals and insisted upon retention of its rights gained by conquest and sanctioned by treaty. Its delegation let it be known that unless the peace treaty formally transferred the German holdings to Japan, the delegation would not sign the peace nor would Japan participate in the League of Nations. President Wilson saw no way out of the dilemma except surrender. The Italian delegation had already walked out of the conference and it was feared might not return, while Russia and Germany would not be within the League. If Japan left the conference, an ominous alliance between Japan, outcast Russia, and defeated Germany seemed only too likely. Even more important to the president was the fear that the League of Nations, in his view mankind's best hope, might be moribund as the result of these defections.

The decision to capitulate was Wilson's own. He did consult his fellow commissioners and received the advice of Lansing, Bliss, and White to stand firm on the issue. Lansing used his talents in a vain effort at persuading the Japanese to accept a compromise. When that proved impossible, however, he and the other commissioners advised resistance even if Japan did bolt the conference. In fact, Lansing believed that the Japanese were merely bluffing, that Japan's role as a great power was so new and its position sufficiently precarious that it would not dare affront world opinion by refusing to sign the Treaty and join the League. Subsequent studies have indicated that he was much too sanguine and that Wilson's apprehensions were well founded. House, on the other hand, counseled compliance with the Japanese demands. In accepting that solution, Wilson was consoled by an unsigned Japanese promise to retain only the economic holdings of Germany in Shantung while restoring political and military control to China at an unspecified future date.

The reactions at Paris and abroad were sharp and angry. The Chinese delegation was naturally disappointed and declined to sign the Versailles Treaty. Many idealistic Chinese were most disappointed with the American prophet from whom so much had been expected. Lansing privately branded the president's decision "a calamity and an abandonment of principle."[15] Bliss and White were also deeply depressed and there was talk of resigning or refusing to sign the Treaty. In America the response of many observers, including many heretofore ardent Wilsonians, was one of great disillusionment and condemnation of an apparent compromise with imperialism. Critics distorted the concession to mean an abandonment of thirty or forty million Chinese to Japanese rule and sovereignty. The Shantung settlement, together with Article X of the Covenant, was to be one of the most criticized aspects of the Versailles Treaty in the subsequent debates before the American public. Yet Wilson's retreat had been a realistic acceptance of the inevitable. He had come to realize at last that Japan could not be evicted from Shantung except by a use of force, which neither he nor the American people were willing to do.

15 April 30, 1919, Lansing Desk Diary.

Mere moral condemnation of Japan, by refusing to accede to its demands, would have achieved nothing and perhaps would have destroyed or further weakened the League of Nations. Unfortunately, the president's decision was too late for the maximum gain. If he had permitted Lansing earlier to reach an understanding with Japan on Shantung and Manchuria, the entire controversy probably could have been avoided or reduced in intensity. As it was, Japan appeared to have won a great victory at Wilson's expense. Ironically, in view of the criticism aimed at Wilson, Japan kept its promise and in 1922 restored the Shantung leasehold to Chinese control.

On May 7, the fourth anniversary of the sinking of the *Lusitania,* the formal peace conference began when the bulky Treaty was handed to the representatives of vanquished Germany. At the Trianon Palace at Versailles, before the assembled delegates, Clemenceau curtly informed the German chief delegate, Count Brockdorff-Rantzau, that Germany has asked for peace and the Allies were now ready to give it; fifteen days would be allowed for study of the document, then the German delegates might submit in writing whatever observations they deemed appropriate. The subsequent German reply raised numerous objections to the proposed terms and charged violation of the Pre-Armistice Agreement in regard to territorial losses, reparations, and unilateral disarmament. Although a few relatively minor changes were made, the victorious powers insisted that the Treaty be accepted without further delay or the war would be resumed and Allied armies would march into the heart of Germany. With all avenues of escape closed, the new German republic reluctantly ordered its delegates to sign the dictated peace.

On the appointed day, June 28, an impressive tableau was staged in the Hall of Mirrors at Versailles. Throngs of delegates, visitors, and newsmen overflowed the room and the surrounding gardens. When Lansing arrived for the ceremony, a smiling Clemenceau greeted him with the remark, "This is a great day for France"; the premier then insisted on grasping both of the secretary's hands, for "that is the way France and America should greet each other today."[16] Upon the

---

[16] Lansing Memorandum, June 28, 1919, U. S. State Department, *Papers Relating to the Foreign Relations of the United States, 1919: the Paris Peace Conference,* XI, 599.

arrival of Wilson and Lloyd George, and after the autograph seekers had been satisfied, the two obscure German representatives entered the hall and affixed their signatures to the Treaty. The American and Allied delegations then followed in the signing. President Wilson subsequently admitted to Lansing that he had been so excited by the high drama of the moment that his hand had trembled when attaching his signature. Within an hour the signing was completed and to the thunderous cheers of the waiting multitude the greatest peace conference since the Congress of Vienna had reached its climax. Treaties still remained to be concluded with the other Central powers, but as far as the United States was concerned those were less dramatic and absorbing tasks. That evening, President Wilson bade Paris farewell and departed for America bearing the Treaty with its Covenant of the League of Nations.

Debate about the nature of the Versailles Treaty began even before it had been completed. Many disillusioned idealists branded it a Carthaginian peace, dictated to the beaten foe and designed to keep Germany prostrate indefinitely. Germany was stripped of its colonies, navy, and merchant marine; deprived of extensive territories inhabited by Germans, in violation of the principle of self-determination; and forced to acknowledge its war guilt while assuming the burden of large but as yet unfixed reparations. Moreover, Germany alone was to be disarmed and left to the mercy of a vengeful France. Why, many asked, had the Fourteen Points been so flagrantly violated? The answer of some critics was expressed by John Maynard Keynes, a British economist at the peace conference and a former admirer of Wilson. In *The Economic Consequences of the Peace,* published in 1920, Keynes attributed the failure to Wilson's moral collapse at Paris. The Philosopher-king from the West, he wrote, had turned out to be merely a stubborn Presbyterian theologian in politics, whose very rigidity of mind and lack of detailed preparation had rendered him vulnerable to the agilities of Lloyd George and the cynical determination of Clemenceau. The president had been confused and deceived by these adept Old World leaders and, obsessed with his dream of a league of nations, had sacrificed most of his own Fourteen Points. After the outbreak of World War II, scholars became less concerned with whether Wilson had achieved all that was possible in behalf of a liberal peace and instead began to criticize the Wilsonian peace pro-

[margin note: German losses]

gram as too idealistic for the painful realities of the modern world. George F. Kennan, in a series of stimulating lectures on American diplomacy since 1900, summed up the view of the realists who deplored the marriage of war hysteria and utopian idealism with which Wilson and his fellow Americans had turned World War I into a holy crusade without conflict and injustice.

The judgment of most students of the period, however, is that neither the disillusioned liberals nor the realistic critics have presented a balanced and fair appraisal of Wilson's efforts at Paris. It was true that the Wilsonian peace program was highly idealistic and was only sketchily outlined in his wartime addresses. Yet that which in the abstract appears visionary sometimes can be eminently practical in application. Thus the principle of self-determination, regardless of the many difficulties in applying it to concrete cases, expressed the realization that any peace treaty which did not accord a very large measure of satisfaction to nationalistic aspirations was doomed to an early demise. Wilson realized, perhaps not as much as he should have, that he would experience great difficulty in implementing his goals against the more narrowly conceived national interests of the Allies at the peace conference. Far from being unprepared, he had created a body of scholars, the Inquiry, to gather information and suggest solutions for the problems likely to arise at the peacemaking.

At Paris, Wilson drove himself almost to the point of exhaustion in conscientious application to the tasks of the conference. He consistently revealed a depth of knowledge and understanding beyond that of his counterparts, Lloyd George, Orlando, and Clemenceau. In retrospect, he appears to have been far more realistic than Clemenceau in his opposition to excessive reparations and efforts to dismember Germany, and the same was true of his objections to many of the boundary changes proposed by the various powers at the conference. Wilson undoubtedly was an idealist at Paris, but he combined with idealism a high degree of practicality and stood firmly for a reasonable and workable peace.

The Versailles Treaty was harsh in many of its provisions and it definitely fell short of a complete realization of the liberal peace goals. Wilson had experienced a defeat in the reparations settlement, though he hoped that American participation in the commission which would determine the actual amount Germany would pay could keep the total bill to a reasonable level. Only Germany was disarmed, but the Covenant of the League did pledge future efforts at significant general reductions. The demilitarization and occupation of the Rhineland and French exploitation of the Saar Valley seemed draconian in German eyes, yet France in view of the past was entitled to reasonable safeguards against a renewed invasion. Moreover, Wilson had successfully defended his principles when he and Lloyd George dissuaded France from insisting on the dismemberment of Germany. The peace undoubtedly would have had an even poorer prospect of permanence if German nationalism had been affronted by partition.

Self-determination, although necessarily transgressed in certain areas because of the intermixtures of population and considerations of economic and strategic factors, was generally honored in the drawing of the boundaries of the new states. Italy had been conceded some areas not inhabited by a majority of Italians, but Wilson had resisted the claim to Fiume, vital to the new state of Yugoslavia, even to the point of an open rupture with the Italian delegation. As for Shantung, it was more an apparent than a real defeat, whatever the political repercussions in America. The mandate solution for Germany's colonies in one sense only put a respectable facade over their acquisition by the victors; yet the new system subjected the mandatory powers to legal and moral restrictions and it symbolized the end of the era of nineteenth-century imperialism. Finally, Wilson undoubtedly regarded the creation of the League of Nations as more than justifying all the defeats and compromises at Paris. Whatever the defects of that global collective security organization which time was to reveal—it broke down in the 1930s primarily because it was not supported—it did offer man's best hope for a more secure and progressive world and it would probably not have been achieved, or at least not then, without the American president's determined efforts. A peace admittedly less than perfect would be preserved and improved, Wilson hoped, through the operations of the League.

II WILSON AND THE NEW DIPLOMACY AT PARIS

Documents

WOODROW WILSON ON THE LEAGUE AND THE NEW DIPLOMACY

The following documents, presented in chronological order, are selected to reveal some of Wilson's ideas on such matters as the League of Nations, the Mandates, the Fiume dispute and the Shantung question. How do these statements by Wilson relate to his negotiating record as described by Smith?

WILSON ON THE LEAGUE

President Wilson's Address before the Second Plenary Session of the Peace Conference: Paris, January 25, 1919

In this speech Wilson concisely presented his hopes for a liberal transformation of world politics through the League of Nations.

I consider it a distinguished privilege to open the discussion in this Conference on the League of Nations. We have assembled for two purposes—to make the present settlements which have been rendered necessary by this War, and also to secure the Peace of the world not only by the present settlements but by the arrangements we shall make in this Conference for its maintenance. The League of Nations seems to me to be necessary for both of these purposes. There are many complicated questions connected with the present settlements which, perhaps, cannot be successfully worked out to an ultimate issue by the decisions we shall arrive at here. I can easily conceive that many of these settlements will need subsequent reconsideration; that many of the decisions we shall make will need subsequent alteration in some degree, for if I may judge by my own study of some of these questions they are not susceptible of confident judgments at present.

It is, therefore, necessary that we should set up some machinery by which the work of this Conference should be rendered complete. We have assembled here for the purpose of doing very much more

[handwritten margin note: arrangements within the league]

From United States Department of State, *Papers Relating to the Foreign Relations of the United States: The Paris Peace Conference, 1919*, 13 vols. (Washington, D.C., 1942–1947), III, pp. 178–180, 765–766; V, pp. 129–130; VI, pp. 48–50, 281, 284–285.

41

than making the present settlement. We are assembled under very peculiar conditions of world opinion. I may say without straining the point that we are not representatives of Governments, but representatives of peoples. It will not suffice to satisfy Governmental circles anywhere. It is necessary that we should satisfy the opinion of mankind. The burdens of this War have fallen in an unusual degree upon the whole population of the countries involved. I do not need to draw for you the picture of how the burden has been thrown back from the front upon the older men, upon the women, upon the children, upon the homes of the civilized world, and how the real strain of the War has come where the eye of Government could not reach, but where the heart of humanity beats. We are bidden by these people to make a peace which will make them secure. We are bidden by these people to see to it that this strain does not come upon them again, and I venture to say that it has been possible for them to bear this strain because they hope that those who represented them could get together after this war, and make such another sacrifice unnecessary.

It is a solemn obligation on our part, therefore, to make permanent arrangements that justice shall be rendered and peace maintained. This is the central object of our meeting. Settlements may be temporary, but the actions of the nations in the interests of peace and justice must be permanent. We can set up permanent processes. We may not be able to set up permanent decisions, and therefore, it seems to me that we must take, so far as we can, a picture of the world into our minds. Is it not a startling circumstance for one thing that the great discoveries of science, that the quiet study of men in laboratories, that the thoughtful developments which have taken place in quiet lecture-rooms, have now been turned to the destruction of civilization? The powers of destruction have not so much multiplied as gained facility. The enemy whom we have just overcome had at its seats of learning some of the principal centers of scientific study and discovery, and used them in order to make destruction sudden and complete; and only the watchful, continuous cooperation of men can see to it that science, as well as armed men, is kept within the harness of civilization.

In a sense, the United States is less interested in this subject than the other nations here assembled. With her great territory and

FIGURE 2. An expected Arrival. From the Brooklyn *Citizen*, December 1918. (Historical Pictures Service Chicago)

her extensive sea borders, it is less likely that the United States should suffer from the attack of enemies than that many of the other nations here should suffer; and the ardor of the United States —for it is a very deep and genuine ardor—for the Society of Nations is not an ardor springing out of fear and apprehension, but an ardor springing out of the ideals which have come to consciousness in the War. In coming into this war the United States never thought for a moment that she was intervening in the politics of Europe, or the politics of Asia, or the politics of any part of the world. Her thought was that all the world had now become conscious that there was a single cause which turned upon the issues of this war. That was the cause of justice and liberty for men of every kind and place. Therefore, the United States would feel that her part in this war had been played in vain if there ensued upon it merely a body of European settlements. She would feel that she could not take part in guaranteeing those European settlements unless that guarantee involved the continuous superintendence of the peace of the world by the Associated Nations of the World.

Therefore, it seems to me that we must concert our best judgment in order to make this League of Nations a vital thing—not merely a formal thing, not an occasional thing, not a thing sometimes called into life to meet an exigency, but always functioning in watchful attendance upon the interests of the Nations, and that its continuity should be a vital continuity; that it should have functions that are continuing functions and that do not permit an intermission of its watchfulness and of its labor; that it should be the eye of the Nation to keep watch upon the common interest, an eye that does not slumber, an eye that is everywhere watchful and attentive.

And if we do not make it vital, what shall we do? We shall disappoint the expectations of the peoples. This is what their thought centers upon. I have had the very delightful experience of visiting several nations since I came to this side of the water, and every time the voice of the body of the people reached me through any representative, at the front of its plea stood the hope for the League of Nations. Gentlemen, select classes of mankind are no longer the governors of mankind. The fortunes of mankind are now in the hands of the plain peoples of the whole world. Satisfy them, and you have justified their confidence not only, but established peace. Fail to satisfy them, and no arrangement that you can make would either set up or steady the peace of the world.

. . . We would not dare compromise upon any matter as the champion of this thing—this peace of the world, this attitude of justice, this principle that we are masters of no people but are here to see that every people in the world shall choose its own master and govern its own destinites, not as we wish but as it wishes. We are here to see, in short, that the very foundations of this war are swept away. Those foundations were the private choice of small coteries of civil rulers and military staffs. Those foundations were the aggression of Great Powers upon small. Those foundations were the holding together of Empires of unwilling subjects by the duress of arms. Those foundations were the power of small bodies of men to work their will upon mankind and use them as pawns in a game. And nothing less than the emancipation of the world from these things will accomplish peace. . . .

WILSON ON MANDATES

Secretary's Notes of a Convention Held at the Quai d'Orsay, Paris, January 28, 1919

Here Wilson defends his conception of mandates against the views of the British Dominions and the European Allies.

President Wilson agreed with Mr. Balfour that there were many points to be cleared up. He admitted that the idea was a new one, and it was not to be expected that it would be found developed in any records or statements. He agreed with what Mr. Lloyd George said were the views of his Colonial Department, viz., that the difficulties were more imaginary than real. In the first place, the composition of the League of Nations, whenever spoken of heretofore, had left the lead to the Great Powers.

Taking the case mentioned by Mr. Balfour where an area contained a German population inclined to intrigue, the mandatory would certainly not be a friend of Germany's; and even if the latter should eventually qualify and be admitted to the League of Nations, at least during a generation her disposition and efforts would be so well known that no responsible man would be misled by them.

He wished that he could agree with Mr. Lloyd George that there was no great difference between the mandatory system and M. Simon's plan. The former assumed trusteeship on the part of the League of Nations; the latter implied definite sovereignty, exercised in the same spirit and under the same conditions as might be imposed upon a mandatory. The two ideas were radically different, and he was bound to assume that the French Colonial Office could not see its way to accept the idea of the mandatory.

He pointed out that Australia claimed sovereignty over German New Guinea; the Union of South Africa over German South-West Africa, and Japan over the leased territory of Shantung and the Caroline Islands; while France claimed a modified sovereignty over the Cameroons and Togoland under certain terms. Here they were at this stage when the only acceptance had been on the part of the Imperial British Government with respect to the area taken from Germany by troops under the direct authority of the Government in London. This was an important exception in which he rejoiced, but it appeared to be the only exception to the rejection of the idea of trusteeship on the part of the League of Nations.

They must consider how this treaty would look to the world, for as it looked to the world it would be, since the world would not wait for explanations. The world would say that the Great Powers first portioned out the helpless parts of the world, and then formed a League of Nations. The crude fact would be that each of these parts of the world had been assigned to one of the Great Powers.

He wished to point out, in all frankness, that the world would not accept such action; it would make the League of Nations impossible, and they would have to return to the system of competitive armaments with accumulating debts and the burden of great armies. There must be a League of Nations, and they could not return to the *status quo ante*. The League of Nations would be a laughing stock if it were not invested with this quality of trusteeship. He felt this so intensely that he hoped that those present would not think that he had any personal antagonism. To secure it no sacrifice would be too great. It was unfortunate that the United States could not make any sacrifice in this particular case as she held none of the territiories in dispute. But her people would feel that their sacrifices in coming into the war had been in vain, if the men returning home only came back to be trained in arms and to bear the increased burden of competitive armaments. In that case the United States would have to have a greatly increased navy and maintain a large standing army. This would be so intolerable to the thought of Europe, that they would see this great wave from the East which would involve the very existence of society, gather fresh volume, because the people of the world would not permit the parcelling out among the Great Powers of the helpless countries conquered from Germany. He felt this so solemnly that he urged them to give it careful thought.

He desired the acceptance of the genuine idea of trusteeship. He regarded this as a test of their labors, and he thought the world would so consider it. He thought it would be most unfortunate if they were, in the instance, to give the world its initial cold bath of disappointment. . . .

WILSON ON SHANTUNG

Notes of a Meeting Held at President Wilson's House in the Place des Etats-Unis, Paris, April 22, 1919

Here Wilson defends his New Diplomacy in the context of the Shantung controversy with Japan.

President Wilson pointed out that in the circumstances he was the only independent party present. He would like to repeat the point of view which he had urged on the Japanese Delegation a few days before. He was so firmly convinced that the Peace of the Far East centered upon China and Japan that he was more interested from this point of view than any other. He did not wish to see complex engagements that fettered free determination. He was anxious that Japan should show to the world as well as to China that she wanted to give the same independence to China as other nations possessed; that she did not want China to be held in manacles. What would prejudice the peace in the Far East was any relationship that was not trustful. It was already evident that there was not that relationship of mutual trust that was necessary if peace was to be ensured in the Far East. What he feared was that Japan, by standing merely on her treaty rights, would create the impression that she was thinking more of her rights than of her duties to China. The world would never have peace based on treaty rights only unless there were also recognized to be reciprocal duties between States. Perhaps he was going a little too fast in existing circumstances but he wished to emphasize the importance in future that States should think primarily of their duties towards each other. The central idea of the League of Nations was that States must support each other even when their interests were not involved. When the League of Nations was formed then there would be established a body of partners covenanted to stand up for each other's rights. The position in which he would like to see Japan, already the most advanced nation in the Far East with the leadership in enterprise and policy, was that of the leader in the Far East standing out for these new ideas. There could be no finer nor more politic role for her. That was what he had to say as the friend of Japan. When he had seen the Japanese Delegates two days ago he had said that he was not proposing that Kiauchau should be detached from the treaty engagements but that it should be ceded to the Powers as trustees with the understanding that all they were going to do was to ask how the treaties were to be carried out and to offer advice as to how this could best be done by mutual agreement. The validity of treaties could not be called in question if they were modified by agreements between both sides. What he was after was to attain a more detailed definition as to how Japan was going to help China as well as to afford an opportunity for investment in railways, etc. He had hoped that by pooling their interest the several nations that had gained foothold in China (a foothold that was to the detriment of China's position in the world) might forego the special position they had acquired and that China might be put on the same footing as other nations, as sooner or later she must certainly be. He believed this to be to the interest of everyone concerned. There was a lot of combustible material in China and if flames were put to it the fire could not be quenched for China had a population of four hundred million people. It was symptoms of that which filled him with anxiety. Baron Makino and Viscount Chinda knew how deep-seated was the feeling of reverence of China towards Shantung which was the most sacred Chinese Province and he dreaded starting a flame there because this reverence was based upon the very best motives and owing to the traditions of Confucius and the foundations of intellectual development. He did not wish to interfere with treaties. As Mr. Lloyd George had remarked earlier, the war had been partly undertaken in order to establish the sanctity of treaties. Although he yielded to no-one in this sentiment there were cases he felt where treaties ought not to have been entered into.

[margin, rotated: Wilson's idea]

WILSON ON THE TREATY OF LONDON

Notes of a Meeting Held at President Wilson's House in the Place des Etats-Unis, Paris, May 26, 1919

In this selection Wilson confronts the Italian delegation on the Adriatic issues and the Treaty of London.

President Wilson said that he feared they were somewhat in danger of getting into a cul de sac. He wanted very earnestly to point out to his Italian colleague the situation as it presented itself to him as a whole. We could not move in two opposite directions at once, and yet the Italians appeared to be trying to do so. The Treaty of London was made in circumstances which had now altogether altered. He was not referring now to the fact of the dissolution of the Austro-Hungarian Empire, but to the partnership of the world in the development of peace, and the attention which had been directed by plain work-a-day people to this partnership as a basis of peace. When the Treaty of London had been entered into, there had only been a partnership between a few Great Powers—Russia, France, Great Britain, with Belgium and Serbia, against Germany, Austria and Turkey. As Belgian and Serbian soil had been violated, the only voluntary partners were France, Great Britain and Russia. He understood that these Powers had wished to induce Italy to become a partner, and for this reason had entered into the Treaty of London. At that time the world had not perceived that the war was a matter of common concern. He knew this because his own people had gone through this phase. He himself, probably before most of his people, saw the effect that the war was going to have on the future destinies and political development of the world. Slowly, at first very slowly, the world had seen that something was being done which cut at the roots of individual liberty and action. When that was realized, there was a common impulse to unite against the Central Empires. Thus, there came into the war many peoples whose interest was absolutely separate from any territorial question that was European in character. They came in for motives that had no connection with territory or any advantage. They sought only the emancipation of the world from an intolerable threat. Then there came new ideas, and the people of the world began to perceive that they had a common purpose. They realized that it was not only Belgium and Serbia, but all the small States that were threatened. Next there was a realization of the rights of minorities and small groups of all kinds. The light broadened out into a perception of the final settlement that was at hand. It was about this time that he himself had made his address to Congress on the results of the war. His own address had taken place, he thought, three days after Mr. Lloyd George's address to the House of Parliament. The only difference between the two addresses was that he summed up his in 14 points. Both his speech and that of the Prime Minister of Great Britain contained the same line of thought and ideas. They stated in their speeches what was coming into the consciousness of the world. When the Armistice was reached, his own statements had been accepted as the basis not only of the Armistice, but also of the peace. These ideas had by this time taken possession of all the world, and even the Orient was beginning to share them. Then came the League of Nations as a practical thing—up to then, it had been regarded as of academic interest—and the nations of the world desired to achieve peace on that basis; hence, when the Peace conference began, the whole platform of the Peace had been laid down. This platform had no relation to the ideas which belonged to the old order in European politics, namely, that the stronger Powers could dispose of the weaker. Great Britain and France had no right because they were strong to hand over peoples who were weak. The new conception did not admit of this. If these principles were insisted on, they would violate the new principles. There would then be a reaction among the small nations that would go to the very heart of the Peace of the world: for all these small nations, when they saw other nations handed over, would say, "Our turn will come next." One of the reasons for which the United States people had gone to war was that they were told that the old-fashioned methods were dead. Hence, if Italy insisted on the Treaty of London, she would strike at the roots of the new system and undermine the new order. The United States would be asked under the Covenant of the League of Nations to guarantee the boundaries of Italy, and they could not do so if this Treaty were insisted on. There was one question which would not be susceptible of solution. If Italy insisted on the Treaty of London, as M. Clemenceau had pointed out, we could not ask Yugoslavia to reduce her army below the point necessary to maintain her

FIGURE 3. The Message. From the Omaha *World Herald.* (Historical Pictures Service, Chicago)

safety against Italy. Yugoslavia would never do it. It would be impossible to use force against her—against the very power whose violation had caused the outbreak of the present war. This process could not be repeated to accomplish the ends the Italians had in view. If he was to be the spokesman and the spiritual representative of his people, he could not consent to any people being handed over without their consent. But he could consent to any people being handed over who stated that they wished to be. He was willing that Italy should have any part on the eastward slope of the Istrian Peninsula whose population would vote to be attached to Italy. Only he could not assent to any population being attached that did not so vote. He wanted to point out to M. Orlando that Great Britain and France could not hand over any part of Yugoslavia to Italy, and that it could not be a legal transaction, except in accordance with the general

peace: that is to say, only in the event of all parties being in agreement. It was constantly urged in the Italian Press and by Italian
spokesmen that they did not want to abandon the Italians on the
other side of the Adriatic. Was it not possible to obtain all she desired
by means of a plebiscite? There would be no risk to Italy to leave the
operation of a plebiscite to be carried out under the League of Nations. Italy herself would be a member of the League of Nations, and
there would be no possibility of her being treated unfairly. If Italy did
not take advantage of this, she would be establishing her enemies on
her eastern borders. Thus there would be a beginning again of the
evils that had arisen in the Balkans. Beyond the boundaries of Italy
would be the Yugoslavs with their eyes turned towards the population which had been placed under Italy by the powerful Western nations. It was impossible for Italy to adopt both methods. Either she
must abandon the new methods altogether, or else she must wholly
abandon the old methods and enter into the new world with the new
methods under conditions more hopeful for peace than had ever before prevailed.

WILSON ON ROUMANIA AND HUNGARY

Notes of a Meeting Held at President Wilson's House in the Place des Etats-Unis, Paris, June 10, 1919

Here Wilson opposes Roumanian incursions into Hungary in the summer of
1919. At this time Hungary, a fragment of the defeated Austro-Hungarian
Empire, was under a Bolshevik regime led by Béla Kun. Roumania, an ally of
the Entente during the war, had intervened for counterrevolutionary and
territorial motives.

President Wilson said that the Council had been much concerned
with the military operations continuing in and about Hungary. The
part of it which had attracted the principal attention was the movement of the Magyars against Czechoslovakia. The information of the
Council, which might possibly not be wholly correct, was to the effect
that this was due to the movement of the Czechoslovaks, threatening
the principal coal mines of Hungary. Behind them there were understood to be other causes that had contributed largely to the situation.
Some time past General Franchet d'Esperey had drawn a line beyond

which the Roumanian forces were not to pass. Nevertheless the Roumanian forces had passed the line. Then a second line had been drawn, and again they had passed beyond it, thus declining to obey the orders of the Allied Commander-in-Chief under whom their army had been placed. It was this second advance which had caused the downfall of Karolyi who, more than any other Hungarian, was supposed to be friendly to the Entente. . . .

Mr. Lloyd George asked whether Roumania had claimed Debreczen.

M. Bratiano said he did not. The Roumanian Army was on the Theiss for military reasons.

Mr. Lloyd George pointed out that the Army on the Theiss was halfway between the proposed eventual frontier and Budapest. This was the way to make Bolshevism.

M. Bratiano said that Mr. Lloyd George misunderstood the matter. The Roumanians had been attacked on the Versailles line and they had advanced to the Theiss solely for military reasons. He explained the whole of these incidents on a map. The evidence in regard to the Bolshevist activities of the Karolyi Government was very definite. Radkowski, who was now Commandant of Kieff, had been at the head of these activities.

Mr. Lloyd George said it would take a great deal to convince him that Karolyi had encouraged the Bolshevik movement.

M. Bratiano regretted that he could not convince Mr. Lloyd George. This was a matter on which probably his information was better than that of Mr. Lloyd George.

The movement had been begun before the time of Karolyi by the Germans. There had been a regular Bolshevik organization established in Mackensen's time. The whole machinery of the movement was quite familiar to the Roumanians. Part of the plan had been to connect the Bolsheviks of Hungary with the Bolsheviks of Russia, across Roumania as part of the German war machine. Of this he had substantial proofs.

President Wilson said he had no doubt intrigues of this kind had been started by Germany. Unquestionably Germany had tried to make the situation in Eastern Europe impossible for the Allies. It was, however, one thing to stir up trouble by means of propaganda and another to do it by aggression. The Allies must see that they do not contribute to it by giving anyone just ground to dread them. As an example, he mentioned that in the United States there was an organization known as the Industrial Workers of the World which was largely and [*an?*] anarchistic organization of laborers but one that was opposed to agreements with anyone. When opportunity offered they took action by means of sabotage. The policy of the United States Government had been to check this by ensuring, as far as possible, that no grievances should exist among the army of working people. He would not say that there were no grievances but where these grievances had been removed the activities of the Industrial Workers of the World had been checked. The right thing, therefore, must be done. Whatever the reasons might be, it was certain that under the terms of the armistice the Roumanian troops had no right on the Theiss. So long as they remained there they were helping to create Bolshevism in Hungary even more than propaganda would. This situation was one of provocation to Hungary. He was surprised at what had been told him as to the Roumanian and Czechoslovak Delegations knowing nothing of the proposed boundaries for them. They certainly ought to be informed, and he could only presume that the reason was that only the initial processes had been passed through. The first question was to settle boundaries and have some understanding in regard to them which could be observed. When the boundaries were settled, he thought the Bolshevist support would be weakened. As a result of this afternoon's meeting, he hoped that they would come to an understanding as to what was right in respect to the positions the armies should occupy and as to the action that the armies should take. With all respect, he would say that the Roumanian troops had no right in Hungary, and if he himself had the misfortune to be Hungarian he would be up in arms against them, and so would anyone. . . .

John Maynard Keynes
THE ECONOMIC CONSEQUENCES OF THE PEACE

John Maynard Keynes was a world-famous international economist who helped to develop the concept of deficit finance to combat depressions. In 1919 he was a representative of the British Treasury at the Paris Peace Conference and came to believe that the Versailles Treaty was an economic, political and moral disaster. The following bitter portrait of Wilson was written in his book of the same title, destined to be the best-known critique of Versailles.

But if the President was not the philosopher-king, what was he? After all he was a man who had spent much of his life at a university. He was by no means a businessman or an ordinary party politician, but a man of force, personality, and importance. What, then, was his temperament?

The clue once found was illuminating. The President was like a Nonconformist minister, perhaps a Presbyterian. His thought and his temperament were essentially theological, not intellectual, with all the strength and the weakness of that manner of thought, feeling, and expression. It is a type of which there are not now in England and Scotland such magnificent specimens as formerly; but this description, nevertheless, will give the ordinary Englishman the distinctest impression of the President.

With this picture of him in mind, we can return to the actual course of events. The President's program for the world, as set forth in his speeches and his notes, had displayed a spirit and a purpose so admirable that the last desire of his sympathizers was to criticize details—the details, they felt, were quite rightly not filled in at present, but would be in due course. It was commonly believed at the commencement of the Paris Conference that the President had thought out, with the aid of a large body of advisers, a comprehensive scheme not only for the League of Nations, but for the embodiment of the Fourteen Points in an actual Treaty of Peace. But in fact the

FIGURE 4. The Doubtful Dove. Wilson: "You can fly when I know you are genuine."
From *Campana de Gracia* (Barcelona). (Historical Pictures Service, Chicago)

President had thought out nothing; when it came to practice his ideas were nebulous and incomplete. He had no plan, no scheme, no constructive ideas whatever for clothing with the flesh of life the commandments which he had thundered from the White House. He could have preached a sermon on any of them or have addressed a stately prayer to the Almighty for their fulfillment; but he could not frame their concrete application to the actual state of Europe.

He not only had no proposals in detail, but he was in many respects, perhaps inevitably, ill-informed as to European conditions. And not only was he ill-informed—that was true of Mr. Lloyd George also—but his mind was slow and unadaptable. The President's slowness amongst the Europeans was noteworthy. He could not, all in a minute, take in what the rest were saying, size up the situation with a glance, frame a reply, and meet the case by a slight change of ground; and he was liable, therefore, to defeat by the mere swiftness, apprehension, and agility of a Lloyd George. There can seldom have been a statesman of the first rank more incompetent than the President in the agilities of the council chamber. A moment often arrives when substantial victory is yours if by some slight appearance of a concession you can save the face of the opposition or conciliate them by a restatement of your proposal helpful to them and not injurious to anything essential to yourself. The President was not equipped with this simple and usual artfulness. His mind was too slow and unresourceful to be ready with *any* alternatives. The President was capable of digging his toes in and refusing to budge, as he did over Fiume. But he had no other mode of defense, and it needed as a rule but little maneuvering by his opponents to prevent matters from coming to such a head until it was too late. By pleasantness and an appearance of conciliation, the President would be maneuvered off his ground, would miss the moment for digging his toes in, and, before he knew where he had been got to, it was too late. Besides, it is impossible month after month in intimate and ostensibly friendly converse between close associates, to be digging the toes in all the time. Victory would only have been possible to one who had always a sufficiently lively apprehension of the position as a whole to reserve his fire and know for certain the rare exact moments for decisive action. And for that the President was far too slow-minded and bewildered.

He did not remedy these defects by seeking aid from the collective wisdom of his lieutenants. He had gathered round him for the economic chapters of the Treaty a very able group of businessmen; but they were inexperienced in public affairs, and knew (with one or two exceptions) as little of Europe as he did, and they were only called in irregularly as he might need them for a particular purpose. Thus the aloofness which had been found effective in Washington was maintained, and the abnormal reserve of his nature did not allow near him anyone who aspired to moral equality or the continuous exercise of influence. His fellow-plenipotentiaries were dummies; and even the trusted Colonel House, with vastly more knowledge of men and of Europe than the President, from whose sensitiveness the President's dullness had gained so much, fell into the background as time went on. All this was encouraged by his colleagues on the Council of Four, who, by the break-up of the Council of Ten, completed the isolation which the President's own temperament had initiated. Thus day after day and week after week, he allowed himself to be closeted, unsupported, unadvised, and alone, with men much sharper than himself, in situations of supreme difficulty, where he needed for success every description of resource, fertility, and knowledge. He allowed himself to be drugged by their atmosphere, to discuss on the basis of their plans and of their data, and to be led along their paths.

These and various other causes combined to produce the following situation. The reader must remember that the processes which are here compressed into a few pages took place slowly, gradually, insidiously, over a period of about five months.

As the President had thought nothing out, the Council was generally working on the basis of a French or British draft. He had to take up, therefore, a persistent attitude of obstruction, criticism, and negation, if the draft was to become at all in line with his own ideas and purpose. If he was met on some points with apparent generosity (for there was always a safe margin of quite preposterous suggestions which no one took seriously), it was difficult for him not to yield on others. Compromise was inevitable, and never to compromise on the essential, very difficult. Besides, he was soon made to appear to be taking the German part and laid himself open to the suggestion (to which he was foolishly and unfortunately sensitive) of being "pro-German."

After a display of much principle and dignity in the early days of the Council of Ten, he discovered that there were certain very important points in the program of his French, British, or Italian colleague, as the case might be, of which he was incapable of securing the surrender by the methods of secret diplomacy. What then was he to do in the last resort? He could let the Conference drag on an endless length by the exercise of sheer obstinacy. He could break it up and return to America in a rage with nothing settled. Or he could attempt an appeal to the world over the heads of the Conference. These were wretched alternatives, against each of which a great deal could be said. They were also very risky—especially for a politician. The President's mistaken policy over the Congressional election had weakened his personal position in his own country, and it was by no means certain that the American public would support him in a position of intransigency. It would mean a campaign in which the issues would be clouded by every sort of personal and party consideration, and who could say if right would triumph in a struggle which would certainly not be decided on its merits? Besides, any open rupture with his colleagues would certainly bring upon his head the blind passions of "anti-German" resentment with which the public of all allied countries were still inspired. They would not listen to his arguments. They would not be cool enough to treat the issue as one of international morality or of the right governance of Europe. The cry would simply be that, for various sinister and selfish reasons, the President wished "to let the Hun off." The almost unanimous voice of the French and British press could be anticipated. Thus, if he threw down the gage publicly he might be defeated. And if he were defeated, would not the final peace be far worse than if he were to retain his prestige and endeavor to make it as good as the limiting conditions of European politics would allow him? But above all, if he were defeated, would he not lose the League of Nations? And was not this, after all, by far the most important issue for the future happiness of the world? The Treaty would be altered and softened by time. Much in it which now seemed so vital would become trifling, and much which was impracticable would for that very reason never happen. But the League, even in an imperfect form, was permanent; it was the first commencement of a new principle in the government of the world; truth and justice in international relations could not be established in a few months—they must be born in due course by the slow gestation of the League. Clemenceau had been clever enough to let it be seen that he would swallow the League at a price.

At the crisis of his fortunes the President was a lonely man. Caught up in the toils of the Old World, he stood in great need of sympathy, of moral support, of the enthusiasm of masses. But buried in the Conference, stifled in the hot and poisoned atmosphere of Paris, no echo reached him from the outer world, and no throb of passion, sympathy, or encouragement from his silent constituents in all countries. He felt that the blaze of popularity which had greeted his arrival in Europe was already dimmed; the Paris press jeered at him openly; his political opponents at home were taking advantage of his absence to create an atmosphere against him; England was cold, critical, and unresponsive. He had so formed his *entourage* that he did not receive through private channels the current of faith and enthusiasm of which the public sources seemed dammed up. He needed, but lacked, the added strength of collective faith. The German terror still overhung us, and even the sympathetic public was very cautious; the enemy must not be encouraged, our friends must be supported, this was not the time for discord or agitations, the President must be trusted to do his best. And in this drought the flower of the President's faith withered and dried up.

Thus it came to pass that the President countermanded the *George Washington*, which, in a moment of well-founded rage, he had ordered to be in readiness to carry him from the treacherous halls of Paris back to the seat of his authority, where he could have felt himself again. But as soon, alas, as he had taken the road of compromise, the defects, already indicated, of his temperament and of his equipment, were fatally apparent. He could take the high line; he could practice obstinacy; he could write Notes from Sinai or Olympus; he could remain unapproachable in the White House or even in the Council of Ten and be safe. But if he once stepped down to the intimate equality of the Four, the game was evidently up.

Now it was that what I have called his theological or Presbyterian temperament became dangerous. Having decided that some concessions were unavoidable, he might have sought by firmness and address and the use of the financial power of the United States to secure as much as he could of the substance, even at some sacrifice of the letter. But the President was not capable of so clear an understanding with himself as this implied. He was too conscientious. Although compromises were now necessary, he remained a man of principle and the Fourteen Points a contract absolutely binding upon him. He would do nothing that was not just and right; he would do nothing that was contrary to his great profession of faith. Thus, without any abatement of the verbal inspiration of the Fourteen Points, they became a document for gloss and interpretation and for all the intellectual apparatus of self-deception, by which, I daresay, the President's forefathers had persuaded themselves that the course they thought it necessary to take was consistent with every syllable of the Pentateuch.

The President's attitude to his colleagues had now become: I want to meet you so far as I can; I see your difficulties and I should like to be able to agree to what you propose; but I can do nothing that is not just and right, and you must first of all show me that what you want does really fall within the words of the pronouncements which are binding on me. Then began the weaving of that web of sophistry and Jesuitical exegesis that was finally to clothe with insincerity the language and substance of the whole Treaty. The word was issued to the witches of all Paris:

> *Fair is foul, and foul is fair,*
> *Hover through the fog and filthy air.*

The subtlest sophisters and most hypocritical draftsmen were set to work, and produced many ingenious exercises which might have deceived for more than an hour a cleverer man than the President.

Thus instead of saying that German-Austria is prohibited from uniting with Germany except by leave of France (which would be inconsistent with the principle of self-determination), the Treaty, with delicate draftsmanship, states that "Germany acknowledges and will respect strictly the independence of Austria, within the frontiers which may be fixed in a Treaty between that State and the Principal Allied and Associated Powers; she agrees that this independence shall be inalienable, except with the consent of the Council of the

League of Nations," which sounds, but is not, quite different. And who knows but that the President forgot that another part of the Treaty provides that for this purpose the Council of the League must be *unanimous.*

Instead of giving Danzig to Poland, the Treaty established Danzig as a "Free" City, but includes this "Free" City within the Polish customs frontier, entrusts to Poland the control of the river and railway system, and provides that "the Polish Government shall undertake the conduct of the foreign relations of the Free City of Danzig as well as the diplomatic protection of citizens of that city when abroad."

In placing the river system of Germany under foreign control, the Treaty speaks of declaring international those "river systems which naturally provide more than one State with access to the sea, with or without transshipment from one vessel to another."

Such instances could be multiplied. The honest and intelligible purpose of French policy, to limit the population of Germany and weaken her economic system, is clothed, for the President's sake, in the august language of freedom and international equality. . . .

André Tardieu
THE TRUTH ABOUT THE TREATY

André Tardieu had a distinguished diplomatic career in France during the interwar years. At the Paris Peace Conference Tardieu was a member of the French Chamber of Deputies and he worked closely with Georges Clemenceau in the course of the negotiations. The following selection contains his comments about the personal and intellectual characteristics of the "Big Three" Allied leaders. To what extent might the differences between the views of Tardieu and Keynes reflect the broader Anglo-French divisions at Paris discussed by Smith?

This was the heroic period of the Conference; . . . From March 24 to May 7 [1919], the whole Treaty was put into shape: territorial, financial, economic and colonial clauses alike. Every morning and every afternoon, the four men met together, usually on the ground floor of the Hotel Bischoffsheim. In the garden an American "dough-boy" stood sentry, wearing the insignia of the Conference, white scales on a blue ground. At other times the meetings were held at the Ministry of War in M. Clemenceau's dark and comfortless office. Habit had created its own laws. In the afternoon each man took the same seat he had occupied in the morning. Sir Maurice Hankey, Secretary of the British War Cabinet, and Professor Mantoux, head in-terpreter of the French delegation, were the only others present. The plenipotentiaries and the experts came only from time to time. The tone was conversational. Neither pomp nor pose. Signor Orlando spoke but little; Italy's interest in the Conference was far too much confined to the question of Fiume, and her share in the debates was too limited as a result. It resolved itself into a three-cornered con-versation between Wilson, Clemenceau and Lloyd George—an amaz-ing contrast of the three most widely different natures that it is possible to conceive. Always sincere and straightforward, these interviews were at times almost tragic in their solemn simplicity and would then relax into something approaching gaiety when agreement was in sight. History will record with approval that even in the most difficult hours the "Four" always spoke the truth, the whole truth and nothing but the truth.

I shared their life too closely to be able to judge them. Who better than I knows their shortcomings? I have no taste to blame them; for I saw them give the very best of their great minds to their task, and what more can one ask? I have no right to praise them. I shall but try to redress, in as few words as may be, the wrong done by the out-rageous pen of a subordinate and disgruntled employee. I shall brush aside the legend that one of these three men hoodwinked the others. In France it has been said that Clemenceau was the dupe of Wilson and of Lloyd George; in the United States that Wilson was the play-thing of Lloyd George, and in England Mr. Keynes has written that M. Clemenceau turned the trick alone. This childish and contradictory explanation, convenient to politicians, must be abandoned. The ex-aggerated honor or the insult which it implies to the three leaders must be repudiated. The truth is that from the first day to the last, with a deep desire to reach agreement, the discussion proceeded foot by foot. I have already explained why.

The discussion between men whose national and individual temperaments were utterly opposed was naturally exceedingly keen. President Wilson discussed like a college professor criticizing a thesis, sitting bolt upright in his armchair, inclining his head at times towards his advisers, developing his views with the abundant clearness of a didactic logician. Mr. Lloyd George argued like a sharpshooter, with sudden bursts of cordial approval and equally frequent gusts of anger, with a wealth of brilliant imagination and copious historical reminiscences; clasping his knee in his hands, he sat near the fireplace, wrapped in the utmost indifference to technical arguments, irresistibly attracted to unlooked-for solutions, but dazzling with eloquence and wit, moved only by higher appeals to permanent bonds of friendship, and ever fearful of parliamentary consequences. As for M. Clemenceau, his part in the discussion was thoroughly typical and in very many instances his views prevailed. His arguments instead of being presented by deductive reasoning like those of Mr. Wilson or of exploding incidentally like those of Mr. Lloyd George— proceeded by assertions weighty, rough-hewn and insistent, but clothed with gentle words that did him credit and refulgent with emotion which at times was overpowering. Mr. Keynes has had the face to find fault with him for seeking first of all to place France beyond the reach of German aggression: it is the criticism of a man who has understood nothing of the history of Europe during the past fifty years and whose insular egoism cannot grasp what invasion means.

This period of history is closed. Most of the men who dominated it are retired. This gives me the greater freedom to say that the lesson of the war was not lost upon them, that despite their deep differences of opinion they were animated by an all-powerful unity of purpose, by a spirit of real understanding. "We entered here united," M. Clemenceau used to say, "we must leave here brothers." France and her spokesman did all they could to bring this about. They had a hard time of it. To give effect by common agreement to the essential bases of peace—restitution, reparation and guarantees—what toil and labor therein lay! Complete harmony crowned their work with success. It is easy to pretend that the policy of France was a "punic" policy: the mark of the beast is upon our devastated region and tells on which side were the Carthaginians. It is easy to taunt President Wilson with having adapted his principles to the pressing demands of reality, although as a matter of fact they were not his principles alone but the principles of all of us and not one of them was violated: this brand of sarcasm comes from those who in the solitary seclusion of their firesides build in their own minds an imaginary world from which living, suffering and achieving humanity is arbitrarily banished. It is easy to make capital out of Mr. Lloyd George's contradictions: no one has suffered more from them than France. But in justice it must be added that in the most serious times those who knew how to talk to the British Prime Minister could always bring him back to fundamental principles. The infinite sensitiveness of his mind, his passionate love of success, led him to improvise arguments which did not always bear examination or were too exclusively pro-British. But when a man who enjoyed his respect answered the bold suggestions of his quick brain with those permanent truths which he had momentarily deserted, he came back to them when the time arrived for final decision. These three men, for whom needless to say I have not the same personal feeling, forced upon me the same conviction about them all; the conviction that in their unheard-of task they managed to maintain and make even closer the bonds that bind our three countries, the breaking of which would spell disaster to civilization. They only did so with great difficulty. In their search for essential unanimity, they sometimes discovered that they neither knew one another well nor understood one another fully. Nevertheless they reached agreement, and reached it by open, straight and honest paths. This I assert, and I assert it because I was there and others who have said the contrary were not. . . .

III WILSON AND THE GERMAN QUESTION AT PARIS

Seth P. Tillman

ANGLO-AMERICAN RELATIONS AT THE PARIS PEACE CONFERENCE

Seth P. Tillman is currently a member of the staff of the Senate Foreign Relations Committee. His analysis of the Peace Conference carefully documents the existence of Anglo-American agreement on a number of key issues. He also shows, however, that Wilson and Lloyd George often failed to coordinate their similar approaches to Germany. The following sections deal with the questions of German borders and reparations. Does Tillman's analysis support or refute Keynes' critique of Wilson's methods at the Peace Conference?

. . . Lloyd George and Colonel House conferred privately in an anteroom at the Quai d'Orsay on March 12 [1919]. The Prime Minister said that he was seriously troubled by the French demand for the Rhine frontier. He recognized, he said, that it would take time for the League of Nations to become a strong organization, and he was therefore prepared to offer a pledge of British assistance to France in case of invasion, in lieu of an occupation and the detachment of the Rhineland. Lloyd George asked if the United States would join Great Britain in such a guarantee. House said that he did not know.

Lloyd George conferred secretly with Wilson on the morning of March 14, the day of the President's return, and told him of the gravity of the French situation and of his proposed military guarantee to France. The President agreed to join in the guarantee, and in a secret meeting that afternoon at the Crillon, Wilson and Lloyd George offered to Clemenceau [treaties of guarantee committing Great Britain and the United States to come to the assistance of France against German invasion, on condition that France give up its demands for the occupation and detachment of the Rhineland.] In making this significant offer, the President and the Prime Minister were proposing a revolutionary innovation in the historical relations between their nations and the continent of Europe.

Clemenceau, though perhaps more pleased with the guarantee offer than he cared to show, gave no immediate answer to Wilson and Lloyd George. On March 17, he handed to the President and

From Seth P. Tillman, *Anglo-American Relations at the Paris Peace Conference of 1919* (copyright © 1961 by Princeton University Press), pp. 179–193, 240–244, and 352–362. Reprinted by permission of Princeton University Press. Footnotes deleted.

the Prime Minister a note accepting the guarantee proposal only if coupled with a thirty-years' Allied occupation of the Rhineland and the complete demilitarization of Germany to a line 50 kilometers east of the Rhine, with any German violation to be regarded as an act of aggression. The note called further for the creation of an Anglo-French-American commission of inspection to oversee German compliance with these terms and also demanded that France be given the right to reoccupy German territory in the event of German violations after the end of the thirty years' occupation.

Although Wilson and Lloyd George resolutely opposed the proposals contained in the French note of March 17, the French clung to their demands and their intransigence now cast an atmosphere of crisis and pessimism over the Peace Conference. "The President," wrote House in his diary on March 22, "looked worn and tired. . . . From the looks of things the crisis will soon be here." Lloyd George was greatly distressed and decided to withdraw for a few days of meditation. "I am going to Fontainebleau for the week-end," he told Lord Riddell, "and mean to put in the hardest forty-eight hours' thinking I have ever done." Lloyd George conferred at Fontainebleau with General Smuts, Sir Henry Wilson, Sir Maurice Hankey, and Philip Kerr and produced a document which expressed British thinking on all of the major problems awaiting settlement.

The Fontainebleau Memorandum of March 25 declared that any effort to hold Germany down by harsh and unjust terms of peace would surely fail. As to the French Rhineland proposals, Lloyd George wrote: "I cannot conceive of any greater cause of future war. . . ." The Prime Minister proposed as a "guiding principle of the peace" that "as far as is humanly possible the different races should be allocated to their motherlands, and that this human criterion should have precedence over considerations of strategy or economics or communications. . . ." Until the League has established its effectiveness, it was asserted, an Anglo-American guarantee to France against aggression was essential. Outlining a broad set of proposed peace terms, Lloyd George suggested as to the Rhineland that it be demilitarized but not separated from Germany, while the Anglo-American guarantee to France would be automatically invoked if German forces crossed the Rhine without the consent of the League Council. As to Germany's western frontier, the memorandum called for German cessions to restore the French frontier of 1814, or alternately, French use of the Saar coal mines for a period of ten years.

The paradoxical nature of Anglo-American relations at the Peace Conference is evidenced by the fact that Lloyd George's statesman-like document was conceived and issued unilaterally, although it contained scarcely a clause to which President Wilson could not have wholeheartedly subscribed. Indeed, the key point of the memorandum, that injustice in the hour of triumph is the cause of future wars, was also one of the President's most cherished principles. Yet the President and the Prime Minister apparently did not even consider a joint statement of their common ideas although such a common front would certainly have strengthened the diplomatic positions of both. One possible explanation for this is that Wilson and Lloyd George, while wholly in accord over the French Rhineland claims, were at this time in sharp disagreement over the reparations question. A more fundamental explanation that suggests itself is the mutual temperamental alienation of the two statesmen which again and again in the course of the Peace Conference led them to strike parallel but never common diplomatic postures.

Lloyd George sent his document to Wilson and Clemenceau on March 26. Clemenceau had Tardieu, who saw the Fontainebleau Memorandum as the latest manifestation of Lloyd George's "parliamentary obsession," prepare a contentious reply, to which Lloyd George in turn responded in angry and caustic terms. So far as is known, President Wilson did not specifically reply to or comment on the Fontainebleau Memorandum.

The French demands and the Anglo-American counterproposals were vigorously debated in the Council of Four on March 27. President Wilson appealed for moderation, urging Clemenceau not to give Germany cause to seek revenge, while Lloyd George, with some lack of tact, recalled to Clemenceau how in 1815 Castlereagh and Wellington had restrained Prussia from destroying France. But Clemenceau was unmovable. "The Germans," he said, "are a servile people who need force to uphold an argument." France needed security, declared the Premier, and since the League of Nations did not provide military sanctions, France had to seek them elsewhere —an equivalent, in short, for the seas which protected England and

America. Agreeing now to the demilitarization of Germany to a line 50 kilometers east of the Rhine as demanded in the French note of March 17, President Wilson asserted that this, coupled with the military guarantee of Great Britain and the United States, would fully satisfy the requirements of French security. Clemenceau replied that France could not be satisfied with a *temporary* military guarantee and asked if the guarantee could not be written into the Covenant of the League. Wilson replied that provisions for a particular nation could not be put into a pact of general principles, but he assured Clemenceau that Britain and the United States would be fully prepared to come to the assistance of France against unprovoked German aggression.

While Clemenceau was thus contesting the adequacy of the proffered Anglo-American guarantee, the American Commissioners were registering opposition to it. Henry White told Colonel House that he and Lansing and Bliss regarded the proposed military alliance as "extremely unfortunate" and "absolutely fatal to the success of the League of Nations."

The deadlock among the heads of government gave rise to speculation that the Peace Conference might break up. "The time has not yet come," said President Wilson; "we cannot risk breaking up the Peace Conference—yet." But apparently he had begun to consider American withdrawal.

The question of French security was again fruitlessly debated in the Council of Four on March 31. Clemenceau now demanded the occupation as a guarantee of reparations payments and Marshal Foch argued that the Rhine was the essential strategic frontier of all of the western powers. Without it, he averred, the Anglo-American guarantee would be inadequate, for the German generals would attempt to defeat France before Anglo-American power could be brought to bear. Wilson and Lloyd George offered vigorous but vain resistance. The deadlock at this juncture seemed quite unbreakable.

The Saar Struggle, the Crisis of April, and the League of Nations Solution

Besides their strategic demands for the Rhine frontier and the occupation of the Rhineland, the French made special demands in regard to the heavily industrialized and coal-producing but German-populated Saar valley. The French eastern frontier of 1814 had included part of the district within France, but it had been entirely German since 1815, and its population had an unquestionable German affinity. The French, however, made a strong claim for the Saar on grounds of reparation. The German Army had despoiled and flooded the French coal mines at Lens and Valenciennes, and Great Britain and the United States readily agreed that France was entitled to restitution from the rich Saar coal fields. The problem was to give France the coal without giving her the German population.

As early as February 21, a group of British and American experts had agreed that France was entitled to full ownership of the Saar coal mines. It was felt, however, that some special regime would be essential to avoid imposing French sovereignty on the Saarlanders. But the Saar problem was not considered in earnest by the heads of governments until the end of March.

The Council of Four took up the Saar issue on March 28. André Tardieu appealed for the French frontier of 1814, French ownership of the mines, and a special administration for the mining and industrial areas, basing the French claims on grounds of historical affiliation and reparation. Lloyd George and Wilson readily agreed that France was entitled to economic compensation, but the President vigorously maintained that annexation by France would be a violation of the fundamental principles on which the peace was to be based. Justice, he said, required compensation to France but proper guarantees for the Saar as a whole. Clemenceau argued eloquently for annexation, contending that justice should satisfy "sentiments" as well as "abstract principles." Lloyd George supported the President, appealing to Clemenceau not to repeat the German error of Alsace-Lorraine. The Prime Minister proposed as a compromise the creation of an autonomous Saar state. Wilson objected that it was as much a violation of self-determination to give to a population an independence that it did not want as it was to place it under an alien sovereignty.

With Lloyd George favoring a separate regime, President Wilson stood alone in upholding the right of the Saarlanders to remain part of Germany. Colonel House appealed vainly to the President to avoid the "tactical error" of adhering to a position which was not supported by the British. The French submitted a note on March 29 demanding ownership of the Saar mines, a special political administration, and a fifteen-year French occupation under a League of Nations mandate with a plebiscite to be held at the end of that period. President Wilson rejected these proposals in the Council of Four on March 31, submitting a new plan which agreed to French ownership of mines but again rejected the demand for a separate political administration.

On April 1, Henry Wickham Steed, the British journalist, took it upon himself to attempt to mediate between Wilson and Clemenceau on the Saar issue. He proposed a French mandate over the Saar for fifteen years, to be followed by a plebiscite. France would have the use but not the ownership of the mines, but if at the end of the fifteen years the French mines were found to be irreparable, France would retain control of the Saar mines regardless of the outcome of the plebiscite. Wickham Steed sent his proposal to House, who submitted it to the President with a penciled note in the margin advising Wilson to let Wickham Steed submit the plan to Clemenceau. It is difficult to understand how Wickham Steed, or House, could have supposed that this plan, which was not a compromise but almost a stiffening of the French demands, would be acceptable to President Wilson. Nevertheless, Wickham Steed reports calling at the Crillon on April 2 and being informed by Frazier that the President had flown into a terrible rage upon seeing his proposals. "Then Clemenceau is quite right," Wickham Steed told Frazier. "Your President is an utterly impossible fellow. . . ."

With the French cirsis seemingly insuperable, Bolshevism spreading in Germany, and widespread turmoil elsewhere in Europe, President Wilson by early April seemed almost ready to break off negotiations. Baker told the President on April 2 that he was being widely held responsible for the crisis and Wilson replied: "I know that. . . . But we've got to make peace on the principles laid down and accepted, or not make it at all." On April 3, Wilson fell seriously ill with influenza and for days thereafter lay in bed while the Council of Four, with House sitting in for the President, debated fruitlessly in the next room. The British, who had agreed to a separate political administration for the Saar, provided no support for the President. Baker discussed Lloyd George's attitude with Wilson on April 7, and the President said: "Well, I suppose I shall have to stand alone." Sir William Wiseman privately recommended that the President lay before the Council of Four a draft treaty of peace based strictly on the Fourteen Points and that he threaten to go home unless there were immediate action. If Wilson would offer the inducement of a deferral of all Allied war loans, Wiseman urged, the Allies would be bound to accept an "American peace."

The President summoned the U.S.S. *George Washington* on April 7, authorizing the American Press Bureau to announce this publicly. The announcement had a resounding impact, shocking the French with the prospect of an American departure and the loss of the promised military guarantee. Baker visited the President on the evening of April 7 and left convinced that the summoning of the *George Washington* was not merely a diplomatic bluff. "Well, the time has come to bring this thing to a head," Baker reports the President as saying. ". . . One mass of tergiversations! I will not discuss anything with them any more."

Wilson's stroke produced immediate results. The summoning of the *George Washington* had a "castor oil" effect on the French, Dr. Grayson wrote to Tumulty on April 10, generating more progress in two days than there had been in the previous two weeks. The negotiations from April 8 to April 14 produced basic agreements on the Saar and Rhineland issues, essentially resolving the French crisis.

The deadlock still seemed hopeless when Wilson returned to the Council of Four on the afternoon of April 8. Lloyd George that morning had endorsed the French position on the Saar, proposing to make it an independent entity under League of Nations authority, with a French mandate and customs union, and with French ownership of the coal mines and control of the administration and foreign relations. Wilson now proposed the retention of German sovereignty over the Saar and the establishment of a commission of arbitration composed of three members appointed by the League of Nations and one each by France and Germany to rule on all issues of French economic rights. In fifteen years, under the President's scheme, there would be a definitive plebiscite to settle the permanent sovereignty over the Saar. Clemenceau maintained adamantly that the economic rights of France were incompatible with German sovereignty and Lloyd George agreed that there should be a special regime.

Tardieu submitted a note to the Council on the morning of April 9 which rejected the President's proposal of the previous day, insisting on a special political administration under a French mandate but agreeing to a plebiscite in fifteen years. The British presented a draft plan which was in most respects the same as the Tardieu proposal. Lloyd George recommended the Tardieu plan to the President as embodying a great concession and he urged the President to agree now to a special political administration for the Saar.

President Wilson rejected the Anglo-French proposals but in the afternoon session of April 9 he set forth a new proposal which broke the impasse. Wilson's plan called for a fifteen-year administration of the Saar under a commission appointed by and responsible to the League of Nations. The commission, though instructed to respect local institutions, would be fully endowed with legislative and executive powers and empowered to arbitrate disputes concerning the economic rights of France. During the fifteen-year period, under this plan, German sovereignty would be *suspended* in practice while retained in theory, and at the end of it, a definitive plebiscite would be held. Lloyd George was at once converted. He now gave his enthusiastic support to President Wilson, maintaining that his plan fully met the objections of the French to the retention of German sovereignty. It was agreed that the experts would consider this proposal, and at the end of the discussion Clemenceau allowed that he foresaw agreement on the basis of Wilson's scheme.

In the remaining negotiations on the Saar, Wilson and Lloyd George stood together for the President's plan. It was accepted in principle on April 10 and its details examined on April 10 and 11. At Clemenceau's insistence, it was agreed that the treaty clause would not specifically state that German sovereignty was maintained. The plan as adopted gave France full ownership of the Saar coal mines and a customs union. The essence of the compromise, which rendered the French demands compatible with President Wilson's principles, was the practical suspension but theoretical maintenance of German sovereignty.

The resolution of the Saar crisis was made possible by the prospective existence of the League of Nations. In this as in other substantive issues dealt with by the Peace Conference, the fledgling League served as a vehicle for the accommodation of seemingly irreconcilable positions. The Saar issue also illustrates the rather different motives of Wilson and Lloyd George in resisting the French program for military security. The President was preeminently con- *Amer.* cerned with the principles of justice involved and resisted the Saar *ideas* and Rhineland claims of the French with equal vigor insofar as they would have placed German populations under an alien sovereignty. Lloyd George was primarily fearful of the practical consequences of *Br.* the French designs for European stability and equilibrium, and this *ideas* perhaps explains why he resisted the permanent detachment of the Rhineland with almost greater vigor than the President while raising no objection to French political administration of the Saar. The latter issue, apparently, did not at first seem to the Prime Minister to pose the threat of "another Alsace-Lorraine." Since one way or the other France was to acquire at least temporary domination of the Saar, Lloyd George was not disposed to quibble over the abstract question of sovereignty. He therefore readily accepted the demand for a French mandate, but when the President devised a scheme to give France economic restitution while reserving the right of the Saar-landers later to elect German nationality, Lloyd George enthusiasti-cally accepted the President's plan as a workable synthesis of political realities and Wilsonian abstractions.

The Resolution of the Rhineland Crisis and the Anglo-American Treaties of Guarantee, April 11–29; Other Territorial Issues in Western Europe

The settlement of the Saar crisis was followed by the resolution of the Rhineland issue and the question of French security. The core of the ultimate compromise between the conflicting French *Bargain* and Anglo-American positions was the abandonment by France of plans for the detachment of the Rhineland from Germany in return for binding Anglo-American military commitments to France con-tained in the proposed treaties of guarantee.

The basis of agreement was established with relative ease. In a note handed to the French on April 12, President Wilson reaffirmed the offer of military guarantees to France while warning that these represented the "maximum of what I myself deem necessary for the safety of France, or possible on the part of the United States." Clemenceau refused an Anglo-American proposal to limit the treaties of guarantee to a period of three years and it was agreed that they would be terminated when a majority of the League Council agreed that the League of Nations itself afforded sufficient protection against German aggression. Clemenceau, in turn, agreed to give up all plans for the detachment of the Rhineland from Germany, but he insisted upon the demilitarization of Germany to a line 50 kilometers east of the Rhine and on a fifteen-years' occupation, no longer demanding one of thirty years.

The compromise was consummated in a conference between Clemenceau and Colonel House on April 14. Clemenceau agreed to couple the treaties of guarantee and the demilitarization of western Germany with a fifteen-year, three-stage occupation providing for partial withdrawals of occupation forces at five-year intervals depending upon German compliance with the treaty. In a meeting with House on April 15, the President, although expressing distaste for the occupation provisions, agreed to the total plan, and on the 16th House informed Clemenceau of the President's compliance.

Lloyd George continued to have grave misgivings about the occupation. He was shocked by Wilson's "surrender" of April 15 and suspected that the President's agreement to the Rhineland occupation was part of a bargain with Clemenceau whereby the latter suddenly called off the hitherto sharp attacks on the President by the French press. "I did my best," writes Lloyd George, "to convince President Wilson of the mischievous possibilities of the occupation, but in vain."

Lloyd George capitulated in the meeting of the Council of Four on April 22, agreeing to the fifteen-year occupation. Clemenceau handed round the draft treaty of guarantee, which he and Wilson had agreed to on April 20. President Wilson, perhaps in fear of the possible reaction in the United States to a direct alliance with England, opposed a tri-partite treaty and suggested that two separate treaties be signed, between France and the United States and between France and Great Britain. Lloyd George readily agreed to this arrangement.

At French insistence, the occupation clause of the treaty was further amended on April 29 to permit a delay in the evacuation of Allied forces at the end of fifteen years if the guarantees against

German aggression at that time "are not considered sufficient by the Allied and Associated Governments. . . ." This was designed to meet French fears that the United States Senate might deny its consent to the ratification of the treaty of guarantee.

The agreement on the treaties of guarantee was announced at the Plenary Session of the Peace Conference on May 6. At the end of the session, Wilson and Lloyd George handed letters to Clemenceau expressing their agreement to conclude the guarantee treaties with France and to submit them to their respective legislatures. Lloyd George's letter stipulated that the Anglo-French treaty "will be in similar terms to that entered into by the United States and will come into force when the later is ratified." On the day before the Plenary Session, President Wilson had commented to David Hunter Miller that "Lloyd George had slipped a paragraph into the British note about ratification by the United States and that he [the President] did not think Clemenceau had noticed it."

Woodrow Wilson has been severely criticized for entering into an "entangling alliance" with France. A noted historian has contended that Wilson "probably knew" that the Senate would refuse to consider the guarantee treaty and that it was "a way the diplomatists had to get around a difficult corner." The accusation that Wilson entered the treaty in bad faith is difficult to credit, not only because of Wilson's character, but because the protracted and difficult negotiations which led to the treaty of guarantee suggest a most serious *bona fide* effort to work out an acceptable commitment and certainly do not provide any evidence of bad faith. Moreover, the French, who were left "holding the bag," did not charge Wilson with bad faith. In July 1920, André Tardieu told Colonel Bonsal that he considered such charges unfounded. "I am not so sure of the good faith of Lloyd George," said Tardieu. "Why should he have made the assistance of Britain contingent upon the ratification of the pact by Washington?"

President Wilson did not conceive of the guarantee pact as a conventional alliance. It was, he told the Senate on July 29, 1919, a "temporary supplement" to the treaty, not independent of the League of Nations but under it. Wilson's concept of collective security assumed a world of juridically equal states and he refused to recognize an Anglo-French-American alliance as its nucleus. The guarantee treaties were, to Wilson, a significant but temporary supplement to the League designed to assuage the fears of France.

The rejection of the treaties of guarantee by the United States and Great Britain did much to destroy the possibility of a liberal development of the Versailles system. By throwing France back to the letter of the treaty in her vain quest for security, the United States and Great Britain contributed indirectly to the rise of the spirit of revenge in Germany, which was further encouraged by the absence of an instrument for the automatic reformulation of the coalition which had defeated Germany in 1918.

The Rhineland crisis was over by the end of April. A movement by French generals to overturn the decisions of the Peace Conference by promoting an artificial separatist movement in the Rhineland in late May and early June angered and alarmed British and American statesmen. Wilson and Lloyd George lodged strong protests with Clemenceau, who loyally took strong measures to crush the "Rhineland rebellion," which consequently ended in ignominious failure.

Of all of the territorial changes which took place in 1919, none was settled with greater ease and unanimity than the restoration of Alsace-Lorraine to France. Both Great Britain and the United States had made the restitution of Alsace-Lorraine an integral part of their war aims. The Treaty of Versailles restored Alsace-Lorraine to France as of the date of the Armistice. Both Britain and the United States fully agreed with the French that a plebiscite, as requested by the Germans, would have been "insultingly illegitimate," implying that the German act of 1871 was an open question.

*   *   *

The Struggle for a Fixed Sum in the Council of Four

The failure of the Commission on Reparation of Damage to agree on figures for compensation returned the issue to the Supreme Council. On March 10, Lloyd George, Clemenceau, and House commissioned a special committee of three experts to negotiate anew for agreement on a reparations figure. The experts, Norman H. Davis, Edwin S. Montagu, and Louis Loucheur, met in secret. The three experts agreed on a report which paralleled the position taken by Lamont in the Second Subcommittee, calling for $30 billion as an absolute maximum of reparations, half of which was to be payable in marks. Davis made these recommendations in a private meeting with Lloyd George, Clemenceau, and House in the latter's apartment at the Crillon on March 15. Lloyd George and Clemenceau, according to Davis, were finally persuaded, and Davis left this meeting with the conviction that a tacit agreement had been reached to work out a solution along the line proposed by the experts.

The apparent agreement of March 15 proved illusory. Davis and Loucheur met privately with Wilson, Lloyd George, and Clemenceau on March 18. Montagu had been called home for personal reasons and Lord Sumner and Keynes attended as the British experts. Sumner put forth an argument for heavy reparations, and, according to Davis, President Wilson told Lloyd George he "thought we had reached an agreement in the previous meeting as to substantially what would be done," and the Prime Minister replied that he "did not believe that we had. . . ."

The British, French, and American experts continued their efforts to reach agreement, attempting to devise a flexible schedule of maximum and minimum reparations payments. Between March 19 and March 24, the Anglo-American experts worked out five drafts of reparations clauses, each providing for flexibility of payments by giving the permanent reparations commission limited power to suspend or cancel payments. But the experts, now including both Sumner and Cunliffe for Britain, were unable to agree on figures. Lloyd George told Lamont and Davis on March 22 that he would readily agree to a figure of $25 billion if they could win the agreement of Cunliffe and Sumner, without which he feared that he would be "crucified" at home. Davis advised President Wilson on March 25 that the experts would be unable to submit a unanimous report. "We have agreed substantially upon the form for the peace treaty and upon the plan for its execution," Davis reported, "but we have been unable to arrive at any agreement with Lords Sumner and Cunliffe . . . because these two gentlemen still stand upon their original estimate of 11 billion pounds."

In his Fontainebleau Memorandum of March 25, Lloyd George was vague on reparations, saying that "the duration for the payments of reparation ought to disappear if possible with the generation which made the war," and that "Germany should pay an annual sum for a stated number of years," the amount "to be agreed among the Allied and Associated Powers." The British, French, and American experts submitted proposed figures on March 25: the British figure was Sumner's $55 billion, the French $31 billion to $47 billion, the American $25 billion to $35 billion. In the Council of Four on the same day, President Wilson warned of the danger of setting reparations beyond the reduced capacity of a Germany deprived of much of its territory and resources. Lloyd George replied that he could not forget public opinion and proposed the inclusion of pensions to the families of soldiers killed and incapacitated as a category of reparation.

Lloyd George struck a different posture on March 26, now contesting the reparations figures proposed by both the French and British experts. Pointing to the danger of a German refusal to sign the treaty, Lloyd George averred that it would be as hard for him as for Clemenceau to dispel "the illusions which prevail on the subject of reparations," but that both should serve their countries as best they could. If he were defeated for failing to do the impossible, he declared, his successor would be able to do no better, and he was convinced that the Germans would not sign the provisions as contemplated. The statesmen, he urged, should stand up to their domestic oppositions. President Wilson replied with enthusiasm: "I cannot fail to express my admiration for the spirit which manifests itself in Mr. Lloyd George's words. There is nothing more honorable than to be driven from power because one was right." If reasonable proposals were made and explained, said the President, not a parliament in the world would be able to blame the statesmen for their decisions. Clemenceau then proposed that the experts be asked to devise a plan setting maximum and minimum *annual* payments but not designating a total sum, but President Wilson insisted that the treaty should contain either a total sum or a time limit. Lloyd George averred that he saw no use in reconvening the experts. His own, he said, were unmovable. When he warned Sumner of the danger of Bolshevism if too much were demanded, said Lloyd George, Sumner had replied: "In that case the Germans will cut their own throats; I would like nothing better."

The French Finance Minister, Klotz, proposed in the meeting of March 28 that no final sum be stated in the treaty but that repara-

tions figures be set for only a year or two while a commission calculated the total damages and then set a final figure. Lloyd George
found this a most satisfactory proposal. At this point, John Maynard
Keynes was brought into the discussion, and he proposed that
Germany be confronted in the treaty with a total bill representing the
sum of damages, but that the amount actually to be paid be settled
later on the basis of final determinations as to Germany's capacity
to pay. Wilson vigorously objected to the Klotz plan as a dangerous
proposal asking Germany to open an unlimited credit to the Allies.
Keynes's proposal, said Wilson, was quite different, in that it would
tell Germany what she owed and leave for later decision only the
question of what Germany could in fact pay. Lloyd George professed
to believe that the two plans were reconcilable, but in any case he
favored the Klotz proposal for telling Germany only what the categories of damage were and leaving the figure to be determined by
a commission. The Klotz plan, said Lloyd George, whose resolve of
the 26th had apparently faded, would provide the means to avoid
discussions in their parliaments and would dispel the differences
within the Council. Reiterating that Klotz's proposal was not really
different from that of Keynes, Lloyd George suggested that any differences within the proposed commission be arbitrated by an ap-
pointee of the President of the United States. President Wilson said
that he must reserve judgment on the plan.

President Wilson offered some further resistance to the proposals
of March 28, but the issue was essentially resolved on that date
against the inclusion of a sum of reparations in the treaty. The
decisive factor in the defeat of the fixed sum was undoubtedly the
final position taken by Lloyd George. After showing some inclination
to accept a moderate figure, as in the discussion with the experts
on March 15 and in the Council of Four on March 26, Lloyd George
ended his vacillations by coming down on the side of the French
plan, leaving President Wilson isolated. Throughout the debate on
the fixed sum, there had been two views within the British delegation,
the extremist position of Lords Sumner and Cunliffe, and the moderate position of the Treasury as represented by Keynes. In his
tergiversations of policy Lloyd George made it plain that his own
inclinations were for the moderate view, but the pressures of British
public and parliamentary opinion brought him finally to the side of

improvisation as an easy escape from the pressures exerted by the extremists. In later years, Lloyd George adhered to his view that the decision against the fixed sum was, in the face of the passions of public opinion, a wise one, leaving the determination to the "cooler light of reason and of practical experience. . . ."

Had President Wilson been able and willing to connect a cancellation or mitigation of inter-Allied war debts with the question of a fixed sum of reparations, it is altogether possible that the latter could have been achieved. Sir William Wiseman urged that a deferral of all war loans, to be paid "if and when" the Allies were able, would constitute the great inducement that would end all British opposition to a moderate reparations settlement and make Wilson the "absolute master" of the situation. But such an inducement was rejected by Wilson and his advisers, and if attempted, it almost certainly would have been repudiated by Congress and American public opinion. . . .

*   *   *

On the afternoon of June 2, Lloyd George submitted to the Council of Four the proposals for revision of the draft treaty which the British delegation had agreed upon. He said that the British Empire delegation was unanimous in refusing to invade Germany and reimpose the blockade if their proposals were rejected. British public opinion, said Lloyd George, "wanted to get peace and was not so much concerned about the precise terms." President Wilson asserted that Lloyd George's proposals were of such importance that he wished to consult the American delegates and experts. At the President's request, the meeting scheduled for the next morning was canceled to allow Wilson and Clemenceau to confer with their advisers. Clemenceau objected most strenuously to the British proposals, contending that they created a "very grave" situation. Lloyd George said that if the French refused concessions on the occupation, he "would have no alternative but to go home and put the whole matter before his Parliament." France, he said, should have chosen between the occupation of the Rhineland and the Anglo-American treaties of guarantee. Asked by Wilson for further definition of his reparations proposals, Lloyd George explained his scheme and expressed his recently acquired view that "there was something in the contention that Germany should not be presented with an unknown liability."

"The difficulty," he declared, "was that they did not know what they had to pay."

President Wilson conferred with the American commissioners and technical advisers on the morning of June 3. The President opened the discussion with an account of the British proposals in regard to the eastern frontiers of Germany, reparations, the occupation and German admission to the League. The reparations question was discussed first. Norman Davis, Thomas William Lamont, Bernard Baruch, and Vance McCormick all felt that the British proposals provided an opportunity to revive the fixed sum. President Wilson recalled the failure of earlier efforts to reach agreement on a fixed sum, and Lamont observed that "Mr. Lloyd George kicked over the traces; but now he has come back to the fold." "Now the joke of it is," said Wilson, "that Lord Sumner was one of those who contributed to the unanimous counsel of the British the other day, and he takes a different position now."

President Wilson turned to the other British proposals. As to Germany's eastern frontiers, Robert Howard Lord said that only very minor changes, if any, were warranted. A fair plebiscite for Upper Silesia, he contended, would be won by Poland, but he doubted that a fair plebiscite was possible, owing to the domination of the Polish masses by German capitalists and landowners. As to the occupation of the Rhineland, Wilson observed that the problem was not so much military as one of French public opinion. General Bliss argued for a substantial reduction of the occupation and its immediate termination upon Germany's entering the League. The President thought that the issue would "solve itself" when Germany was admitted to the League. Secretary Lansing asked if it were possible to fix the time of German admittance to the League, and Wilson replied: "I don't honestly think it is. I think it is necessary that we should know that the change in government and the governmental method in Germany is genuine and permanent. We don't know either of them yet."

The discussion turned to general considerations of the justice and expediency of the proposed concessions to Germany. The President said that the question chiefly in his mind was: "Where have they shown that the arrangements of the treaty are essentially unjust?" and not: "Where have they shown merely that they are hard?" For, said Wilson, "they are hard—but the Germans earned that." "I have no desire to soften the treaty," the President affirmed, "but I have a very sincere desire to alter those portions of it that are shown to be unjust, or which are shown to be contrary to the principles which we ourselves have laid down." Herbert Hoover thought that the expediency of inducing Germany to sign the treaty should be the primary consideration in regard to the proposed revisions, "because the weighing of justice and injustice in these times is pretty difficult." "Well," said Wilson, "I don't want to seem to be unreasonable, but my feeling is this: that we ought not, with the object of getting it signed, make changes in the treaty, if we think that it embodies what we are contending for; that the time to consider all these questions was when we were writing the treaty, and it makes me a little tired for people to come and say now that they are afraid the Germans won't sign, and their fear is based upon things that they insisted upon at the time of the writing of the treaty; that makes me very sick. . . . These people that overrode our judgment and wrote things into the treaty that are now the stumbling blocks, are falling all over themselves to remove these stumbling blocks. Now, if they ought not to have been there, I say, remove them, but I say do not remove them merely for the fact of having the treaty signed."

The President's ire was clearly directed against the British. "Here is a British group," he declared, "made up of every kind of British opinion, from Winston Churchill to Fisher. From the unreasonable to the reasonable, all the way around, they are all unanimous, if you please, in their funk. Now that makes me very tired. They ought to have been rational to begin with and then they would not have needed to have funked at the end. They ought to have done the rational things, I admit, and it is not very gracious for me to remind them— though I have done so with as much grace as I could command." "They say that they do not quite understand why you permitted them to do that," said Davis. "I would be perfectly willing to take the responsibility if the result is good," the President affirmed. "But though we did not keep them from putting irrational things in the treaty, we got very serious modifications out of them. If we had written the treaty the way they wanted it, the Germans would have gone home the minute they read it."

Wilson's candid remarks to the American delegates evidence

quite clearly the fundamental differences between himself and Lloyd George not only with respect to the British proposals for revision of the draft treaty but also in the basic approaches of the two statesmen to the entire peace settlement. Lloyd George was governed by considerations of practicality and expediency, above all, in this instance, by his desire to induce Germany to sign the treaty without a renewal of hostilities. The President, on the other hand, was prepared to risk the dangers and inconveniences of a German refusal to sign, nor was he interested in moderation or liberality as such. His objective was justice, or, more accurately, an approach in this world toward a concept of absolute and transcendental justice, and, in his own conception, he was bound to its service not by choice but by compulsion.

The depth of this conviction was never clearer than in a speech which he had delivered on Memorial Day at the Suresnes Cemetery, in which he said: ". . . If I may speak a personal word, I beg you to realize the compulsion that I myself feel that I am under. By the Constitution of our great country I was the commander-in-chief of these men. I advised the Congress to declare that a state of war existed. I sent these lads over here to die. Shall I—can I—ever speak a word of counsel which is inconsistent with the assurances I gave them when they came over? It is inconceivable. There is something better, if possible, that a man can give than his life, and that is his living spirit to a service that is not easy, to resist counsels that are hard to resist, and to stand against purposes that are difficult to stand against, and to say, 'Here stand I, consecrated in spirit to the men who were once my comrades and who are now gone, and who have left me under eternal bonds of fidelity.' "

In the first two weeks of June, the British proposals were debated in the Council of Four. In the service of practical necessity, Lloyd George appealed for concessions to the Germans, and, in the service of principle, Wilson came reluctantly to agree with the Prime Minister. But the basic distrust remained between the two statesmen with their radically different motives. A few days after the meeting of the American delegates, Herbert Hoover appealed to President Wilson to make common cause with Lloyd George, and the President replied sharply: "Lloyd George will not stand up against Clemenceau despite what he says."

**The Debate in the Council of Four on Lloyd George's Proposals
for Revision of the Draft Treaty, June 3–16; The Allied Reply
to the German Counterproposals and the Signing
of the Treaty, June 16–28**

The deliberations of the Council of Four in the first two weeks of
June were concerned with the four categories of revisions proposed
by Lloyd George: the German-Polish border, the reparations settlement, the admission of Germany to the League of Nations, and the
duration and conditions of the Allied occupation of the Rhineland.

On revisions

Lloyd George opened the discussion of the German-Polish frontiers
on the afternoon of June 3 with his proposal for a plebiscite in Upper
Silesia. Wilson reported Lord's contention that the region was dominated by a few German capitalists and landed magnates who would
thwart a free expression of the will of the people. Lloyd George
replied that an Allied occupation would be necessary to prevent
intimidation of the people. His understanding of self-determination,
he said, was "that of the people themselves, and not that of experts
like Mr. Lord." Lloyd George declared himself to be "simply standing
by President Wilson's Fourteen Points and fighting them through."
Wilson replied that he was fully in favor of a plebiscite if there were
assurances of a free vote, and, rather heatedly, that he "could not
allow Mr. Lloyd George to suggest that he himself was not in favor
of self-determination." Lloyd George explained that his concern with
Upper Silesia was motivated by a strong desire to avoid the necessity of Allied forces marching on Berlin, which, he feared, would be
another "Moscow campaign." Wilson said that he was "less concerned with the question of whether Germany would or would not
sign than with ensuring that the arrangements in the treaty of peace
were sound and just." Lloyd George replied that he was "ready to
make any concession that was fair and just, particularly if it would
give the Germans an inducement to sign." Clemenceau vigorously
opposed a plebiscite in Upper Silesia, and Wilson noted that it was
not required by Point 13. Nevertheless, Wilson agreed to a plebiscite
to be conducted under the supervision of an inter-Allied commission,
and the Council agreed that the draft treaty would be amended to
provide for a plebiscite in the portion of Upper Silesia which had
been transferred to Poland. KT Revision

A sharp exchange took place on the morning of June 5 between Lloyd George and Paderewski of Poland. Paderewski bitterly protested the plebiscite decision, contending that it violated promises made to Poland and that it would destroy the faith of the Polish people in the Allies. Lloyd George bluntly accused Poland of ingratitude and imperialist designs. ". . . Not only has she no gratitude," fulminated the Prime Minister, "but she says she has lost faith in the people who have won her freedom." ". . . It fills me with despair," he declared, "the way in which I have seen small nations, before they have hardly leaped into the light of freedom, beginning to oppress other races than their own."

The British and American critics of the draft treaty were impressed with Lloyd George's stand and puzzled by Wilson's apparent reticence. Harold Nicolson, for instance, recorded in his diary on June 5: ". . . Cannot understand Wilson. Here is a chance of improving the thing and he won't take it. Lloyd George, however, is fighting like a little terrier all by himself."

President Wilson gave increasing support to Lloyd George but showed no real enthusiasm for the plebiscite in Upper Silesia. On June 11, he reiterated that the plebiscite was not necessary in principle under Point 13. The Allies, he said, while refusing all sacrifices on their own part, were throwing upon Poland the burden of appeasing Germany. Lloyd George reaffirmed his threat that he would not order British soldiers to fight if the Germans broke with the Peace Conference over the plebiscite. A special committee on Germany's eastern frontiers, which had been constituted on June 3, reported on June 11 that the Poles in Upper Silesia were not free to form their own opinions and recommended, therefore, that the plebiscite be delayed. The American member, Lord, and the French and Italian members, urged a delay of one or two years, while the British member, Headlam-Morley, thought that the plebiscite could be held sooner. President Wilson proposed that the plebiscite be delayed as recommended by the majority of the committee, and the Council agreed. It was further agreed to place Upper Silesia temporarily under the administration of a four-member inter-Allied commission. Wilson explained the plebiscite decision to Paderewski on June 14 as designed to deny Germany any excuse for disturbing the peace. Paderewski pronounced it a "very serious blow to Poland," and

Polish dissent

Lloyd George joined the President in attempting to assuage the Polish leader's distress. After Paderewski left, the Council decided that the plebiscite would be held within six to eighteen months of the establishment of the commission, rather than one or two years as at first agreed.

Starting from an attitude of marked reluctance, Wilson came finally to full support of Lloyd George in regard to the Polish-German frontier. Henry White exercised considerable influence in bringing the President to this stand. In 1923, Wilson said to White's daughter: "But for your father I should have never known the truth about Upper Silesia; the French and the Poles had entirely misled me."

The British proposals in regard to reparations gave rise to a re-newed American effort to secure agreement on a fixed sum. In a memorandum submitted on June 3, Bernard Baruch pointed to the financial advantages of a fixed sum to all of the Allied states. Wilson raised the issue in the Council of Four on the afternoon of June 3, but Lloyd George maintained that "every possible way of arriving at a fixed sum had been attempted, but it had not been found pos-sible." He described his two alternative schemes: a German contract to make full restoration of the devastated areas within a certain time, with a fixed sum to cover all other items, including pensions; or, a German offer within three months of the signing of the treaty of a lump sum in settlement of all reparations claims, with the stipulation that if this were not acceptable to the Allies the original clauses of the treaty would stand. The Council constituted a special committee of Lloyd George, Baruch, and Loucheur to examine the Prime Minister's proposals.

Wilson and his experts continued to press for the determination of a fixed sum of reparations for inclusion in the treaty. Baruch and Lamont conferred with Lloyd George on June 7, appealing to him to reconsider the fixed sum, but he continued to press his own proposals, contending that any fixed sum to which the Allies might agree would be too high for the Germans to accept. "Any figures that would not frighten them," Lloyd George told the Council on June 9, "would be below the figure with which he and M. Clemenceau could face their peoples in the present state of public opinion." President Wilson said that he was "perfectly willing to stand by the treaty pro-vided that it were explained to the Germans, but he had understood that the British and French Governments were desirous of making some concessions as a possible inducement to the Germans to sign." "If we must make concessions," he said, "then he was in favor of perfectly definite concessions." Wilson then read a proposal submitted by the American experts calling for a fixed sum of $25 billion and assurances to Germany of a certain amount of working capital. Lloyd George said that he liked the "crust and the seasoning *No sum* but not the meat" of the American proposal. Wilson agreed to omit *fixed* the fixed sum from the treaty.

Lloyd George's reparations proposals were adopted by the Council of Four. Wilson said on June 10 that the American proposals had been offered only in a spirit of cooperation and that if they were not acceptable they could be withdrawn. Lloyd George declared that he fully agreed with the "spirit" of the American proposals but that all that was needed to induce Germany to sign the treaty was "some general assurance." On June 11, the Council agreed on its reply to the German counterproposals regarding reparations. Although the first of Lloyd George's alternate plans was dropped at the insistence of Clemenceau, the reply included the offer to allow Germany to submit within four months a lump-sum proposal or "any practicable plan" for the restitution of damages, with the Allies to reply to any German plan within two months of its submission.

Lloyd George's vague proposal for the early admission of Germany to the League of Nations was readily accepted by President Wilson. Wilson favored a "general assurance" to Germany of her admission to the League as soon as the Allies were convinced that the changes in her Government were sincere. It was so agreed. The final reply to Germany in regard to the League, adopted on June 12, informed Germany that her immediate admittance was not justified but that if she acted sincerely to meet her obligations under the treaty, she would be admitted to the League "in the near future."

The United States was in essential sympathy with Lloyd George's proposal for the mitigation of the terms of the occupation. Clemenceau appealed to the Council on June 12 to make no changes in the Rhineland settlement, but Lloyd George maintained that Parliament might refuse to accept both the treaty of guarantee and a long occupation of the Rhineland. Clemenceau asserted that a reduction of the period of occupation was impossible. The commission established on May 29 to rewrite the draft convention on the occupation of the Rhineland submitted recommendations which were adopted by the Council on June 13. The concessions adopted were embodied in a declaration on the occupation of the Rhineland signed by Wilson, Lloyd George, and Clemenceau on June 16. The declaration promised that if before the end of the projected fifteen-year occupation Germany has given proof of her good will and satisfactory guarantees to assure the fulfillment of her obligations, the Allied and Associated Powers "will be ready to come to an agreement between themselves for the earlier termination of the period of occupation." The declaration promised further that as soon as Germany fulfilled the disarmament clauses of the treaty, the annual charge to Germany for the cost of the occupation would not exceed $60 million. 3RD Revision

The Anglo-American rebellion against the draft treaty thus came to an end with modest alterations of the treaty in regard to reparations, German admission to the League, and the Rhineland occupation, and with a major alteration in regard to Germany's eastern frontier. The episode illustrates once again the failure of Great Britain and the United States to coordinate strategy in promoting common objectives. Some of the changes advocated by Lloyd George in May and June had been advocated by President Wilson earlier in the Peace Conference and defeated. In June, Wilson thought it too late to make major changes although he lent rather grudging support to Lloyd George. On the crucial issue of reparations, the President did seriously probe Lloyd George's intentions but found him unwilling to go beyond "general assurances" that might induce the Germans to sign the treaty. The British were puzzled by the tepidness of Wilson's support, failing, apparently, to understand the mentality which made the President feel bound to his covenants with Clemenceau, however reluctantly entered, just as he felt bound to his covenants with the enemy under the Pre-Armistice Agreement. Wilson, moreover, felt a profound disgust with the motivations of pure expediency which underlay the British proposals for revision, a sentiment which he revealed without a trace of ambiguity in his conference with the American delegates on June 3. When motives are set aside, however, and consequences considered, it seems quite clear that Lloyd George, and not Wilson, was the principal champion of a settlement both just and expedient in regard to the occupation of the Rhineland and the German-Polish borderlands.

Wilson's own feelings

N. Gordon Levin, Jr.

WOODROW WILSON AND WORLD POLITICS

N. Gordon Levin, Jr., is associate professor of history at Amherst College. The following selection explores the relationships in Wilson's thinking between his German policy, the League of Nations and the problem of Bolshevism.

Two contradictory Wilsonian approaches to the problem of Germany dialectically interacted at the Paris Peace Conference, ultimately to create an ambiguous American policy toward the future role of the leader of the Central Powers. One of these approaches, the reintegrationist tendency, was oriented toward the inclusion of a democratized Germany in a new nonrevolutionary community of liberal nation-states. This reintegrationist orientation, supported ideologically by the President's reformist anti-imperialism of liberal order, was marked by efforts to moderate Allied, and especially French, economic and territorial demands on Germany in the interests of securing world peace and preventing the further spread of Bolshevism. At the heart of the reintegrationist position on Germany was the Wilsonian vision of a universal international commercial and political system, led by American missionary liberalism, and free from both traditional imperialism and revolutionary socialism.

Wilsonian policy at Paris was also marked, however, by an almost equally strong and necessarily conflicting punitive approach toward Germany. If the Administration's reintegrationist tendency was supported in part by the concern that the German Revolution might go too far to the Left and destroy liberal-capitalism along with autocratic-militarism, the punitive tendency was supported paradoxically by the reverse fear that the moderate German Revolution that Wilsonians defended against Bolshevism had not really destroyed the reactionary roots of German militarism. Unwilling to opt for real solidarity with Germany's more revolutionary socialist elements, the Wilsonian decision-makers were often forced, for reasons of policy and diplomatic necessity, to accept various forms of military controls on a probationary Germany which they still distrusted. Moreover, the President's loyalty to France and to the national aspirations of the new Slavic states of Eastern Europe led him to approve territorial demands on Germany which, despite their moderation by comparison with the more extreme French demands, were far in excess of what Germany's moderate-socialist and liberal-nationalist leaders were prepared to accept willingly. These new German leaders had hoped to use Allied fear of Bolshevism and Germany's mild democratization to win a compromise peace and entrance for Germany into a postwar anti-Leninist community of democratic states. Yet, in counting on the reintegrationist tendency of Wilsonian policy to aid them, the German leaders forgot Wilson's commitment to Slavic nationalism. They also underestimated the possibility that Wilsonians would be somewhat influenced by the French desire to place the prime responsibility for containing Bolshevism on the new anti-German states of Eastern Europe that were to be guaranteed by the League of Nations.

Ultimately, the dialectical interplay between these reintegrationist and punitive tendencies in Wilsonian policy at Paris led to a situation in which American power was co-opted into the maintenance of the moderately anti-German settlement which American statesmen had ambivalently helped to create. Convinced that America's liberal-exceptionalism assured no contradiction between his position as leader of a powerful nation-state and his role as spokesman for world liberalism, the President chose to moderate Allied demands by the judicious use of America's economic and political power. If, however, American power could often moderate the peace program of the Allies, it could also, in the absence of any desire on the Administration's part either to challenge the givens of international politics in a revolutionary fashion or to aid Germany excessively, create simultaneously the possibility of its own absorption into the defense of the resulting compromise settlement. Indeed, this absorption of American power into the maintenance of a moderately punitive European settlement had been a dominant goal of British policy at Paris, and the hope of some of the more far-sighted French leaders as well. It is not surprising then, that the League of Nations, a product of the interplay of reintegrationist and punitive tendencies at

[margin handwritten note: German ideas]

Paris, ended by combining the qualities both of a new community of democratic states under international law and of an extension of the Entente alliance against Germany into the postwar period. For Wilson, however, in the last analysis the League legitimized the absorption of American strength into European politics by seeming to contain the promise of the triumph of American-inspired world liberal order over both traditional imperialism and revolutionary-socialism.

*   *   *

Wilsonian Punishment and Control of Germany

One source of the contradiction noted above lay in Wilson's ambivalent attitude toward the German Revolution of 1918–1919. On the one hand, the President, as we have seen, was concerned lest the Revolution go too far to the Left and was, therefore, insistent that Germany be allowed the necessary food, economic relief, and military force to defend her fragile liberal political and economic institutions against revolutionary-socialism. In effect, then, Wilsonians supported the decision of Germany's moderate-socialists, backed by the army and the majority of the German people, to limit the Revolution to the area of formal constitutional democracy while leaving largely untouched the underlying social supports of German traditionalism in the form of conservative civil servants, army officers, Junker landowners, jurists, and large industrialists. Yet, having done all he could to prevent the radical revolutionists from dismantling the German social order root and branch, Wilson could not escape the paradoxical but related problem of the threat to German liberal stability posed by the still powerful German Right. How could Wilson be sure that the mild German Revolution he supported had really destroyed the roots of German militarism?   *Germ. problem for W.*

The evidence suggests that, beginning with his firm demands for German democratization in the pre-Armistice exchange of notes with the Government of Prince Max, the President remained concerned with the threat to Germany's new liberal order from the traditionally militaristic Right throughout the Peace Conference period. On several occasions Wilson revealed a belief that Germany ought not to be admitted to the League of Nations until she had passed through a probationary period, testing the staying power of

FIGURE 5. Upon the Answer Depends the Peace of the World. From the Chicago *Tribune.* (Historical Pictures Service, Chicago)

her new liberal institutions and the sincerity of <u>her complete dis-avowal of militarism</u>. Thus, just as in the President's pre-1917 mediation efforts and in his wartime attempts to appeal to German liberalism, so too, at Paris, a central problem for Wilsonian ideology and policy remained the inherent difficulty of reintegrating a Germany, perceived as extraordinary in its traditional militarism, into a projected liberal-capitalist international community. While it was natural for the Administration to support German liberalism against socialist revolution, could Wilsonians then trust the ability or the will of German liberalism to control the German Right?

In sum, Wilson feared the potential influence of the German Right in the postwar period, but he could not seek a destruction of the German Right by the German Left because, among other reasons, of his concern lest Bolshevism result and Germany be irrevocably lost to world liberal order. Inevitably, then, the President came to accept, with some efforts to moderate its severity, the basic Allied notion of the necessity of establishing postwar military and political control of the German state, a notion which became central both to the nature of the Armistice agreements and to the makeup of the very organizational structure of the Paris Peace Conference itself. The records of one negotiating session at Paris in February 1919 report Wilson as affirming that "he felt that until we know what the German Government was going to be, and how the German people were going to behave, the world had a moral right to disarm Germany, and to subject her to a generation of thoughtfulness."

For dominant French opinion the German Revolution created no real ideological dilemmas since the leading French publicists and decision-makers were convinced that the sociopolitical structure of Germany had been unchanged by the revolution and that, in any event, a unified and democratic Germany could be as great a threat to France as a more traditional Germany. In essence, the French, along with many of Wilson's Republican opponents at home, developed a critique of the German Revolution which, in many of its particulars, was paradoxically close to that of the German revolutionary-socialists themselves. Yet, while the German revolutionists hoped to destroy the German Right from within, Lodge and Clemenceau hoped to contain both Germany and revolution with military force. Wilson, torn between his reintegrationist and punitive orientations toward Germany, ultimately opted for a moderate system of military controls on a probationary German state. The irony was that, by partially accepting the basic assumption underlying the Paris Peace Conference, the assumption that a liberalized Germany was still a suspect nation to be controlled and dictated to rather than negotiated with as an equal, Wilsonians inadvertently played their own role in the creation of a self-fulfilling prophecy about the character of the postwar German state.

Lodge + Fr. aims

Peace treaty helped dictate future Germ.

There is also much evidence to suggest that, whatever his attitude toward German reintegration and the German Revolution, the President approached the Peace Conference with an extremely moralistic attitude of judicious, but nonetheless punitive, righteousness toward Germany. Wilson's desire for a "temper of high-minded justice" in the treatment of postwar Germany definitely ruled out Allied extremism but was not incompatible with a more punitive desire to make the German settlement an example of the harsh wages of international sin. Wilson felt it was possible to combine justice, rationality, and harshness in the creation of a German settlement. Thus, while it is important to emphasize Wilson's reintegrationist-oriented desire for a rational reparations settlement, it is equally important to stress that the issue between the President and the Allies on reparations was in reality a struggle over the method of collection from Germany and not a disagreement over the underlying assumption, accepted by both Wilsonians and the Allies, that a guilty Germany ought to be forced to pay large reparations. On one occasion, Wilson made quite explicit this fusion of rationality and harsh justice:

> He [Wilson] only looked towards reaching a peace and in doing so putting Germany in the position to build up a commerce which would enable her to pay what she ought to pay in order to make good the robbery and destruction she had perpetrated. But if the robber was to be in such a position that he could not pay the penalties would be inoperative. The penalties ought to be operative and real. We ought to see that Germany could put herself in a position where she could be punished.

It could be said that the President's reintegrationist approach toward Germany, modified by his punitive orientation, represented not so much a desire to accept the postwar liberalized German state on terms of equality and solidarity, as it represented an effort to curb Allied extremism just enough to permit Germany to be punished and controlled in a manner that would neither encourage Bolshevism nor prevent a lasting peace. In his Fontainebleau Memorandum, Lloyd George, well aware of the essential reintegrationist concerns over war and revolution, joined Wilson in the comforting assumption that the peace terms "may be severe, they may be stern and even ruthless, but at the same time they can be so just that the country

FIGURE 6. Letting Down a Ladder. From the New York *Evening Mail*. (Historical Pictures Service, Chicago)

on which they are imposed will feel in its heart that it has no right
to complain."

The President's response on May 16, 1919, to a critical letter
from General J. C. Smuts on the final peace terms reveals that,
whatever its contradiction to his reintegrationist approach, Wilson
retained throughout the Peace Conference a moralistic desire to
make Germany an example to mankind of the severe results of international criminality:

> *No apology was needed for your earnest letter of the fourteenth. The
> treaty is undoubtedly very severe indeed. I have of course had an oppor-
> tunity to go over each part of it as it was adopted and I must say that
> though it is in many respects harsh I do not think that it is on the whole
> unjust in the circumstances, much as I should have liked to have certain
> features altered. I am in entire agreement with you that real consideration
> should be given to the objections that are being raised against it by the
> Germans, and I think I find a growing inclination to treat their representa-
> tions fairly. As it happens, they have so far addressed their criticisms only
> to points which are substantially sound. I feel the terrible responsibility of
> this whole business, but invariably my thought goes back to the very great
> offense against civilization which the German state committed and the
> necessity for making it evidence once and for all that such things can lead
> only to the most severe punishment. I am sure you know the spirit in
> which I say these things and that I need not assure you that I am just as
> anxious to be just to the Germans as to be just to anyone else.*

While Wilson was not unwilling to reconsider the terms of the Treaty
in the light of Germany's counter proposals, he was somewhat less
receptive to such a reconsideration than either General Smuts or
the ardent reintegrationists in the American delegation. Indeed, in
May 1919, such committed reintegrationists as Lansing, Hoover,
Bliss, and White were convinced that the terms of the Treaty ought
to be revised in Germany's favor and were, therefore, happy when
Lloyd George was moved by some of his advisers and his own doubts
to call for last-minute revision of some of the harsher terms of the
settlement.

On June 3, 1919, a full meeting of the American Peace Commission was held to consider Lloyd George's proposals. At this meeting, Lansing, Bliss, White, Norman Davis, and Hoover all argued
from a reintegrationist orientation in an effort to win as many concessions for the Germans as possible. Wilson found himself in agree-

ment with the ardent reintegrationists on some issues, especially in matters concerning the reparations settlement and the plans for a continued military occupation of Germany, but the President's remarks to Lansing at one critical juncture of the meeting reveal that Wilson never lost his sense of punitive righteousness when dealing with policy matters relating to Germany:

> *Mr. Lansing was asking me if I did not think that it would be a good idea to ask each of our groups to prepare a memorandum of what might be conceded, and while I do not want to be illiberal in the matter, I should hesitate to say "yes" to that question. The question that lies in my mind is: "Where have they made good in their points?" "Where have they shown that the arrangements of the treaty are essentially unjust?" Not "Where have they shown merely that they are hard?," for they are hard—but the Germans earned that. And I think it is profitable that a nation should learn once and for all what an unjust war means in itself. I have no desire to soften the treaty, but I have a very sincere desire to alter those portions of it that are shown to be unjust, or which are shown to be contrary to the principles which we ourselves have laid down.*

Clearly, whatever his desire to reintegrate Germany into a postwar liberal world order safe from war and/or revolution, the President was less prepared than his most ardently reintegrationist advisers to make concessions to the new Germany in the process.

Finally, it should be noted that, on issues related to Germany's eastern frontiers with Poland and Czechoslovakia, the President was influenced both by his own pro-Slavic biases and by the strategically oriented advice of some anti-German experts serving on the staff of the American Inquiry at Paris. As a result, Wilson accepted territorial arrangements in the East which, if far too moderate by French, Polish, and Czechoslovakian standards, were definitely harsh from the standpoint of the German people assigned, for economic or strategic reasons, to the new Slavic States. Moreover, it is clear that, on Polish frontier issues in particular, Wilson, while in no sense acquiescing in all Polish demands, often stood somewhat closer to the Poles than did Lloyd George, whose Fontainebleau Memorandum had emphasized the dangers from Bolshevism and German nationalism latent in Poland's claims. The crucial point is not that Wilson was oblivious either to the dangers of postwar Polish militarism or to the reintegrationist insights of the Fontainebleau Memorandum,

[margin note: Harsh Slavic terms for Germans]

but rather that the President was not prepared to follow reintegrationist logic if it should lead, by way of appeasing German nationalism in the East, to any compromising of his vision of injustice to long-oppressed Slavic peoples.

Wilsonian Liberalism, the League of Nations, and the German Problem

Up to this point in our discussion, we have chosen, for analytic purposes, to treat separately the Wilsonian reintegrationist and punitive approaches toward Germany at Paris. By way of conclusion, however, it is important to attempt to speak of Wilsonian policy at the Paris Peace Conference in more comprehensive terms capable of subsuming the reintegrationist-punitive dialectic into a larger analytic synthesis. Ultimately we shall see that, for Wilson himself, the League of Nations served the function of resolving whatever contradictions were inherent in his efforts to create a European settlement which would control and punish Germany and which would, at the same time, also insure against war or revolution.

On the eve of the Peace Conference, there were some serious misconceptions in Europe and America as to the probable nature of Wilson's role in postwar world politics. Perhaps most indicative of this situation is the fact that late in 1918 and early 1919 some European political elements expected the President to play an openly radical, if non-Bolshevik, role in European politics. Hopes for some form of open radical solidarity with Wilson against the Entente Establishment were shared by the majority of Europe's social democrats who often found themselves torn between liberal and revolutionary anti-imperialism. Moreover, the Allied governments and the Republican opposition in the United States were concerned in late 1918 that the presence of the President in Europe, which would make direct contact between Wilson and the people probable, might lead to just such an overt Wilsonian-radical union against an extremist peace. Yet such radical hopes and conservative fears proved largely groundless, because they were based on an underestimation of the extent to which Wilsonians, for all their missionary American opposition to Old World imperialism, still remained fundamentally committed to the nonrevolutionary politics of centrist liberalism, to the accepted practices of international relations, and to inter-Allied unity against a defeated Germany. Let us turn then, to a more detailed analysis of the reasons behind Wilson's failure to satisfy his would-be allies among the non-Bolshevik European Left. *W to Leftists*

Part of the problem was that Wilson's supporters on the post-war Left seriously underestimated the extent to which the President and his advisers conceived of the Peace Conference in somewhat conventional terms, as a gathering of victorious Allies meeting to impose just but severe terms on a defeated criminal enemy. Social democratic hopes notwithstanding, Wilson was extremely reluctant at Paris ever to risk either inter-Allied unity or Entente political and military control of Germany in the process of attempting to check Allied extremism. Many European and American nonrevolutionary radicals who hoped that Wilson would use the Peace Conference as a forum from which to launch an anti-imperialist assault on the Allies, failed to comprehend that much of the President's crusading liberalism remained, even in the postwar period, directed primarily at German imperialism in particular rather than at European imperialism in general. Indeed, it is possible, after understanding Wilson's ambivalent attitude toward the German Revolution, to describe the President's reintegrationist critique of Allied extremism operationally as an effort to moderate an essentially punitive peace. In sum, then, the non-Bolshevik radical vision of postwar democratic-socialist solidarity between Wilson, the German revolutionaries, and the Allied Left against both Allied and German imperialism was checked *?* in part by the fact that Wilson ultimately chose moderated Allied *•* military and political power, and not some form of social-democratic solidarity, as his prime response to the threat of German imperialism.

No attack on European imperialism

Yet it must also be clear from what has just been said that, in the maintenance of his reluctance to play a more openly radical role at Paris in opposition to Allied extremism, Wilson's own commitment to the reformist politics of ordered liberalism was as important an element as was his punitive orientation toward Germany. It should be noted that Wilson had, as an historian, looked favorably on Edmund Burke's opposition to the French Revolution, and that the President had interpreted Burke's position as one based on progressive liberal pragmatism and oriented toward "a sober, provident, and ordered progress in affairs." Probably it was in an address delivered

"Ordered liberalism

before the International Law Society at Paris in the spring of 1919
that the President best expressed both his deeply felt opposition to
any form of socio-political radicalism and his sense of the tension
implicit in the role of the moderate reformer who seeks to contain
utopian impulses within the framework of international liberal legality:

> *May I say that one of the things that has disturbed me in recent months
> is the unqualified hope that men have entertained everywhere of immediate
> emancipation from the things that have hampered and oppressed them.
> You cannot in human experience rush into the light. You have to go
> through the twilight into the broadening day before the noon comes and
> the full sun is on the landscape; and we must see to it that those who
> hope are not disappointed, by showing them the processes by which that
> hope must be realized—processes of law, processes of slow disentangle-
> ment from the many things that have bound us in the past. You cannot
> throw off the habits of society immediately any more than you can throw
> off the habits of the individual immediately. They must be slowly got rid
> of, or, rather, they must be slowly altered. They must be slowly adapted,
> they must be slowly shapen to the new ends for which we would use them.
> This is the process of law, if law is intelligently conceived.*

The past must be overcome, but by an evolutionary rather than a
revolutionary process. In the postwar period, then, Wilson did not
hesitate to support the moderate politics of the anti-imperialism of
liberal order against both the passions of Jacobin-like Bolsheviks
and the class-oriented politics of Europe's social democrats. . . .

Since he was unwilling to risk either the control of Germany or
world liberal order by openly moving toward solidarity with the non-
Bolshevik Left in opposition to German and/or Allied imperialism at
Paris, Wilson was forced to devise another policy for the defense of
his international goals. The President needed a moderately reformist
program which would oppose both traditional imperialism and revolutionary-socialism, while remaining well grounded in the twin legitima-
cies of a liberal-capitalist nation-state system and of Allied-American
dominance over Germany. Somehow a program would have to be
devised which, while permitting Germany to be punished and controlled, would nonetheless retain enough reintegrationist features
to assure the gradual reabsorption of Germany into a viable non-
Bolshevik world of liberal order. Moreover, such a program would
also have to be able to legitimize ideologically the co-opting of

American power into the maintenance of a basically anti-German peace settlement, by providing a liberal vision going beyond mere punitive righteousness. Such a program would have to hold out the promise that America's complete involvement in world politics represented not a destruction of America's liberal-exceptionalism, but rather the possibility of restructuring world politics, under the inspiration of America's liberal idealism, into a new international order safe from imperialist war and from socialist revolution. Ultimately, such a program was available to Wilsonians in the form of the League of Nations. It will be important, therefore, to turn now to an analysis of the Wilsonian conception of the League of Nations, in order to understand how, for the President, the League seemed to resolve all the contradictions latent in his policies at the Paris Peace Conference.

The League of Nations issue is perhaps best viewed as an institutional and ideological microcosm containing all the tensions present in the postwar Wilsonian approach to the German question. On one level of analysis, therefore, it could be argued that, along with whatever more purely reintegrationist tendencies it certainly contained, Wilson's attitude toward the League also included his related but somewhat contradictory desire to punish and to control the defeated Germans. In his major address of September 27, 1918, Wilson made it clear that, for him, one of the essential functions of a projected League of Nations would be to enforce just peace terms on a probationary Germany:

If it be in deed and in truth the common object of the Governments associated against Germany and of the nations whom they govern, as I believe it to be, to achieve by the coming settlements a secure and lasting peace, it will be necessary that all who sit down at the peace table shall come ready and willing to pay the price, the only price, that will procure it; and ready and willing, also, to create in some virile fashion the only instrumentality by which it can be made certain that the agreements of the peace will be honored and fulfilled. That price is impartial justice in every item of the settlement, no matter whose interest is crossed; and not only impartial justice, but also the satisfaction of the several peoples whose fortunes are dealt with. That indispensable instrumentality is a League of Nations formed under covenants that will be efficacious. Without such an instrumentality, by which the peace of the world can be guaranteed, peace will rest in part upon the word of outlaws and only upon that word. For

Germany will have to redeem her character, not by what happens at the peace table, but by what follows.

In this connection, it is important to note that Wilson often made clear his belief that Germany ought to be excluded from the League of Nations, for a probationary period, while the Allied democracies made certain that Germany's autocratic political structure and imperialistic foreign policy had both been sufficiently liberalized. Moreover, it is also significant that on many occasions during 1919, the President spoke of the League's important role in guarding Poland and the other newly liberated states of Eastern Europe against any future economic or political aggression from Germany. Then, too, reflecting the interrelatedness of punitive and reintegrationist tendencies among Wilsonians at Paris, it is worth noting that, while Colonel House and General Bliss were more prepared than Wilson to admit Germany to the League immediately, both House and Bliss also saw the League, in part, as a device for controlling Germany.

Wilson and House also argued on occasion that the League of Nations could serve specifically as a defense for France against the threat of another German attack. Indeed, without some emphasis on the League as an anti-German bulwark, it is doubtful that Wilsonians would have been as successful as they were in moderating some of France's most extreme postwar designs on Germany. In a letter responding to Elihu Root's measured opposition to possible American overinvolvement in European politics, David Hunter Miller, the Wilsonian expert on international law at Paris, succinctly conveyed his awareness of the real necesssity of assuring France of America's commitment to the League of Nations, as an instrument of security against German aggression, in order to win French approval of more moderate peace terms:

The question discussed is not only one of the highest political importance but of immediate importance. France does not think that our interest in a future attack of Germany on France is secondary but primary, and feels that that possibility should be the first concern of the world in general and of America in particular, while admitting that no such attack for the next few years is possible. Whether this feeling on the part of France is right or wrong is not the question, for it exists in a degree which it is almost impossible to overstate, and any attempt to limit our responsibility in the matter would defeat the whole Covenant, for France would prefer then to make a different kind of peace with Germany and not to have a League. Certainly without the League we could hardly refuse her the right to make a peace with Germany which would let her feel secure, but such a peace would then be made as would be contrary to everything we have stood for.

David Hunter Miller's analysis of the anti-German security aspects implicit in the League as it emerged at Paris points up for us anew one of the central paradoxes of Wilsonian policy at the Peace Conference. In its efforts to check Allied extremism and to provide for the reintegration of a liberalized Germany into a new nonrevolutionary world order, the Wilson Administration was partly inhibited by the fact that the President, and many of his advisers, retained a punitive and a suspicious orientation toward the postwar German polity. Yet, even when they did disagree on German questions with the British and French, Wilsonians were also inhibited from more direct conflict with the Allies by the fear that an overt U.S.-Entente break might somehow give encouragement to manifest and latent revolutionary-socialist tendencies in postwar Europe. It followed, therefore, that to whatever extent the President and his advisers did choose to oppose Allied, and especially French, extremism at Paris, the Americans were not prepared to rely on the tactic of radical mass mobilization against imperialism. Instead, Wilsonians sought to moderate Allied policies behind the scenes by the implicit and explicit use of America's one viable weapon: namely the threat of the possible withdrawal of the economic, political, and military power of the United States from the immense task of guaranteeing the final European settlement. It must be noted, however, that, paradoxically, the employment of such tactics meant that every concession on the German question which the Administration won in negotiation with the Entente only served to bind American power more securely to the task of guaranteeing the peace settlement. The willingness of Wilson and House, despite the reintegrationist objections of Lansing, White, and Bliss, to join Great Britain and France in a special anti-German security treaty in return for French concessions to moderation in Rhineland negotiations was the classic case in point. In sum, then, part of the American conception of the League of Nations involved anti-German security considerations.

For their own part, unlike Wilson and his advisers, the postwar leaders of France saw the League only as a *de facto* military alliance to protect France from Germany. The French would accept moderation of their demands in the Rhineland only after the United States and Great Britain agreed to sign a special security treaty guaranteeing France against unprovoked German aggression. Thus, so deeply interrelated at Paris were the Wilsonian reintegrationist and punitive orientations toward Germany that, whatever the inherent tension between them, both these approaches often coexisted in the Wilsonian response to such issues as the reparations tangle and the question of the League and French security.

In any event, there is no doubt that on one level Wilsonians were definitely prepared to conceive of the League partly as an instrument for enforcing the final peace terms on Germany, notwithstanding whatever inherent contradiction such a view might involve for the Administration's equally strong desire to reintegrate a democratized Germany into a nonrevolutionary liberal-capitalist world order. In this sense, the Wilsonian orientation toward the League tended to merge well with the world views of such leading British statesmen as Lloyd George, who envisioned the absorption of American power permanently into the maintenance of a peace settlement in Europe which would fuse punitive and reintegrationist features in an uneasy balance. It is also interesting to observe that, during 1919, many security-conscious elements of the French Center and Right moved from opposition to later support of the President, as it became clear that he meant to pledge American power to the protection of France and to the maintenance of the severe peace settlement through the League of Nations and the related security treaty.

Yet if, during 1919, the French and British leaders moved to support Wilson and the League, it is true that, conversely, Europe's democratic-socialists and Left-liberals tended to move from initial support of the President to an increased rejection of Wilsonian policies. Desperate in their search of a way to end imperialism without socialist revolution, many democratic-socialists hoped that Wilson would create a League which, rather than being made up exclusively of the representatives of various foreign offices, would instead reflect the diversity of class and party interests in each member country, and would, thereby, provide a world forum capable both of being strongly influenced by socialist values and of transcending the nation-state system of world politics. However, having underestimated Wilson's loyalty to liberal-nationalist legitimacy, his distaste for any form of socialist politics, and his desire to control Germany by reliance on Allied armed power rather than through more radical means, the democratic-socialists were necessarily disillusioned by the actual League of Nations, which emerged as a union of governments implicitly pledged, in part, to enforce an anti-German peace. Radicals could see clearly that, far from ending such contradictions in world politics as the German question by any sort of revolutionary transformation, the League created by the statesmen at Paris was itself partially based on those very contradictions.

Within the Wilsonian delegation itself, at Paris, a critical approach toward the postwar Allied-American political agreements also developed among such ardent reintegrationists as Lansing, Bliss, White, and Hoover. Convinced of the necessity strongly to oppose the Allies in the interests of a moderate settlement which would strengthen Germany as a bastion of liberal political and economic stability, these committed reintegrationists were often fearful that, in secret negotiations, House and Wilson would allow American power to be absorbed fully by the Allies into the maintenance of a severely anti-German peace capable of producing war or social revolution. Lansing, for one, even went so far as to be deeply critical of the League of Nations, which he saw as basically an alliance of the victorious powers formed primarily to enforce harsh peace terms on Germany. Lansing had envisioned instead a League with no real powers of enforcement which, by immediately including a liberalized Germany and by bringing all nations to pledge allegiance to the principles of liberal-internationalism on an equalitarian basis, could not have implicitly become a postwar extension of the Entente alliance. In part, then, [Lansing, Hoover, and Bliss became somewhat "isolationist" in their reactions to events at Paris, in that they sought to keep America free from entangling economic and political ties to the Allies.] Yet, their "isolationism" was always ambivalent at best, since these ardent reintegrationists also hoped, in their own way, to make possible, under the guidance of a liberal-exceptionalist America uncontaminated by power politics, the creation of a more inclusive international system of political and economic liberalism, safe from either traditional imperialism or Bolshevism.

It is true that at Paris neither Wilson nor House was indifferent either to general reintegrationist criticism of Allied policy or to the desire of the most committed American reintegrationists to defend America's political and economic freedom against possible Allied absorption. At the same time, and to a greater extent than Lansing, Bliss or White, both Wilson and House were also prepared to view the League as a device making possible the involvement of American power in the tasks of controlling Germany and of enforcing the peace settlement. Indeed, Wilson's defense of the League Covenant in America during the summer and early fall of 1919 was partly based on the argument that the League was needed to maintain American-Allied unity in the face of a Germany which had suffered severe but just punishment. This apparent contradiction could be wholly resolved in the realm of ideology, if not so completely in the area of practice, since both House and the President also saw the League of Nations as having strong counterbalancing reintegrationist potentialities.

Along with their more static vision of the League as a defender of the Versailles settlement, both the President and Colonel House also saw the League as a potentially flexible instrument through which the imperfect decisions made at Paris could be readjusted in the future. Unwilling completely to share the view of such reintegrationist critics as Lansing, Wilson and House preferred to view the League more broadly and hopefully as a living liberal institution capable of constant adaptation and growth. "A living thing is born," said Wilson of the League at one point, "and we must see to it that the clothes we put on it do not hamper it—a vehicle of power, but a vehicle in which power may be varied at the discretion of those who exercise it and in accordance with the changing circumstances of the times." Similarly, the President hoped that America's postwar participation in the work of the Reparations Commission would make possible a rational readjustment of the problematic reparations settlement which Wilsonians had been forced to accept at Paris. For Wilson, then, the League was the means of extending to the world scene an American vision of pragmatic and progressive change within the confines of a liberal order.

In this general context it is of interest to note that even such ardent reintegrationists and critics of the Paris settlement as Hoover, Lansing, Bliss, and White were in no sense immune to the notion that the League might prove to be useful in an imperfect world, by assuring some degree of continued international cooperation in the interests of world stability. Lansing's memoirs make clear that, for him, his eventual support of the cause of treaty ratification represented no change of heart from his critical stance at Paris, but rather a sense that American ratification of the Treaty and the League Covenant was necessary to the prevention of social chaos:

> My own position was paradoxical. I was opposed to the Treaty, but signed it and favored its ratification. The explanation is this: Convinced after conversations with the President in July and August, 1919, that he would not consent to any effective reservations, the politic course seemed to be to endeavor to secure ratification without reservations. It appeared to be the only possible way of obtaining that for which all the world longed and which in the months succeeding the signature appeared absolutely essential to prevent the widespread disaster resulting from political and economic chaos which seemed to threaten many nations if not civilization itself. Even if the Treaty was bad in certain provisions, so long as the President remained inflexible and insistent, its ratification without change seemed a duty to humanity.

It is quite probable that, considering his general world view, Lansing had Bolshevism in mind when he referred to a "widespread disaster resulting from political and economic chaos which seemed to threaten many nations if not civilization itself." Ironically, Colonel House, a man whose constant efforts to compromise with the Allies had drawn Lansing's wrath at Paris, had been himself moved to compromise in the interests of a speedy peace partly because of a fear that Bolshevism was growing in the atmosphere of postwar uncertainty. In any event, it could be said that, in the aftermath of the Paris Peace Conference, the differences between Wilson and such reintegrationist critics within the Administration as Hoover and Lansing tended to be submerged in a unified Wilsonian effort to attain both Treaty ratification and the maintenance of world liberal-capitalist stability in the face of intransigent criticism of the Versailles Peace from the Left and the Right in the United States.

In the realm of ideology, Wilson's reintegrationist conception of the League was more powerful than his somewhat contradictory vision of the League as a means for controlling Germany and enforcing the peace settlement. After all, the President did feel that Germany would be admitted to the League after having proved her liberal sincerity, and that Germany's eventual admittance could help to ease certain problems latent in the terms of the Treaty. On September 13, 1919, Wilson clearly affirmed his idea of the future reintegration, after a period of probation, of a truly liberalized Germany:

> *I read you these figures in order to emphasize and set in a higher light, if I may, the substitute which is offered to us, the substitute for war, the substitute for turmoil, the substitute for sorrow and despair. That substitute is offered in the Covenant of the League of Nations. America alone cannot underwrite civilization. All the great free peoples of the world must underwrite it, and only the free peoples of the world can join the League of Nations. The membership is open only to self-governing nations. Germany is for the present excluded, because she must prove that she has changed the processes of her constitution and the purposes of her policy; but when she has proved these things she can become one of the partners in guaranteeing that civilization shall not suffer again the intolerable thing she attempted.*

Thus, Wilson's conception of the League as an inter-Allied instrument to control a justly punished Germany was ultimately transcended by the President's related but broader vision of the League of Nations as an inclusive concert of liberal powers into which a reformed Germany could eventually be reintegrated.

As early as spring 1918 the President had urged that the League ought not to be "an alliance or a group formed to maintain any sort of balance of power, but must be an association which any nation is at liberty to join which is willing to cooperate in its objects and qualify in respect of its guarantees." Similarly, at Paris, Wilson affirmed that "there must now be, not a balance of power, not one powerful group of nations set off against another, but a single overwhelming, powerful group of nations who shall be the trustee of the world." Of course, it is clear that, for a time, the powerful trustees would be the victorious Allied powers, but it is significant, as Colonel House made plain, that one of the reasons for America's rejection of the French plan for an official League army was the Wilsonian concern lest the French succeed in turning the League completely into an anti-German instrument. In sum, then, the basic Wilsonian reintegrationist conception of the League, as an inclusive community of liberal states mutually pledged to defend international law and

League to become ideologically free

one another's territorial integrity, had the potential of ideologically transcending the actual anti-German context from within which the League emerged at Paris.

At one point, while in England late in 1918, the President spoke of the League in terms which contained many of the ambiguities already discussed:

> I wish that it were possible for us to do something like some of my very stern ancestors did, for among my ancestors are those very determined persons who were known as the Convenanters. I wish we could, not only for Great Britain and the United States, but for France and Italy and the world, enter into a great league and covenant, declaring ourselves, first of all, friends of mankind and uniting ourselves together for the maintenance and the triumph of right.

On the one hand, both the direct mention of the Allied powers as forming the moral core of the League, and the reference to stern covenanted unity in "the maintenance and the triumph of right," could imply the creation of a League simply to defend a righteously punitive settlement against Germany. On the other hand, however, such phrases as "and the world" and "friends of mankind" obviously suggest the more inclusive and reintegrationist possibilities of Wilsonian liberal-internationalism.

There can be no doubt that the President saw the League of Nations, in part, as a postwar inter-Allied police force growing naturally out of the progressive nucleus of the Allied-American liberal alliance which had defeated the special reactionary challenge to world liberalism posed by German autocratic imperialism. Yet, beyond the necessary defeat of atavistic German imperialism, there also existed the larger Wilsonian hope to so reorganize world politics as to prevent any other nation from repeating Germany's imperialistic actions in the future. In his defense of the Versailles settlement, the President was concerned not only with reforming and controlling Imperial Germany; he also sought to liberalize the entire imperialistic system of European politics within which an autocratic Germany had simply played the most militant and aggressive single role. The President often combined an argument to the effect that the League was the necessary culmination to the triumph of world liberalism over German imperialism with a broader argument that the League

FIGURE 7. The Fifteenth Point. From *Reynold's Newspaper* (London). (Historical Pictures Service, Chicago)

was also the means by which world liberalism would finally reform the Old World's traditional balance-of-power system.

The point is that, speaking theoretically, Germany's eventual re-integration was latent in the Wilsonian critique of the traditional imperialistic system. Had Wilson joined the French in merely seeking to punish and to control German imperialism alone, the League of Nations would have been only a postwar extension of the Entente alliance. To be sure, the League was, in part, just such a peacetime extension of the anti-German wartime alliance, yet the Wilsonian critique of European imperialism also contained an implicit condemnation both of any continued Allied reliance on the old diplo-

Wilson's League embodies New Diplomacy

macy of the balance of power and of any Allied failure to live up to liberal values in the future. For the President, then, the League Covenant projected the vision of a liberal world order, transcending the historical and traditional restraints of power politics, into which a liberalized Germany could eventually be reintegrated as a full partner.

Wilson conceived the essence of the League as an orderly social contract among the nations. The international social contract represented by the Covenant of the League was to rescue the world from an insecure "Hobbesian" state of nature in which nations could find temporary security only through armaments and the balance of power. The President saw the League Covenant as establishing a new cooperative international society, governed by liberal norms, whose nation-state members would be pledged to substitute public discussion and peaceful arbitration under world law for the reactionary diplomatic practices of secret diplomacy or armed conflict. Indeed, Wilson always put far more emphasis on the universal moral force of world liberal opinion, focused in an association of self-governing states, than he did on the armed power of the League members.

In Wilson's new "Lockeanized" international environment, in which formerly hostile nations had been theoretically transformed into equal law-abiding liberal world citizens, all countries, weak and strong alike, were to eschew power politics and were also to covenant together, under Article X of the League of Nations Covenant, to defend each other's legal rights and territorial integrity. On one occasion, the President pithily expressed his orderly liberal desire to transform a world political system in which, historically, might had made right, by remarking that he hoped "to make a society instead of a set of barbarians out of the governments of the world." The League Covenant, then, ultimately represented for Wilson the fulfillment of America's historic mission to lead the Old World away from the traditional war-producing diplomacy of the balance of power to an harmonious American-inspired liberal world order of international responsibility under law. In the eyes of the President the League Covenant was the embodiment of American and world liberalism's final triumph over the imperialistic and atavistic restraints of the pre-liberal historical past.

There can be little doubt that, without his faith that the League offered a new liberal beginning in world politics, in which the concept of a universal concert of powers replaced the old notion of a balance of power, the President would not have been willing to involve the United States so permanently in European affairs. Given Wilson's missionary conception of the universality of America's liberal-nationalism, the League legitimized for him the involvement of American power in world politics by permitting him the assumption that, far from being absorbed as another competing element into the traditional global political reality, American strength was enabled, by the League, to enter world politics at the very moment that world politics was transcended by liberal-internationalism. For Wilson America's involvement in world affairs was inseparably joined with America's effort to lead a liberal anti-imperialist transformation of global reality through the League of Nations. In a theoretical sense, then, the League may be seen as Wilson's answer to reintegrationist critics, such as Hoover and Lansing, who feared lest Allied absorption of America's political and economic power might end hopes for the establishment of an American-inspired world of liberal-capitalist harmony.

For Wilson, the ultimate mission of a liberal exceptionalist America was to lead the rest of the world, without socialist revolution, to a universal liberal triumph over all elements of pre-bourgeois reaction and atavistic imperialism. The war years had seen a strengthening of the President's faith that, under his leadership, the United States was fulfilling this historic destiny by uniting America, the Allies, and common peoples of all countries in a liberal people's war on behalf of freedom and the creation of a new anti-imperialist world order. In the postwar period as well, Wilson was more than ever certain that it was the duty of the American state to continue to act selflessly as the leader of world liberalism in the effort to create a new international system free of power politics and Europe's traditional balance of power. In this connection, it is not surprising that the President saw the American-inspired League of Nations as a logical extension, to the entire world, of America's effort, under the Monroe Doctrine, to keep European reaction out of the Western Hemisphere. In essence, therefore, Wilson saw a powerful postwar America as the leader of the liberal opinion of the world, as the selfless and trusted arbiter of international problems, and as the disinterested defender of a new world order against both traditional imperialism and revolutionary socialism. For the President, America's political, economic, and military self-interest was inseparably joined to America's missionary idealism, in the Wilsonian struggle for international liberal stability.

In the final analysis the League of Nations proved to be the central element in the Wilsonian vision of an Americanized postwar world order in which the contradictions of international politics would be resolved in a new liberal harmony. While it is true that the League provided a means to enforce a severe peace on Germany, it is also true that, for Wilson, the League held out the promise of the eventual reintegration of a reformed Germany into an American-inspired liberal-capitalist world order safe from war and/or socialist revolution. Moreover, by maintaining the basic legitimacy of the nation-state system, the League was a logical expression of Wilson's effort, based on his ideology of American liberal-exceptionalism, to combine the leadership of world liberal anti-imperialism with his somewhat contradictory position as the leader of the military powerful American nation-state. Finally, by permitting Wilson to link ideologically American nationalism with liberal-internationalism, the League was the culmination of the President's vision of an orderly American-inspired reform of the traditional world political-economy. Such Wilsonian international reform, by using the League to establish a universal liberal-capitalist stability without class conflict, would ultimately defeat both atavistic imperialism and revolutionary socialism, the two mutually reinforcing barriers to the final realization of America's true national interest and pre-eminence in a liberal world order.

Documents

WILSON AND GERMANY AT PARIS

The following documents, arranged chronologically, are presented as evidence of Wilson's approach to the German question at the Paris Peace Conference.

CABLE FROM COMMISSIONER HENRY WHITE TO SENATOR LODGE ON DANGER OF BOLSHEVISM IN POSTWAR GERMANY

The Commission to Negotiate Peace to the Acting Secretary of State

Paris, 8 January, 1919.

For Senator Lodge from Mr. Henry White. Feel I should no longer delay laying before you condition which has been gradually forcing itself upon our Delegation and which now dominates entire European situation above all else; namely: steady westward advance of Bolshevism. It now completely controls Russia and Poland and is spreading through Germany. Only effective barrier now apparently possible against it is food relief, as Bolshevism thrives only on starvation and disorder. Consensus of opinion is that joint military occupation which has been suggested by France for Poland, even if practical would not solve problem. Confidentially Paderewski has sent us a most urgent appeal for assistance in Poland where conditions he says are desperate. I consider it therefore of utmost importance that President's request for hundred million appropriation for relief be granted at once. Impossible to inaugurate Peace Conference under proper auspices without previous adequate provision to cope with situation. Aside from stoppage of Bolshevism, I understand there is in United States considerable surplus of food accumulated at high prices maintenance whereof guaranteed by our government or assurance under its auspices and that it is necessary to dispose of this surplus in order to relieve warehouse and financial facilities as well

From United States Department of State, *Papers Relating to the Foreign Relations of the United States: The Paris Peace Conference, 1919*, 13 vols. (Washington, D.C., 1942–1947), II, p. 711; III, pp. 708–709, 901, 1001–1002; IV, pp. 417–418; V, pp. 232–233, 800–801; XI, pp. 568–569; XI, pp. 198, 218–220.

as prevent serious fall in prices with radical break in market which would cost our country more than the appropriation asked for. The appropriation is not for the purpose of advancing money to Germany which will pay on a cash basis for any food sent there. It is too late I fear to stop Bolshevism in Russia and Poland, but there is still hope of making Germany, Roumania and certain other areas effective barriers. . . .

WILSON ON GERMAN DISARMAMENT

Records of Sessions of the Supreme War Council Held at the Quai d'Orsay, Paris, on January 24, February 7, and February 12, 1919

Meeting of January 24, 1919. Marshal Foch replied that the controlling parties would only be allowed to see what the Germans wished them to see. Undoubtedly, guarantees could be taken by seizing arms, but it was doubtful whether they would give them all up. In addition, munition factories could be taken over, but it would be quite impossible to occupy them all. Our own line of action could not be based on the estimate of the military situation existing in Germany at any given time, because it would be impossible to say what the actual military strength of Germany at the time really was. . . . To sum up, he maintained that clauses relating to demobilization, including the surrender of arms and the seizure of munition factories, could be entered in the armistice, but it would be very dangerous to base our policy on the assumption that these conditions would be fulfilled. He urged, therefore, that the Allied Governments should make no reductions in the agreed strengths of the armies of occupation, at all events before the 31st March next.

President Wilson asked that the following aspect of this matter be considered before coming to a conclusion. It had been stated that the officers of the German army had no control over their men. Consequently, even if remobilization were ordered, it probably could not be carried out. They had also been told that the men were merely hanging round the depots in order to be fed. It was admitted that it would be very difficult for Germany to establish any credit until she could resume her economic life. Obviously this was difficult under present conditions; meanwhile, the number of unemployed must increase, and would still further increase if demobilization were hastened. The increase of unemployment would widen the soil for the seeds of Bolshevism, and so create a Germany with which it would be impossible to deal at all. Moreover, sooner or later the Allies would be compelled to trust Germany to keep her promises. When peace would be signed, should we still be compelled to maintain a great army of occupation to make sure that Germany would keep her promises? In the Peace Treaty, Germany might agree to maintain a smaller army; should we be compelled to keep an army on her border to ensure the fufilment of this promise? The real solution of the question lay in an early peace. Peace would bring with it a settlement of the many questions which were troubling Europe, which now consisted of a seething body of an uncertain and fearful people who did not know what fate awaited them. He put forward these considerations, though he realized they did not lead to a definite conclusion.

Mr. Lloyd George agreed with President Wilson that the only satisfactory solution of the difficulty would be the making of peace. But they, in Great Britain, were compelled to face the problem of demobilization at once. It was a very serious problem. Great Britain was not a military nation like France, and the people were not disciplined. Therefore, he felt compelled at once to say that he was doubtful whether Great Britain could contribute the troops asked for. At any rate, he could give no undertaking. He would, without further delay, have to discuss the question with his advisers in order to arrive at an immediate conclusion. He admitted that it might be best to put off the decision until the signing of the Peace Treaty; but they could not do that in Great Britain. Some means must, therefore, be devised for reducing their effort.

Marshal Foch's argument really meant that Germany could never be trusted, and, therefore, that the armies of occupation could never be materially reduced. On the other hand, he thought they had in food, raw material, and the seizure of arms, better means of controlling the situation in Germany. As long as it was a question of fighting, they had had no difficulty with the British troops. But, now that the soldiers were standing to their arms, whilst many of their comrades were being demobilized and were able to obtain good employment at high rates of pay, the feelings of discontent were bound to arise, which made matters extremely difficult. . . .

President Wilson said that he did not think the German people would be willing to take up arms again, nor that Germany could in her present condition possibly carry out an organized war against organized Governments. He would ask that a draft resolution be drawn up embodying in explicit terms the proposals made by Mr. Lloyd George. This resolution could then be submitted to the meeting, and brought under discussion. He thought they should at the same time study a scheme to relieve unemployment in Germany. In his opinion, Bolshevism was the greatest danger, and the only real protection against it was food and industry. Consequently, whilst demobilizing the German Army, they should take steps to protect themselves against the greater danger of Bolshevism. . . .

Meeting of February 7, 1919. President Wilson said that the last time armistice conditions had been discussed, he had thought it his duty to oppose any addition to the armistice terms. He thought that the council should have known what it was doing when the armistice was drawn up, and that it was not sportsmanlike to attempt to correct now the errors that had then been made. It was quite clear to him that the Allies were running a grave risk of bringing about a situation when, having made a threat, they might be challenged to carry it out. He understood that the Allies already controlled in the occupied districts of Germany 26 million out of 32 million tons of the iron production of Germany. He was afraid that the control of the factories by officers, as proposed, would prove insufficient, and that it would become necessary to occupy more territory, with the result that the military commanders would require more troops. It had already been suggested by Mr. Lloyd George that, as Germany was paying for the army of occupation, it would clearly be to her interest to reduce this burden. It must also be remembered that if the demobilization of the German Army were imposed on a large scale, Germany would have forced on her a large body of unemployed, who would add to the element of unrest and be a danger to Germany and to the Allies. It was, therefore, to the interest of the latter to give Germany the means of renewing her economic life, not only for the purpose of reducing the number of unemployed, but also to enable her to pay the reparations which the Allies had a right to expect. He, therefore, proposed the institution of a civil commission to meet a similar German commission, to negotiate with them and to say— that if Germany would reduce her forces and yield a proper proportion of her mischievous equipment, the Allies would reduce their army of occupation, reducing the charges therefore; they would at the same time relax the blockade to allow the passage of sufficient raw materials, except for armaments, to enable her to renew her economic life.

He thought in that way the Allies would avoid doing the improper thing of exacting terms, without running the risk of renewing war and of bringing about an intolerable state of affairs.

Meeting of February 12, 1919. President Wilson said that after reflecting on the morning's proceedings he had come to the conclusion that the difference of opinion was reduced to one point. That point was one of great importance. Mr. Balfour had made the difficulty quite clear by saying that we should not delay until our forces were so reduced that we could not compel the Germans to accede to our demands. This was the point that he had himself sought to make clear. By reducing our forces month by month, and by renewing the armistice month by month, we might be led to a stage at which Germany could resist with some prospect of success. He wished to be sure the danger point was past before reducing the Allied forces to the extent mentioned in the morning. Should trouble arise, he would be quite willing to re-mobilize the American forces, but this might be difficult, and it would certainly be a lengthy process, as the troops would have scattered to their homes. The longer we dealt with the Germans on this plan, the longer their hopes would have to grow. This might lead them to a false sense of self-confidence, and the German Government's forces might consolidate in a way which it was not at present possible to forecast, and the ancient pride and boastfulness of Germany might gain a new lease of life. The point under discussion in the morning concerning which no agreement had been reached was the question whether the military terms of peace could be isolated from the other conditions of peace. Peace, it had been said, was one fabric with one pattern. The plan of general disarmament, which had been alluded to, seemed to render it difficult as a provisional measure to prejudge what should be the relative strengths of national forces. Disarmament contained two elements—(1) the maintenance of an adequate force for internal police; (2) the national contribution to the general force of the future League of Nations. At present we did not contemplate that Germany should make any contribution to the latter force. We need therefore not take that element into consideration. All we need contemplate was the amount of armed force required by Germany to maintain internal order and to keep down Bolshevism. This limit could be fixed by the military advisers. In general, he felt that until we knew what the German Government was going to be, and how the German people were going to behave, the world had a moral right to disarm Germany, and to subject her to a generation of thoughtfulness. He therefore thought it was possible to frame the terms of Germany's disarmament before settling the terms of peace. He was encouraged in this belief by the assurance that the military advisers could produce a plan in forty-eight hours. It might take more than forty-eight for the heads of Governments to agree on this plan. It was not his idea that the armistice should be protracted very much longer, but a definite term could not be fixed until the Governments had matured their judgment concerning the disarmament of Germany. Once this point was settled, the Germans could be given short notice to accede to our demands under pain of having the armistice broken. The main thing was to do this while our forces were so great that our will could not be resisted. The plan he proposed would make safety antedate the peace. He thought that this brought the two views into accord as regards the purpose in the minds of both parties to the morning's debate. . . .

M. Clemenceau said that the purpose pursued by President Wilson was exactly the same as his own. He was therefore prepared to accept his proposal. Before doing so, however, he would like more precise information on certain points. We were to ask the experts to state as quickly as possible the conditions of the disarmament of Germany. The American experts, President Wilson had said, were ready. The French were also ready.

Mr. Balfour remarked that the English were ready, too.

WILSON ON THE POLISH-GERMAN BORDER

Secretary's Notes of a Conversation Held at the Quai d'Orsay, Paris, March 19, 1919

Mr. Lloyd George said that though the British delegates had adopted the conclusions, they had done so reluctantly. They regarded them as a departure from the principles of the Fourteen Points which had been adopted by the Allies. In some parts of the territory assigned to Poland the argument of political colonization did not apply. We were told, moreover, that a region colonized with Germans as far back as the eighteenth century should be restored to Poland. But because fifty years ago some capitalists had built a railway that was convenient to the Poles, the area surrounding it must be ascribed to Poland, in spite of the undoubted German nationality of the population. M. Cambon had said that a corridor to the sea was necessary to Poland. He had nothing to say against this. The Vistula was a navigable river, and must remain the principal artery for commerce. There were, moreover, other railways. A railway could be removed, but a long-settled population was not removed with the same ease. He thought that in accepting these proposals the Council would be abandoning its principles and making trouble, not only for Poland, but for the world. Wherever it could be shown that the policy aimed at reversing the German policy of Polish expropriation the decision might be accepted by the Germans, but the areas he had in mind would be represented as "Germania Irredenta" and would be the seed of future war. Should the populations of these areas rise against the Poles, and should their fellow-countrymen wish to go to their assistance, would France, Great Britain and the United States go to war to maintain Polish rule over them? He felt bound to make this protest against what he considered to be a most dangerous proposal.

President Wilson said that the discussion had brought out a difficulty which, it had been said, would be met in many cases, and he had not reached a definite conclusion in his own mind on the particular point under discussion. He hoped that the discussion would be carried far enough to bring out all its elements. Everywhere in Europe blocks of foreign people would be found whose possession of the country could be justified by historic, commercial and similar arguments. He acknowledged that the inclusion of two million Germans in Poland was a violation of one principle; but Germany had been notified that free and safe access to the sea for Poland would be insisted upon. The Allied and Associated Powers were therefore not open to the reproach that they were doing this merely because they had the power to do it. This was one of the things they had fought for. The difficulty was to arrive at a balance between conflicting considerations. He thought Mr. Lloyd George was misinformed in saying that the river carried the largest proportion of the commerce. He would find that the railroad along the river carried the greater, or at least an equal amount, of the traffic.

Mr. Lloyd George pointed out that he was referring not to the railroad along the river, but to the one further to the east.

President Wilson said that the proposal would, however, leave in German hands territories abutting on the westerly railroad at several points.

M. Cambon said that the direct line to Warsaw through Mlawa was quite near the frontier proposed by the Committee. Mr. Lloyd George had mentioned the Vistula as the main artery of traffic. Marienwerder dominated the Vistula as well as the railway lines, and anyone holding that place commanded the valley.

M. Pichon pointed out that there were only two lines of railroads from Dantzig to supply twenty millions of people. One of these was through Thorn and the other through Mlawa. The latter passed east of Marienwerder, this was the one referred to by Mr. Lloyd George. Both were indispensable to the economic life of Poland.

Mr. Lloyd George admitted that the line from Mlawa was important, but did not regard it as essential for access of Poland to the sea.

President Wilson said that it must be realized the Allies were creating a new and weak state, weak not only because historically it had failed to govern itself, but because it was sure in the future to be divided into factions, more especially as religious differences were an element in the situation. It was therefore necessary to consider not only the economic but the strategic needs of this state, which would have to cope with Germany on both sides of it, the eastern fragment of Germany being one of a most aggressive character. There was bound to be a mixture of hostile populations included in either state. The Council would have to decide which mixture promised the best prospect of security. He was afraid himself of drawing the line as near the Dantzig-Thorn railway line as Mr. Lloyd George suggested. He, however, felt the same anxieties as Mr. Lloyd George. The desire might arise among the Germans to rescue German populations from Polish rule, and this desire would be hard to resist. It was a question of balancing antagonistic considerations. He had wished to bring out the other elements in the problem.

WILSON ON GERMAN REPARATIONS

Notes of Two Meetings Held at President Wilson's Residence, Place des Etats-Unis, Paris, April 25 and May 21, 1919

Meeting of April 25, 1919. President Wilson said that one aspect was constantly in his mind in regard to the whole of the Treaty with Germany. When the German plenipotentiaries came to Versailles they would be representatives of a very unstable Government. Consequently, they would have to scrutinize every item, not merely to say that it was equitable, but also as to whether it could be agreed to without their being unseated. If the present Government were unseated, a weaker Government would take its place. Hence the question had to be studied like a problem of dynamics concerning the action of forces in a body in unstable equilibrium. Any special restrictions on their nationals which they could not meet by corresponding restrictions would place them in difficulties. The Treaty would hit them very hard since it would deprive them of their Mercantile Marine; would affect their international machinery for commerce; would deprive them of their property in other countries; would open their country by compulsion to enterprising citizens of other countries without enabling their enterprising citizens to try and recover their position in foreign countries. He did not think that the fact had been sufficiently faced that Germany could not pay in gold unless she had a balance of trade in her favor. This meant that Germany must establish a greater foreign commerce than she had had before the war if she was to be able to pay. Before the war the balance of trade in Germany's favor had never equalled the amounts which she would now have to pay. If too great a handicap was imposed on Germany's resources we should not be able to get what Germany owed for reparation. Moreover, if the business world realized that this was the case the securities on which the payment of reparation would depend would have no value. If this reasoning was sound it provided a formidable argument. He only looked towards reaching a peace and in doing so putting Germany in the position to build up a commerce which would enable her to pay what she ought to pay in order to make good the robbery and destruction she had perpetrated. But if the robber was to be in such a position that he could not pay, the penalties would be inoperative. These penalties ought to be operative and real. We ought to see that Germany could put herself in a position where she could be punished. At the present time we were sending food to Germany but she would not be able to pay for that for more than about two months. . . .

Meeting of May 21, 1919.   President Wilson said he would like to intimate to the Germans that the experts of the Allied and Associated Powers were now ready to discuss with their Experts in regard to Financial and Economic Conditions.

M. Clemenceau thought it would weaken the Allied and Associated Powers.

President Wilson said that his object was to demonstrate to Europe that nothing had been left undone which might have induced the Germans to have signed. If they did not sign it would involve sending troops into the heart of Germany and their retention there for a long period. Germany could not pay the costs of this occupation which would pile up the expenses to people who were already protesting against the burden of occupation. People would ask if there was anything reasonable left undone which might have averted this. There would be no loss of dignity by carrying out this plan. The experts of the Allied and Associated Powers would merely explain the meaning of some parts of the Treaty of Peace which, in his view, the Germans had failed to understand. If our Experts could show that no heavier burden had been laid on the German people than justice required, it might make it easier for the German Delegates to explain to their own people.

M. Clemenceau thought that this would serve the objects of the Germans. He agreed that they would probably leave without signing, but when troops began to move, they would sign soon enough. They wanted some excuse with their own people to make them sign.

Mr. Lloyd George thought that sufficient excuse would be given if some concession could be gained. He had nothing particular in mind but there might be some concession which did not matter very much which could be made. The question would not be decided until the German answer to our proposals was available. He had in his mind that they would make proposals perhaps about coal.

M. Clemenceau said we had a very strong answer on this. He had seen some extraordinary effective figures of M. Loucheur's.

Mr. Lloyd George thought they might also make proposals about restoration. He thought before deciding this question, it would be better to await the German reply and to keep an open mind on the subject.

President Wilson said that the letter which had just been considered gave a conclusive reply to the German letter but provided no ray of hope. It merely said that the Treaty was right and nothing more. He had understood that the experts who had discussed with the German Financial Experts at Villette found Herr Melchior a very sensible man. Melchior was now one of the German Delegates, and he was a representative of the kind of people in Germany who wanted to get their industries going again, and he wanted to avoid the chaos and confiscations of property and looting which had occurred elsewhere. These people wanted to get their country started again, and they would listen to what our experts had to say. The United States Experts had, all along, said that the present scheme of reparation would not yield much. This was Mr. Norman Davis' view, and Mr. Keynes, the British expert, shared it. He himself wanted the Allies to get reparation. He feared they would get very little. If it could be shown to Melchior that the Reparation Commission was allowed to consider the condition of Germany and to adjust the arrangements accordingly from time to time, it might enable him to persuade the German people.

M. Clemenceau said that President Wilson was right, but he did not want to be placed in the position of a man who was begging a favor. He preferred Mr. Lloyd George's idea, of waiting until the German comprehensive reply was received. This would be our *morceau de résistance.*

SECRETARY OF STATE LANSING ON THE TREATY OF PEACE

Memorandum by the Secretary of State, Paris, May 8, 1919

Both for personal and substantive reasons Secretary of State Lansing became disaffected from Wilson's diplomacy at Paris. The following document reveals that Lansing's view of the Versailles Treaty was close to that of John M. Keynes.

The terms of peace were yesterday delivered to the German plenipotentiaries, and for the first time in these days of feverish rush of preparation there is time to consider the Treaty as a complete document.

The impression made by it is one of disappointment, of regret, and of depression. The terms of peace appear immeasurably harsh and humiliating, while many of them seem to me impossible of performance.

The League of Nations created by the Treaty is relied upon to preserve the artificial structure which has been erected by compromise of the conflicting interests of the Great Powers and to prevent the germination of the seeds of war which are sown in so many articles and which under normal conditions would soon bear fruit. The League might as well attempt to prevent the growth of plant life in a tropical jungle. Wars will come sooner or later.

It must be admitted in honesty that the League is an instrument of the mighty to check the normal growth of national power and national aspirations among those who have been rendered impotent by defeat. Examine the Treaty and you will find peoples delivered against their wills into the hands of those whom they hate, while their economic resources are torn from them and given to others. Resentment and bitterness, if not desperation, are bound to be the consequences of such provisions. It may be years before these oppressed peoples are able to throw off the yoke, but as sure as day follows night the time will come when they will make the effort.

This war was fought by the United States to destroy forever the conditions which produced it. Those conditions have not been destroyed. They have been supplanted by other conditions equally productive of hatred, jealousy, and suspicion. In place of the Triple Alliance and the Entente has arisen the Quintuple Alliance which is to rule the world. The victors in this war intend to impose their combined will upon the vanquished and to subordinate all interests to their own.

It is true that to please the aroused public opinion of mankind and to respond to the idealism of the moralist they have surrounded the new alliance with a halo and called it "The League of Nations," but whatever it may be called or however it may be disguised it is an alliance of the Five Great Military Powers.

It is useless to close our eyes to the fact that the power to compel obedience by the exercise of the united strength of "The Five" is the fundamental principle of the League. Justice is secondary. Might is primary.

The League as now constituted will be the prey of greed and intrigue; and the law of unanimity in the Council, which may offer a restraint, will be broken or render the organization powerless. It is called upon to stamp as just what is unjust.

We have a treaty of peace, but it will not bring permanent peace because it is founded on the shifting sands of self-interest.

WILSON ON TREATY REVISION

Stenographic Report of a Meeting between the President, the Commissioners, and the Technical Advisers of the American Commission to Negotiate Peace, Hotel Crillon, Paris, June 3, 1919

A meeting of Wilson and his leading advisers to consider the last-minute revisions in the Treaty proposed by the British in response to German objections.

The President: Gentlemen, we have come together in order that we may hear from you on the question of the German counterproposals. We all have moving recollections of the struggles through which we have gone in framing the treaty, and the efforts we made that were successful, and the efforts we made that were unsuccessful to make the terms different from what they are, and I have come here not to express an opinion but to hear opinions, and I think perhaps the best course to follow will be to get a general impression from each other as to which parts of the German counter-arguments have made the greatest impression upon us.

Just as a guide, I find that the parts that have made the greatest impression on our British colleagues are the arguments with regard to the eastern frontier with Poland, the parts with regard to reparations, the parts about the period of occupation, together with the point about the League of Nations, their impression being that the Germans might very well be given reasonably to expect that the period of their probation would not be long in the matter of admission into the League. Those are the four points, the four subjects upon which the German counterproposals have made the deepest impressions upon them. That might be the start.

The reparation is the biggest point. That involves leftovers of the financial clauses. I would be glad to hear from anyone of our financial group who would like to express himself on that point.

Mr. Norman H. Davis: We feel that the Germans have really given us a basis for getting together properly on reparation, by coming back with a fixed sum. It is a rather rigid fixed sum, which can be modified and made more workable. There is a considerable possibility of getting together there, if we can get the French to agree upon a fixed sum. As you know, we have always insisted on the necessity of having a fixed sum, because by leaving it indefinite we had to give considerable powers to the Reparations Commission, and that is what seems to worry the Germans more than anything else— the powers given to the Reparations Commission, which, as they claim, are rather destructive than constructive, and if we come back and make a fixed amount, it will be possible to do away with the functions of the Reparations Commission which most worry the Germans, and it will avoid the necessity of interfering with their internal affairs, and so on. . . .

The President: . . . Mr. Lansing was asking me if I did not think it would be a good idea to ask each of our groups to prepare a memorandum of what might be conceded, and while I do not want to be illiberal in the matter, I should hesitate to say "yes" to that question. The question that lies in my mind is: "Where have they made good in their points?" "Where have they shown that the arrangements of the treaty are essentially unjust?" Not "Where have they shown merely that they are hard?'', for they are hard—but the Germans earned that. And I think it is profitable that a nation should learn once and for all what an unjust war means in itself.

I have no desire to soften the treaty, but I have a very sincere desire to alter those portions of it that are shown to be unjust, or which are shown to be contrary to the principles which we ourselves have laid down.

Take the Silesian question, for example: we said in so many words in the documents which were the basis of the peace, that we would make a free Poland out of the districts with Polish population. Now where it can be shown that the populations included in Poland are not indisputably Polish, then we must resort to something like a plebiscite. I agree with Dr. Lord that in the territory like northern Silesia the sincerity of the plebiscite might be questioned—in fact it might be very difficult to have a plebiscite that was a real expression of opinion, and therefore we would have to go by what we believed was the preponderance of the wishes of the population.

But I believe that where we have included Germans unnecessarily, the border ought to be rectified. Or where we have been shown to have departed from our principles, then we must consider what adjustments are necessary to conform to those principles.

Take Poland's access to the sea. For strategic reasons our Polish experts—the group of Allied experts—recommended a corridor running up to Dantzig and it included some very solid groups of German populations. We determined in that case to leave the Dantzig district to the Germans and to establish a plebisicite.

Where the railway track from Dantzig to Warsaw runs, notwithstanding the capital strategic importance of that railway to Poland, that railway is to remain German if its population votes to remain German.

I think that we have been more successful than I supposed we could possibly be in drawing ethnographic lines, because races are terribly mixed in some parts of Germany where we tried to draw the line. But wherever we can rectify them we ought to rectify them.

Similarly, if the reparations clauses are unjust because they won't work—not because they are putting the heavy burden of payment upon Germany (because that is just)—but because we are putting it on them in such a way that they cannot pay, then I think we ought to rectify that.

I put it this way: We ought to examine our consciences to see where we can make modifications that correspond with the principles that we are putting forth.

Secretary Lansing: That is what I say, Mr. President, but I should not confine it to "injustice"; where we have made a mistake I should not say it was an injustice. I should say that where it is something that is contrary to good policy that I do not think that is unjust; I simply think that we made an error, and we ought to correct it. That was my idea of what modifications should be suggested; not that we would adopt them, but to say whether it was wise to adopt them, so that we would have something in writing, something to work with. It is all in the air now.

The President: The great problem of the moment is the problem of agreement, because the most fatal thing that could happen, I should say, in the world, would be that sharp lines of division should be drawn among the Allied and Associated Powers. They ought to be held together, if it can reasonably be done, and that makes a problem like the problem of occupation look almost insoluble, because the British are at one extreme, and the French refusal to move is at the opposite extreme.

Personally I think the thing will solve itself upon the admission of Germany to the League of Nations. I think that all the powers feel that the right thing to do is to withdraw the army. But we cannot arrange that in the treaty because you cannot fix the date at which Germany is to be admitted into the League. It would be an indefinite one.

Secretary Lansing: Would that be done only by unanimous consent?

Mr. Hoover: The document provides that on two-thirds vote of the Council she should be admitted.

Secretary Lansing: But France, being on the Council, would have the decision.

Colonel House: I agree with the President: let Germany in, and when she gets in, the other follows. . . .

IV WILSON AND BOLSHEVISM AT PARIS

George Frost Kennan
RUSSIA AND THE PEACE CONFERENCE

George Frost Kennan has had brilliant careers as both a diplomat and an historian. From 1947 to 1950 he served as Director of the State Department Policy Staff and was appointed Ambassador to the USSR in 1952. In recent years he has written extensively in the areas of Russian history and the history of Soviet-American relations. He is presently a Professor in the Institute for Advanced Study, at Princeton. The following selection presents Kennan's critical perspective on Allied policy in Russia during the Paris Peace Conference. What alternative policies do you think might have been followed by Wilson and the Allies on the Russian problem at Paris?

Wilson came to Paris . . . at the end of 1918, profoundly disturbed about the Russian problem and most anxious to see something done that would put an end to the Russian civil war and bring Russian representatives to the Peace Conference.

Lloyd George shared this view. As the opening of the conference approached, he became increasingly convinced, to use his own words, "that world peace was unattainable as long as that immense country [Russia] was left outside the Covenant of Nations."[1] He would have gone far to bring about Russian representation at the conference.

Not so Clemenceau. He was firmly against Russian representation. The World War—France's conflict with Germany—was for him the only important issue. Russia, as he saw it, had betrayed France in the war. She had thereby excluded herself as a partner in the peace talks. The peace to be concluded did not concern her. His concern was not that Bolshevism should be fitted into the new world order; it was that Bolshevism should be destroyed or, if this was not possible, that a quarantine zone should be erected around it.

In the weeks just preceding the opening of the Peace Conference, the Soviet government repeatedly attempted to convey to the Allies its desire for an immediate and peaceful termination of the interven-

[1] David Lloyd George, *The Truth about the Peace Treaties* (London: Victor Gollancz Ltd., 1938), I: 315.

tion and for the establishment of normal political and commercial relations with the Western countries. The Bolshevik leaders were now well aware that none of their Russian opponents would be able to hold out in the absence of Allied military support. They were therefore willing to make serious concessions in order to get the foreign troops out. The Sixth All-Russian Congress of Soviets, convening immediately after the Armistice, addressed to the Allied governments a formal appeal for peace, which was followed up by telegrams to the Allied governments and various proclamations of the same tenor. Shortly thereafter, Litvinov was sent out to Stockholm to try to establish contact with the Allied governments. He succeeded in speaking there with one or two subordinate British and American agents. This occurred just at the time the Paris Conference was convening. Litvinov assured these Allied representatives that the Soviet government was anxious for peace and was prepared to compromise on all important points, including the Russian state debt to the Allies, protection to foreign enterprises in Russia, and the granting of new concessions. It was against the background of these far-reaching assurances, together with the dismal prospects for the Allied intervention, that the Allied statesmen initiated their discussion of the Russian problem in Paris at the beginning of 1919.

Lloyd George described as follows the situation as it existed at the outset of the conference:

> *Personally I would have dealt with the Soviets as the* de facto *Government of Russia. So would President Wilson. But we both agreed that we could not carry to that extent our colleagues at the Congress, nor the public opinion of our countries which was frightened by Bolshevik violence and feared its spread. . . .*[2]

Other expedients had therefore to be pursued. We can see today, with the advantage of hindsight, that the real possibilities open to the Allied statesmen for doing anything constructive about Russia at the conference were extremely limited. Nothing the Allies could have done would have served to overthrow the Bolsheviki or to make them anything else than what they were. The Allies could not top the Russian civil war, nor could they assure the victory of those they regarded

---

[2] Ibid., p. 331.

FIGURE 8. The Next Menace to Be Overcome. From the Dayton *News*. (Historical Pictures Service, Chicago)

as their friends. They could not create a friendly, well-behaved Russia and bring its representatives to Paris. The best they could have done, at that moment, would have been to trade a withdrawal of the Allied forces from Russia for a promise on the part of the Russian Communist leaders to grant an amnesty to those Russians who had collaborated with those forces and thus offended the Soviet government. It is true that such an amnesty would not have had any very enduring effect: the amnestied Whites would certainly not have ceased to oppose Soviet power, and the Soviet authorities would soon have found ways of punishing them for doing so. But such an arrangement would at least have given the Allied governments a reasonably graceful means of exit from what was, in the best of circumstances, a most embarrassing and unprofitable involvement.

It will be useful for us to examine why not even this modest minimum could be achieved by the Allied representatives at the Paris Conference.

There were really five different attempts at the Paris Peace Conference to do something about the Russian problem. First there was an invitation to the warring factions in Russia to send representatives to a conference with Allied delegates on the Island of Prinkipo in the Sea of Marmara. Secondly, there was a brief and valiant personal effort by Mr. Winston Churchill to bring things to a head and to compel the Bolsheviki either to cease hostilities at once or to suffer a greatly increased Allied military effort against them. Thirdly, there was an attempt by the American and British governments to sound out the Soviet leaders by sending a secret diplomatic agent, Mr. William C. Bullitt, to Moscow to talk to them. Fourthly, there was a project, initiated by Herbert Hoover with the collaboration of the Norwegian explorer, Fridtjof Nansen, to get food to the hungering Russian population on terms that would force a clarification of the political situation. Finally, after all of these other starts had failed, there was an attempt to create a new rationale for supporting the anti-Bolshevik factions in Russia by pinning them down to a public statement of liberal and democratic purposes.

I should like to examine each of these initiatives in turn, as briefly as possible, and to attempt to identify the reasons for their failure. We will find these reasons instructive and revealing, I think, not just for the failures of Allied statesmanship at that moment but also for some of the later problems of the Western relationship to Soviet power.

First of all, the Prinkipo invitation.

It was Lloyd George who took the initiative, at the outset of the conference, in proposing that representatives of all the warring factions in Russia be invited to Paris to consult with the Peace Conference, on the condition that they first cease hostilies against one another. This suggestion was immediately snagged on Clemenceau's violent objection. He flatly refused to receive any Bolshevik delegates in Paris. He would resign, he said, rather than do it. This disposed of Lloyd George's proposal.

Wilson, who had favored the British proposal, then suggested that the Russian representatives be invited to meet with the Allied delegates at some other place than Paris. It was suggested that a suitable place would be the Island of Prinkipo in the Sea of Marmara. Travel to that place, it was argued, would not involve the transit of the Soviet delegates through any third country. Clemenceau disapproved of the whole idea, but said he would go along for the sake of solidarity. He suggested that Wilson should draw up an appropriate proclamation. This Wilson proceeded to do. His draft was accepted by the others, including Clemenceau, and was immediately published to the world.

The proclamation was a characteristically Wilsonian document, full of wholly sincere professions of disinterestedness and of a desire to serve the Russian people. Like the original British suggestion, it envisaged a truce in the Russian civil war as a prerequisite for the Prinkipo Conference: if the parties would not stop fighting, their representatives would not be received. February 15—a day only three weeks off—was named as the opening date for the conference.

This proposal was a naive one. What the Bolsheviki and their Russian opponents were interested in was each other's total destruction. There was no room here for amicable discussion. Since the document stemmed from Wilson's pen, it would be easy to assume—and some have done so—that the proposal was only another reflection of the naive American conviction that man is a reasonable animal, dominated by good will. Wilson was much laughed at for this step. But it was quite unjust to charge him with the authorship of it. It was in a meeting of the Imperial War Cabinet in London on the last day of December 1918 that the idea had its origin. The Americans, actually, were not particularly sanguine about it. Wilson's Secretary of State, Robert Lansing, wired privately to his deputy in the State Department that nothing was likely to come of the proposal; it had been adopted only because military intervention was a failure; the alternative would have been to remain silent and let things take their course. This, Lansing said sadly, would have satisfied no one.

Lansing's pessimism was wholly justified. The invitation was flatly rejected by the Russian Whites. Their representatives in Paris had been quietly encouraged by the French, behind Wilson's back, to decline the invitation. They appear, in fact, to have been assured by the French that they needn't worry—they would continue to have Allied support even if they turned down the invitation. This action on the part of the French did not remain concealed from the President; and it may be presumed to have been one of the things that did not particularly endear his Continental colleagues to him.

The Soviet reply, while not wholly negative, was evasive about the truce, and somewhat insulting in its language, after the fashion of early Soviet diplomatic communications to capitalist governments. This, together with the refusal of the anti-Bolshevik groups to sit down at a table with the Communists, was sufficient to kill the proposal.

The two replies—Communist and non-Communist—were delivered to the conference on February 12. President Wilson was scheduled to leave for the United States two days later, for an absence of several weeks. This combination of facts—the failure of the Prinkipo plan and the President's imminent departure—caused considerable perturbation in the British government, particularly among those members of the Cabinet who did not share Lloyd George's skepticism about the usefulness of the intervention and who wanted to see some incisive action agreed upon at once. Plainly, if Wilson got away before any new decisions were taken, things would just drag on, and there would be many weeks more of uncertainty and inaction. Lloyd George was detained in London at that moment, by political difficulties at home. It appears to have been decided, in the light of this fact, that Mr. Churchill should go over to Paris, attend the last meeting of the Council of Ten on the day of Wilson's departure, and attempt to get the President's agreement to some definite and incisive course of military action in Russia, as an alternative to Prinkipo.

Just how and why it was that Mr. Churchill (who disagreed with

Lloyd George thoroughly on everything having to do with the Russian question) should have been selected for this mission, is unclear. Lloyd George said in his memoirs that "Mr. Churchill very adroitly seized the opportunity . . . to go over to Paris and urge his plans upon the consideration of [the others]."[3] The uninitiated American historian may be permitted to wonder whether Lloyd George himself did not adroitly seize the opportunity to let Mr. Churchill work off some of his steam against Wilson's glacial aversion to everything that had to do with military intervention, and against the complete unwillingness of any of the other Allies to put up money or forces for an expanded military effort in Russia.

In any case, Mr. Churchill did join the session on the day of Wilson's departure. It was, of course, a full and busy day. The senior statesmen were preoccupied with many other matters. It was not until about seven o'clock in the evening, when everyone was tired and the dinner hour was pressing, that the talk got around to Russia. In these circumstances, the discussion was unavoidably cursory and inconclusive.

We come up at this point, incidentally, against one of the basic reasons why the statesmen at Paris failed in their effort to deal with the Russian problem. I have in mind here the inherent defects of what we might call "summit diplomacy"—of the effort to transact important diplomatic business by direct meetings between senior statesmen. These defects are many. The multitude of ulterior problems that press upon a prime minister or a head of state is so great that no single subject, especially one not regarded as of primary importance, is apt to receive detailed and exhaustive attention. Nor can the senior statesmen stay with a problem for any great length of time. Their time is precious; other responsibilities take them away. In the present instance the very fact that both Wilson and Lloyd George were obliged to leave the conference at this juncture and, incidentally, that Clemenceau was seriously wounded by a would-be assassin four days later, shows clearly how the treatment of any important international subject is endangered when its negotiation is left to those who hold the supreme positions.

In any case, to return to our narrative: on the late afternoon of

[3] Ibid., p. 368.

February 14, at the meeting of the Council of Ten, with Wilson fidgeting to get off to the railway station, Churchill brought up the Russian question and emphasized the need for clearing up at once the uncertainty resulting from the inconclusive outcome of the Prinkipo proposal. He pointed particularly to the deterioration of the military situation of the anti-Bolshevik forces in Russia and to the weakened morale of the Allied units there. To this Wilson responded by saying that the Allied troops were doing no good in Russia; they did not know for whom or for what they were fighting; the groups they were supporting showed no political promise; they ought to be withdrawn at once. As for Prinkipo: if Russian delegates could not be brought to the West, perhaps an effort could be made to get in touch with them through informal representatives.

Churchill stressed, in reply, the debt of loyalty the Allies owed to the anti-Bolshevik forces with whom they were associated. Wilson admitted that this was a dilemma, but pointed out, very truly, that the Allied forces would have to leave Russia someday: it was no good putting off the day of reckoning.

On this inconclusive note, the session of the fourteenth ended. For three days after Wilson's departure, Churchill continued to press, in the absence of both Lloyd George and Wilson, for issuance of a ten-day ultimatum to the Bolsheviki to stop the fighting, with the understanding that if it was not accepted, the Supreme War Council would see what could be done about overthrowing the Soviet government by force of arms. But the report of these suggestions, relayed to Lloyd George and Wilson, drew indignant protests from both of them. Neither would entertain the thought of anything like an intensified military effort in Russia. Mr. Churchill was obliged to retire in frustration. Immediately after Churchill's return to England, Clemenceau was shot. With that, all three of the top figures were out of action. Discussion of the Russian problem at the senior level stopped for several weeks. Intensified intervention, as a means of dealing with the Russian situation, had been proposed, and in effect rejected by the conference.

Wilson, in the discussion on the day of his departure, had hinted at the desirability of getting in touch with the Soviet leaders through informal representatives. This was not an empty phrase. What he had in mind, unquestionably, was an idea which had been suggested to

Colonel House by the well-known American journalist, Lincoln Steffens. Steffens had suggested the dispatch of a private exploratory mission direct to Moscow. The idea commended itself to House and evidently to Wilson. Mr. William C. Bullitt, an attaché of the American delegation at the Peace Conference, was selected for the task. Steffens was to go with him. Mr. Bullitt, you will recall, was destined fourteen years later to be the first American ambassador to the Soviet Union. He was, at the time of his first visit to Russia in 1919, twenty-eight years old, liberal in his views, brilliant, inexperienced, and greatly excited.

The British were informed of the project and evidently approved of it. At a later date Lloyd George and his private secretary, Mr. Philip Kerr (later Marquess of Lothian), denounced Bullitt's subsequent revelations about this mission as a tissue of lies; and Lloyd George conveyed the impression that he had nothing to do with it. It is possible that Bullitt may have been unintentionally inaccurate in some of his statements. But he did produce, on this later occasion, the text of a private note handed to him by Mr. Kerr before his departure for Russia, to which was appended a list of the conditions upon which Kerr personally thought it would be possible for the Allied governments to resume normal relations with Russia. These included a general cessation of hostilities, an amnesty to Russians who had fought on the Allied side, and the eventual withdrawal of the Allied forces. It was, perhaps, improper for Bullitt to make public this note, as he subsequently did; but I am not aware that its authenticity has ever been denied. It was with this document in his pocket that Bullitt set off for Moscow. One can only regard his visit, therefore, as having British as well as American sanction.

The Americans said nothing to the French about Bullitt's mission. They were under the impression that the French had deliberately sabotaged the Prinkipo proposal behind the scenes, and they did not wish this second effort to be similarly frustrated.

Bullitt and Steffens arrived in Moscow in mid-March. They were well received. Bullitt had talks with Lenin and others of the Soviet leaders. Both men were favorably impressed by the evidences of discipline and singleness of purpose on the part of the Soviet government, and by the sincerity of the desire of the Soviet leaders to put an end to the civil war and the intervention. They obtained from Lenin, after some discussion, the draft of a document having the form of an Allied proposal to the Soviet government. Bullitt was assured that if this proposal were actually made by the Allied governments not later than April 10, it would be accepted by the Soviet leaders.

It was probably an unwise method of procedure, on Bullitt's part, to return with such a document. It left to the Allied governments no latitude of negotiation. By taking cognizance of the document, they would obviously place themselves in a position where they could only take it or leave it. Any alteration in its text at the Allied end would have given the Soviet government formal grounds for refusing to accept it. Nevertheless, it was in substance not an offer to be lightly rejected from the Allied standpoint. It did provide for a cessation of hostilities between the various existing governments and factions in Russia, for a raising of the Allied blockade, for the opening up of the channels of communication, for a withdrawal of Allied troops and a termination of Allied military support for any Russian groups. Most important of all, it promised a general amnesty for those who had supported the Allies.

The Allies, as subsequent events were to demonstrate, would have been well out of it on these terms. It is a pity they were not accepted. But this was not to be. Bullitt, having wired his findings from Helsinki, got back to Paris in the last days of March, bursting with the importance of what he had accomplished. To his astonishment and chagrin, he found that the whole situation had changed. The senior statesmen, now back in Paris, were locked in a series of Herculean disagreements on questions of the treatment of Germany. These days constituted, in fact, the first great crisis of the conference. Bullitt seems to have reached the scene just at the time when passions were at their peak and the strain on everyone was the greatest.

Whether Wilson and Lloyd George ever gave serious attention to the proposals with which Bullitt had returned does not appear from the records. Wilson, pleading a headache, refused to receive him and shunted him off to Colonel House, saying to House that he himself had a single-track mind and simply could not take on the Russian problem in addition to what he was already thinking about. Bullitt was profoundly offended by this brush-off, and sneered ever afterwards about the President's headache. But here he was probably unjust. The episode occurred within a day or two of Wilson's nervous and physical collapse, at the beginning of April. He may well have had a headache on the day in question.

Bullitt appeared before the other members of the American delegation at the conference, and spent a day talking with them. The following morning, according to his own statement, he had breakfast with Lloyd George, General J. C. Smuts, Sir Maurice Hankey, and Kerr. He later cited Lloyd George and Smuts as having been strongly in favor of a solution along the lines embodied in the Soviet proposal, but Lloyd George, he said, was frightened by the attacks being launched against him in England from the Conservative side over the Russian question. Waving a copy of the *Daily Mail,* Lloyd George said—still according to Bullitt—"As long as the British press is doing this kind of thing how can you expect me to be sensible about Russia?"[4] He expressed doubt that Bullitt's tale would be believed. He talked of sending some prominent Conservative to Russia to find out for himself and to tell the public what the Bolshevik attitude was.

From this point on the matter seems to have bogged down completely. Colonel House passed Bullitt on to some of his own subordinates who were actually averse to the Bullitt proposals and had a wholly different idea as to what ought to be done. The April 10 deadline proposed by the Soviet government was allowed to pass without and Allied reaction. This, of course, obviated the entire proposal; for, once the deadline was passed, the Soviet government was no longer committed. If anything were now to be done, the matter would have to be entirely renegotiated.

In the ensuing days the Bullitt mission was the subject of insistent queries in the House of Commons on the part of alarmed Conservatives, partisans of the intervention, who had heard rumors of Bullitt's trip and of the proposals with which he had returned, and who feared that the British government might be on the point of accepting them. On April 16, Lloyd George, temporarily back in London, took the bull by the horns, appeared in the House of Commons, and made a major policy statement on the Russian question. He was then asked by one of the members whether he could make any statement on the approaches or representations alleged to have been made to his gov-

[4] *The Bullitt Mission to Russia: Testimony before the Committee on Foreign Relations, United States Senate, of William C. Bullitt* (New York: B. W. Huebsch, 1919), p. 66.

ernment by persons acting on behalf of such government as there
was in central Russia. To this Lloyd George replied that they had had
nothing authentic—no such approaches at all. But he did think he
knew to what the Right Honorable Gentleman referred:

> *. . . There was some suggestion that a young American had come back
> from Russia with a communication. It is not for me to judge the value of
> this communication, but if the President of the United States had attached
> any value to it he would have brought it before the conference, and he
> certainly did not.*[5]

Lincoln Steffens, who had accompanied Bullitt on his trip, heard
somewhere that Lloyd George's reason for washing his hands of
Bullitt in this way was to protect himself against the French, who,
having learned of the Bullitt mission, were now accusing Lloyd George
of having gone behind their back. This sounds quite plausible.

Bullitt, in any case, being unaccustomed to the cruelty of politics
and perhaps to the personal amorality which is the concommitant of
high political authority, was doubly stung by this public denial. His
cup of bitterness overflowed. He was disillusioned anyway with the
form the Peace Treaty was assuming under the hammering of the
European Allies. He blamed Wilson for surrendering his ideals. A few
weeks later he resigned, reproaching Wilson bitterly with having "so
little faith in the millions of men, like myself, in every nation who had
faith in you."[6] When the journalists asked him what he proposed to
do, he said he was going to go down to the Riviera and lie on the
sands and watch the world go to hell. Some months later he spilled
his own story, with passionate indiscretion, to a senatorial committee
anxious to discredit the President in the fight over the League.
Neither Wilson nor his British friends ever forgave him for doing so.

The reasons for the failure of the Bullitt mission lie to some extent
in the partiality of Colonel House's entourage to another idea, which
remains to be discussed. But I think it worth noting, before we go on
to that, the other factors that led to Bullitt's failure. One of these was
certainly the general atmosphere of confusion that attends any large
multilateral gathering of senior statesmen—in other words, the char-

[5] Ibid., p. 94.
[6] Ibid., p. 97.

acteristic inadequacy of summit statesmanship, which I talked about earlier. Closely connected with this was the great difficulty which is always involved in any attempt of a coalition of sovereign governments to negotiate with a single hostile political entity, particularly in a confused and rapidly moving context of circumstance. This is something that requires centralization of authority, complete privacy of decision, and a highly disciplined mode of procedure. These are not the marks of coalition diplomacy. Their absence is something that has bedeviled the statesmanship of the Western democracies down to the present day.

An even more important cause of Bullitt's misfortune was no doubt the domestic-political situation in England, which did not permit Mr. Lloyd George to do what he thought would have been sensible about the Russian problem. Here you get into another of the characteristic disadvantages of democratic diplomacy—the fact that a system of government under which the executive power is sensitively attuned to the waves of popular sentiment, and of parliamentary opinion, is one which finds it difficult to adjust rapidly and incisively to a complicated and fast-moving series of circumstances, especially when controversial domestic issues are involved. De Tocqueville once observed that "a democracy can only with great difficulty regulate the details of an important undertaking, persevere in a fixed design, and work out its execution in spite of serious obstacles."[7] All this was doubly true of the representatives of democratic governments who struggled with the Russian problem at the Peace Conference in 1919.

But there was another reason for the failure of the Bullitt mission. At the time of Bullitt's return to Paris a new proposal was being entertained in the entourage of Colonel House. House's leading subordinates were evidently influenced by the anti-Bolshevik feeling that predominated in the State Department and in the Allied social circles generally, and contrasted strongly with the realistic appreciation shown by Wilson and Lloyd George for the dangers of the intervention.

The scheme which, during Bullitt's absence in Russia, had begun to commend itself to these gentlemen was one which centered around the person and activities of the future American president, Herbert

[7] Alexis de Tocqueville, *Democracy in America* (New York: Alfred A. Knopf, 1948), I: 235.

Hoover. Hoover was at that time Director of the Commission for Relief in Belgium, an American organization which had functioned with spectacular success during the war in getting food relief to the population of German-occupied Belgium. Hoover, a mining engineer by training, had been given complete control of this operation. He had plenty of money at his disposal. He had been able to draw on members of the executive staffs of American businesses all over Europe, now displaced by the war. He was a ruthless and effective administrator; and his organization, unencumbered with the usual burdens of governmental bureaucracy, was able to do an effective and impressive job.

As the war came to an end, Hoover's organization moved into other areas of Europe, bringing urgent food relief to the peoples, and particularly to children and other specially needy portions of the population. Hoover was, in fact, made Food Administrator for the Allies generally. This position gave him in many situations considerable political power; and he did not fail to make this influence felt in a number of instances, in the interests of the success of his program.

To people who were impressed with Hoover's operations, and the power that had gravitated into his hands, it was only a step to the assumption that if he could move into Russia with a food relief program, as he had done into various parts of central Europe, he would be able to extort an end of the civil war on terms favorable to Allied interests, as a price for the food relief. Whether this would involve the fall of the Soviet regime was, I think, not clear in the minds of most people who entertained the idea; but it was assumed that at least the Russian Communists could be confronted with the choice between moderating their behavior and their principles of conduct, or accepting the onus of denying the proffered food to a Russian population, large parts of which were already starving.

On March 28, 1919, just after Bullitt's return to Paris, President Wilson received a long letter from Hoover recommending the establishment of a relief commission for Russia along the lines of the Belgian one. The plan was not, I hasten to explain, the result of any friendly sentiments on Hoover's part toward the Soviet regime. Hoover, whose experience as a mining engineer had included service in Russia before the war, had no friendly feelings toward the Bolsheviki. It was his view that the Allies should insist, as part of the price for their support of such a scheme, that the Bolsheviki cease hostilities against their opponents in Russia and stop their propaganda abroad. Communist political activity was now beginning to make serious headway in other countries of Europe and to be a source of real worry to a great many upstanding people. Just one week before Hoover wrote his letter, the Communists had seized power in Hungary, where Hoover's Food Administration was attempting to organize a relief action. Hoover no doubt shared the horror which many people were now experiencing on their first contact with this new doctrine and their realization of what it might mean for Europe. Thus he took pains to specify that his plan did not involve any recognition of what he called "the Bolshevik murderers" any more than England, in supporting the Belgian relief program, had entered into a relationship with a hostile Germany. His idea was that a neutral figure should be placed in charge of the program; the latter should publicly ask for Allied support; the Allies should then state the conditions on which they would support the program. These conditions would be such as to place the Soviet government, as I have just suggested, before the choice of falling in with general Western desiderata or accepting the onus of denying the food to the Russian people.

The idea of using food as a weapon was one which had a very strong appeal to the American mind. It appealed to some of the most dangerous weaknesses in the American view of international affairs, and had, in my opinion, a most pernicious influence on American thinking. Since the money and the food would be donated by Americans, the action could always be portrayed to people at home as an altruistic and benevolent one, and made to contrast favorably with that evil and awful thing called "power politics" of which the European countries were presumed to be chronically guilty. No use of force was involved. No troops had to be kept on foreign soil as sanctions for this diplomacy. One was relieved of the sordid ordeal of political negotiations and compromise. One simply defined one's conditions and left it to the other fellow to take it or leave it. If he accepted, all right; if he declined, so much the worse for him.

It was, of course, true that anyone making such an offer had a perfect right to define the conditions of it. It is also only fair to recognize that the conditions laid down by Hoover's organization were moderate

American public thought

and reasonable, and usually essential to the successful operation of the program. In no instance were they ones that sought any territorial acquisitions or other illicit gains for the United States. A certain basic decency of the whole procedure was assured by the very mildness of the aspirations of an America still deeply rooted in the tradition of isolationism.

But the farther you got away from the orderly and liberal forms of society prevailing on Europe's Atlantic seaboard, and the closer you came to the more primitive political conditions of eastern Europe, the more difficult it became to define conditions for the distribution of food that were not simultaneously conditions for the adjustment of domestic political realities. To insist on the fair and impartial distribution of food was to insist on moderation and liberality of political behavior generally; but to insist on this, in terms of Russia and eastern Europe, could be the most violent and outrageous of interventions in the domain of domestic political affairs. People in that part of the world were inclined to ask: What was the use of having power if you could not deprive your enemies of food and channel it to your friends?

Wilson, very much preoccupied by the crisis over the German problem to which the Peace Conference itself had, by April 1919, advanced, turned Hoover's letter over to Colonel House. Hoover, meanwhile, who was not the man to doubt that any recommendation of his would be instantly accepted, had proceeded to implement his idea by summoning Fridtjof Nansen to Paris, and asking him to accept the titular leadership of the proposed Relief Commission for Russia. Nansen, after agreeing to do this, was persuaded to support Hoover's letter with another letter of his own to the Big Four senior statesmen at the conference. The text of this letter, incidentally, had been drafted for him by Hoover. In this letter, Nansen formally proposed the relief action which Hoover had suggested, and asked on what conditions the Allied governments would approve it.

Nansen's letter was delivered to the members of the Council of Four on April 3. This was one of the darkest and most dramatic days of the Peace Conference. It was the day on which President Wilson, worn with strain and frustration, collapsed and took to his bed for a period of some days. On the previous day, April 2, the awkward questioning about the Bullitt mission had begun in the House of Commons.

There was more of this questioning on the third; and the spokesman for the government felt obliged to assure the House that "the Allied Governments had received no proposals for an honorable understanding with the present rulers of Russia"[8]—a statement which might have been technically defensible but was certainly quibbling. We may be fairly sure that Lloyd George had by this time made it clear to Wilson and Colonel House that there could, in these circumstances, be no question of a follow-up on the Bullitt proposals. Wilson's illness precluded any discussion of them, anyway, at the top level.

House, encouraged by his subordinates, therefore seized on the letter from Hoover and Nansen as a means of evading Lenin's offer. Here was an alternative scheme which, if successful, appeared to spell less risk for the Allies, and could bring no embarrassment if it did not succeed. House charged his subordinates with the task of preparing a reply to Nansen. He disposed of Bullitt by suggesting to him that the Allied reply to Lenin could be embodied in the terms of the Nansen proposal, and suggested that he merge his efforts with those who were handling the Hoover-Nansen initiative.

House's subordinates at once produced, for Bullitt's edification, a draft which—unbeknownst, apparently, to Bullitt—also had proceeded from Hoover's pen.

Bullitt tried his best to work into the letter to Nansen something resembling a response to Lenin's proposals; but without success. The most he was permitted to do was to polish up Mr. Hoover's somewhat jerky prose. This edited version was duly laid before the Big Four, who signed it as a formal communication of the Peace Conference, and dispatched it to Dr. Nansen on April 17. It was at once released to the public, and was splashed over the headlines of the world press. In it, the Allied statesmen welcomed the Nansen proposal and went on to define the conditions on which they would be prepared to support it. A cessation of the hostilities in Russia was stipulated; but in contrast to Lenin's proposals, nothing was said about any withdrawal of the Allied forces. Distribution and transportation within Russia, it was said, would have to be under the supervision of the proposed Relief Commission; but, subject to this

[8] *The Parliamentary Debates*, House of Commons, 5th Series, Vol. 114, col. 1351.

supervision, the distribution of the food in Russia was to be "solely under the control of the people of Russia themselves." The people in each locality—Dr. Nansen was told—

> . . . should be given, as under the regime of the Belgian Relief Commission, the fullest opportunity to advise your Commission upon the methods and the personnel by which their community is to be relieved.[9]

Was there ever, one wonders, any greater nonsense than this curious document, bearing the signatures of Orlando, Lloyd George, Wilson, and Clemenceau? The provision for supervision of all Russian transportation by the Relief Commission meant simply taking one great and vital branch of economic and military administration out of the hands of the Russian government entirely. This the Soviet government could never have accepted without a disastrous collapse of its prestige. But beyond this, how could the people of any Russian locality act as a collective entity in such matters, even assuming that experience and tradition had fitted them to do so, unless they were in some way organized and represented for this purpose? This meant elections—elections of public bodies with real power. But the Russia of the spring of 1919 was, God knows, in no condition to conduct elections of any kind. It was ravaged by hunger and cold and confusion and a civil war which had now advanced to the utmost degree of bitterness and commitment on both sides. Who was to organize such elections? Who was to stand guard over their impartiality? Who was to see and to count the ballots? Where was the Russian whose detachment toward the civil war was so great and so generally recognized that others would consent to place their lives and that of their families in his power by handing to him a secret ballot? The very suggestion of local community action of this sort reflected a terrifying naïveté as to what the Russia of that hour was really like.

Nansen took the letter from the Big Four and tried to transmit it by wire to Lenin. Despite the fact that Clemenceau had signed it, the French government's radio station refused to send it. Again, as in the case of the Prinkipo proposal, the French were sabotaging the very measures to which Clemenceau had agreed. Cap in hand, Nansen went from one of the Allied governments to the other, vainly trying to

---

[9] *The Memoirs of Herbert Hoover*, Vol. I: *Years of Adventure, 1874–1920* (London: Hollis & Carter, 1952), p. 416.

find one that would consent to transmit the note the Allied statesmen had themselves signed. He finally got it sent, apparently through German channels. It was not until May 4 that the Soviet government picked it up, as it had picked up the Prinkipo proposal, from the air waves.

What were the Soviet leaders to make of such a communication? A resignation of their powers over food distribution, over the transportation system, and over local government, coupled with the continued presence of the foreign troops in Russia, would plainly spell the end of their regime. The deadline for acceptance of the proposals they had handed to Bullitt had long since lapsed. They were now doing better in the civil war, both militarily and politically, than they had done in March. They needed the food, needed it badly, in fact; but they were in no mood to entertain Western schemes which concealed under the mask of a food relief program the destruction of their political system.

The reply which they sent was signed not by Lenin but by Chicherin. It was polite enough in its tone of address to Nansen personally; but it was unsparing in its denunciation of the Allied note. It was clear that the Soviet leaders smelled, in the provision for a cessation of hostilities, an Allied effort to trick them of the military victory in the civil war which they were quite confident would be theirs if there were no increase in the Allied military effort against them. To require a cessation of hostilities meant, Chicherin pointed out in the reply, to prevent the belligerent who had every reason to expect successes from obtaining those successes. This, he went on to say, was a purely political act. It had nothing to do with food relief. Nansen's humanitarian intentions were being obviously abused, he charged, by the Allied governments. The Soviet government had repeatedly offered to discuss a cessation of hostilities; it was still ready to do so, but only if there could be a discussion also of the true reasons why the war was being waged against it—and a discussion with its real adversaries, the Allied governments, not just with the puppets of those governments: the Russian Whites. The Bolsheviki were prepared to meet at any time with Nansen and his collaborators; but they could not accept the Allied conditions.

While all this was going on, the Big Four had begun to discuss the attitude they should adopt toward Kolchak. It was Wilson who raised the question on May 9, a few days before Chicherin's reply was received. The effort of the American troops to maintain a detached and neutral position vis-à-vis the warring Russian factions had by this time aroused the ire both of the Allied governments and of Kolchak and his followers and associates, who simply could not understand why the Americans should refuse to participate in the effort to over-throw the Bolsheviki. There was a growing danger of clashes be-tween the American forces and the Russian Whites. Wilson brought this to the attention of the Peace Conference, and said that he thought the situation could not go on much longer. Either the Amer-ican expeditionary force must be instructed to support Kolchak, or it must be withdrawn at once. The American government had little con-fidence in Kolchak. Therefore he, Wilson, favored the withdrawal of the American contingent.

Lloyd George pleaded for a postponement of the decision. He was under the impression, as were the French, that Kolchak was doing very well indeed: that he had the Communists on the run, that if one only waited a little while the Bolsheviki would be finished. Kolchak would then be easy to deal with.

As we know today, this was not so at all. The high-water mark of Kolchak's spring offensive had really been passed some two to three weeks earlier. By the time this discussion took place in Paris, Kolchak was not only again on the defensive, but he had begun that retreat which was to lead, within the year, to his political and per-sonal destruction. The reason why the statesmen in Paris did not know this was that they were making the same mistake the Americans were destined to make forty years later in the case of the Chinese civil war: they were drawing their information exclusively from the side which they wanted to see win. The Allies had no observers, at this point, on the Bolshevik side. They *had* had observers there some months earlier, but these had been lightheartedly sacrificed to the interests of the intervention itself. The Allied governments were now paying the penalty for this sacrifice, in the form of very poor and un-reliable information about Russian conditions. It was a heavy price.

Wilson himself was not much impressed with these optimistic re-ports of Kolchak's progress. He continued to favor withdrawal of the American troops. But his spirit had by this time been broken in the battle over the Versailles Treaty. He yielded reluctantly, in the end, to Lloyd George's opinion, observing sadly that the British had more experience with intervening in remote countries than had the Americans. And as a result of Wilson's yielding on this point, the American forces remained in Siberia almost a year longer than would otherwise have been the case. Wilson did suggest, however—and the suggestion was favorably received—that an effort might at least be made to pin Kolchak down to some sort of public assurance that he would, in the event of his political and military success, introduce a liberal and democratic system of government in Russia.

It was this suggestion that the statesmen had on their minds when Chicherin's reply to the Nansen proposal was laid before them, on May 20. Nansen wanted to accept the Soviet offer. He proposed to send his own representatives to Stockholm for discussions with the Bolshevik delegates. Wilson thought there was merit to some of Chicherin's points, and would probably have wished to encourage Nansen. But Clemenceau, once more, refused to hear of it. It was clear, he said, that Bolshevik power was now on the decline. The Communists had rejected Nansen's offer—founded on pure humanitarianism. What could you do with such people?

No one had any very good answer to this; and the discussion degenerated into a desultory post-mortem over the manner in which they had all become involved in this miserable Russian situation in the first place. Lloyd George said the British objective in the intervention had been the restoration of the eastern front; but this had necessitated collaboration with the Russian Whites; one could not now leave them in the lurch. Wilson recalled that the Americans had gone into Siberia only in order to help the Czechs get out; but when they got there, the Czechs had refused to leave. His own sense of frustration, he indicated, was complete. For the first time, he said, he had ceased to experience any chagrin over the fact that they had never had a policy toward Russia; there was no policy that they could have had.

There is something very sad in this confession. For two long years, the Russian situation had lain close to Wilson's heart. Earnestly he had hoped to demonstrate, in his handling of Russian matters, the principles to which he was so profoundly attached. It was he who had said, after all, in the Fourteen Points speech, that the treatment of Russia by her sister nations would be the acid test of their good will,

of their comprehension of her needs, of their own intelligent and un-
selfish sympathy. Now all these high hopes lay in the dust.

Actually, in this sad confession Wilson was close to the heart of
the matter. The beginning of wisdom, in the Russian question of
1919, was the recognition that there was nothing more the Allied
governments could accomplish by the retention of their forces in
Russia.

But Wilson was in a lone and helpless minority. There was no
further discussion of Chicherin's reply. Nansen was left, for the
moment, to die on the vine. Instead of pursuing the Nansen project,
the senior statesmen went on to order the drafting of the communication to Kolchak, asking him to clarify his democratic intentions. By
May 26, the draft, prepared by Mr. Philip Kerr, was ready and approved. It was dispatched that very day and, again, was made public.

This document, representing the last action to be taken at the
Peace Conference on the Russian question, opened with the extraordinary proposition that the time had come for the Allied and Associated Powers to make clear "once more" the policy they proposed
to pursue in regard to Russia. (Unkind critics might well have asked
on what previous occasion they had made this clear.) The note then
went on to promise to the doomed Kolchak, whose power was already rapidly disintegrating, the assistance of the Allies in munitions,
supplies, and food, to the end that he might install his regime as the
government of all Russia. He was asked, however, to give assurances
that he would, if successful, convene a constitutional convention;
that he would permit free local elections; that he would not attempt
to restore the old order; that he would make certain concessions in
the nationalities problem; that he would bring Russia into the League
of Nations; and that he would agree to assume the indebtedness of
former Russian governments.

The principal purpose of this note was simply to provide a moral
and political basis for the participation of the United States government in the supplying and provisioning of Kolchak. The British had
already given all they could. The French and Italians had nothing to
give.

The answering note represented, of course, an empty gesture.
Paper promises were a dime a dozen during the Russian civil war.
The issuance of the desired assurances cost Kolchak precisely noth-

ing. The reply, actually, was largely drafted for him by the French and British representatives at his headquarters, who thought they knew what President Wilson wished to hear. Very soon after this reply was received in Paris, the decline of Kolchak's fortunes became too obvious to be longer ignored. Wilson, who had never been convinced that things were as they had been represented to him, sent his own representative to Siberia to find out the true facts. This representative, the American ambassador to Japan, Mr. Roland Morris, reported that, without direct reinforcement by an Allied contingent of at least fifty thousand men, Kolchak could not possibly maintain himself, and that further shipments of supplies and munitions would simply be wasted. This killed the whole project, so far as the United States government was concerned. Kolchak proceeded rapidly to his early and tragic demise.

With this, the last of the efforts of the Peace Conference to deal with the Russian problem passed into history, devoid, like all the earlier ones, of any positive result. And not only, let us note, had no positive goals been achieved, but the Allies had succeeded in forfeiting, in the course of their handling of this problem, the only favorable and useful possibility that did lie, briefly, before them: a deal with the Soviet government that would have permitted a relatively graceful and early withdrawal of the Allied forces from the Russian scene, by agreement with the Soviet government, on the basis of a stipulated amnesty for those Russians who had collaborated with the Allied forces.

Arno J. Mayer
POLITICS AND DIPLOMACY OF PEACEMAKING

Arno J. Mayer is a professor of history at Princeton University. He is the author of several books and articles dealing with the interaction of domestic

From *Politics and Diplomacy of Peacemaking*, by Arno J. Mayer. Copyright © 1967 by Arno J. Mayer. Reprinted by permission of Alfred A. Knopf, Inc., and George Weidenfeld & Nicholson.

politics and diplomacy in modern Europe. The following selection conveys Mayer's view that the Paris Peace Conference was imbedded in the broader context of a left-right conflict throughout European politics, and he examines Wilson's role at Paris in relation to that conflict.

The Russian Revolution came as a timely reminder of the costs of military exhaustion and defeat under conditions of mounting political tensions. Otherwise both the Allies and the Central Powers might well have held out for unconditional surrender. Had it not been for the demonstration effect of the Bolshevik Revolution neither side would have considered the Wilsonian points as an acceptable basis for armistice negotiations. In the event the Armistice was concluded just in time to limit the political consequences of military defeat in Central and East Central Europe to less than revolutionary proportions. But even with this eleventh-hour finish the legacy of disruption and convulsion was far from negligible.

Granted, neither Germany nor Austria went Spartacist; and Hungary remained Bolshevik for only 133 days. Even so, particularly since Allied policies contributed to this outcome, it would be wrong to dismiss the danger of revolution as having been at best a sham or at worst a conspiracy. Admittedly, the social and political carriers as well as the precipitants of unrest varied in composition and intensity from country to country, and from month to month. But, the fact remains that there were grave disorders, rebellions, and strikes throughout defeated Europe, notably because politicians and labor leaders had ready-made organizational weapons with which to capitalize on political instability, unemployment, food shortages, and runaway prices.

In her diary Beatrice Webb raised a question that haunted Europe's political class, including the chief statesmen, throughout the Peace Conference: "Are we confronted with another Russia in Austria, possibly even in Germany—a Continent in rampant revolution . . . ?"[1] For General Smuts Europe was reduced to her "original atoms," with no hint of the "new political forms" within which these might be joined.[2] Curiously, it was the conservative liberal and legal-

[1] Margaret I. Cole, ed., *Beatrice Webb's Diaries, 1912–1924* (London: Longmans, Green, 1952), pp. 133–134, entry of November 4, 1918.
[2] Cited in David Hunter Miller, *My Diary at the Conference of Paris*, 21 vols. (privately printed; New York: Appeal Printing Company, 1924), III, p. 36.

istic David Hunter Miller who stressed, quite properly, that whereas the peacemakers of 1814–1815 only had to reconcile disputes "between well-known and established powers," those of 1918–1919 had to bring about "order out of chaos in practically all of Europe east of the Rhine, and north of the Danube, as well as restoration and a new life in various other parts of Europe and Asia."[3] Likewise, Walter Lippmann noted the absence of "stable government anywhere east of the Rhine," warning that no one knew "what Germany would be, nor Russia, nor the twenty odd nationalities of Eastern Europe and New Asia."[4] With good reason Woodrow Wilson acknowledged the wisdom and necessity of postponing the Conference "until there were governments in Germany and Austria-Hungary which could enter into binding agreements."[5] While Smuts exuberantly proposed that the League be made the trustee of the politically untrained peoples "left behind by the decomposition of Russia, Austria, and Turkey,"[6] Wilson and his advisers did their best to press the Allies into helping the "receiver" and successor governments of the defeated empires to consolidate themselves.

Of course, even without the force of the Soviet Russian example and the activities of local Bolshevik parties this chaos would have developed and caused concern. But as it was, the Bolshevik regime, by its mere survival as well as through its flaming manifestoes, provided encouragement to all far-Left radicals and stirred especially independent socialists into greater militancy. In addition, Lenin offered food to the Ebert-Scheidemann government, sent the Radek mission to Berlin, charted the Third International in early March 1919, and built up the Red Army. Counterrevolutionaries in particular vastly exaggerated the scope and aggressive nature of these steps, thereby making the specter which was haunting Europe doubly terrifying.

Naturally not only the Big Four or Five but also the experts within each delegation differed among themselves in their estimates of the nature and seriousness of the revolutionary threat, and hence in their

---

[3] Memorandum by Miller, dated November 21, 1918, cited in *F.R., P.C., 1919*, I, 354–357.
[4] Walter Lippmann, *The Political Scene: An Essay on the Victory of 1918* (New York: Holt, 1919), p. 31.
[5] Wilson to Edward Mandell House, November 10, 1918, cited in *F.R., P.C., 1919*, I, p. 128.
[6] Cited in Miller, *Diary*, III, p. 36.

prescriptions for containing it. Moreover, as in 1792–1794, the coherence and unity of the counterrevolutionary crusade were undermined by rival national interests, uneven material capabilities, and shifting domestic pressures. Even so, in spite of these grave dissonances, the Paris Peace Conference made a host of decisions, all of which, in varying degrees, were designed to check Bolshevism: the victors made territorial concessions to Poland, Rumania, and Czechoslovakia for helping to stem the revolutionary tide beyond their own borders; they gave military assistance and economic aid to these and other border lands as well as to the Whites for their armed assault on Soviet Russia and Hungary; they stepped up their direct military intervention in Russia; they rigorously enforced the blockade against Bolshevik Russia and Hungary; they rushed economic assistance to Austria and the successor states to help stabilize their governments; and they drafted the charters of the International Labor Organization (I.L.O.) and the League of Nations with a view to immunizing the non-Bolshevik Left against the ideological bacillus of the Bolshevik Revolution.

Some of these measures constituted a defensive containment policy, a *cordon sanitaire* calculated to prevent the Revolution from spreading beyond Bolshevik-controlled areas; other measures were aimed at the outright overthrow of Lenin and Béla Kun. But all alike were decided, orchestrated, sanctioned, or condoned by the peacemakers in Paris. Furthermore, all alike—intentionally or unintentionally—contributed to sparing defeated Europe further revolutionary infections. During the pivotal year of 1918–1919, when defeated Europe was most vulnerable, the armed intervention, reinforced by the blockade, forced Lenin to exhaust his scarce military and economic resources in defensive operations. Outside Russia he was reduced to countering the massive material intervention by the Allies with ideological appeals.

At the time, the outcome of this first round in the international civil war of the twentieth century seemed to be very much in the balance. According to Ray Stannard Baker, "at all times, at every turn in the negotiations, there rose the specter of chaos, like a black cloud out of the east, threatening to overwhelm and swallow up the world. There was no Russia knocking at the gates of Vienna! At Vienna, apparently, the revolution was securely behind them; at Paris it was always with them."[7] At one time or another every delegation played on this fear of the Bolshevik specter for its own purposes, thereby making the threat even more pervasive than it needed have been.

The uses and abuses of this spuriously inflated bogy of Bolshevism were as numerous then as they are today. With intermittent support from Lloyd George, President Wilson sought to convince Georges Clemenceau that Germany would succumb to Spartacism unless the Allies promptly lifted the blockade and proffered moderate peace terms. Back home, when Congress threatened to refuse his first major foreign aid bill, Wilson reluctantly but successfully frightened Capitol Hill with tales of the horrors of Bolshevism sweeping over the entire European continent.

Naturally, the vulnerable "receiver" governments of Germany, Austria, and Hungary were the most boisterous advocates of this Wilson line, insisting that should their countries be swallowed up by Bolshevism the advancing flood would not stop at the borders of the victor nations. Ironically, the German government itself diminished the blackmail value of Spartacism by repressing it sternly at home and by fighting Bolshevism eagerly in the *Baltikum*. On the other hand, Count Michael Károlyi invited the Bolsheviks into the Hungarian government in order to make his threats more credible. As for the Poles and the Rumanians, they received vast amounts of financial, economic, and military aid from the Allies for their assault on Soviet Russia and Soviet Hungary. Roman Dmowski and John Bratiano, supported by Ferdinand Foch and Winston Churchill, styled themselves as selfless champions of anti-Bolshevism, all the time extorting exorbitant territorial annexations for their counterrevolutionary services. Even Eleutherios Venizelos, whom Harold Nicolson mysteriously paired with Lenin as "the only two great men in Europe,"[8] was not above trading on the Bolshevik scare; neither were Thomas Masaryk and Eduard Beneš.

In brief, at one time or another most delegations at the Paris Peace Conference wielded the specter of Bolshevism as a weapon and a threat. In each instance the assault on or containment of Bolshevism was calculated to advance a government's foreign policy goals while

---

[7] Ray Stannard Baker, *Woodrow Wilson and World Settlement,* 3 vols. (Garden City, N.Y.: Doubleday, Page, 1923), I, p. 102.
[8] Harold Nicolson, *Peacemaking, 1919* (New York: Harcourt, Brace, 1939), p. 271.

at the same time fortifying its political position at home. *Contra communismo saepe; pro patria et politica semper.*

This twin assignment of stabilizing governments throughout defeated Europe and of containing if not destroying the Russian Revolution called for day-to-day consultations, decisions, and directives. Here, then, was one of the chief sources of that "vast quantity of executive work which was thrust upon the Conference of Paris and which found no parallel at Vienna."[9] Once the Paris Conference is placed in its historical context this executive work can no longer be deplored as a festering diversion from the real stuff of diplomacy, from negotiations of frontier adjustments, colonial redistributions, and reparations. In fact, this diversion, which vastly complicates diplomacy, may yet turn out to be the essence of peacemaking in an era of international civil war. It certainly deserves more than passing mention that the peacemakers of 1918–1919 manipulated blockades, wielded military and economic aid, and ordered counterrevolutionary military interventions. Properly to carry out this assignment of preventing Europe "from going to smash under [their] feet," they established the Supreme Economic Council, the Directory for Relief, the Blockade Committee, and the Supreme Council.[10]

The tight interlocking of international and domestic policies in both defeated and victor nations complicated the diplomacy and peacemaking still further.

Since in the defeated nations governments had to be formed before plenipotentiaries could be sent to the Paris Peace Conference, foreign policy platforms became decisive weapons in the struggle for political control. In November 1917 the Bolsheviks had seized power in Russia primarily though not exclusively on a promise of immediate peace; and they were determined to maintain themselves in power without external aid until fellow revolutionary regimes could come to their rescue.

After the Armistice, in Germany, Austria, Hungary, and the successor states, rival political parties, notably those which eventually

[9] Webster, "The Congress of Vienna 1814–1815 and the Conference of Paris 1919," p. 6.
[10] Baker, *World Settlement*, II, p. 365. Cf. André Tardieu: *La Paix* (Paris: Payot, 1921), pp. 118–119; Winston Churchill, *The Aftermath* (London: Macmillan, 1941), pp. 143–144; Nicolson, *Peacemaking*, pp. 117–118, 139; Paul Birdsall, *Versailles Twenty Years After* (New York: Reynal and Hitchcock, 1941), p. 57.

formed or controlled the governments, claimed that they were best qualified to secure favorable terms from the Big Four. The essential corollary of this pledge was the insistence that successful performance in the peace negotiations was the passkey to domestic rehabilitation, reconstruction, and reform.

But whereas in Russia the Bolsheviks had seized power from below, in Germany, Austria, and Hungary inveterate power elites invited the leaders of the nonrevolutionary forces of movement to act as receivers for bankrupt regimes. They pressed Friedrich Ebert, Friedrich Adler, and Károlyi into accepting these receiverships, not only because at home each was an ideal foil against revolutionary and anarchist excesses, but above all also because each was alone likely to inspire confidence in the Allies, notably in Wilson.

The promise and, in the case of Austria, the fulfillment of Allied goodwill and aid played a crucial role once these provisional governments tried to transform their receiverships from above into popular mandates from below. The Social Democrats and their collaborators forewarned the electorates—and the Allies punctuated these warnings—that in case of chaos or revolution their countries could expect neither food, nor credits, nor favorable peace terms, with the result that there would be massive starvation, especially in the large cities. On the other hand, they promised that provided order was maintained and reformist republican regimes established, the victors, under pressure from Wilson and the Allied Left, would provide economic aid and grant moderate peace terms. By mid-January the triumph of the parties of the July Coalition in the campaign for the German Constituent Assembly best attested to the nature and successful application of this political formula. Within two months Károlyi's withdrawal in favor of Béla Kun, which was precipitated by the peremptory Vix Note, demonstrated the failure of the same formula in Hungary.

Just as the peacemakers could ill afford to ignore this interplay of national international politics in the defeated countries, they could not ignore it in their own. 1814–1815 the peace was negotiated "in elegant and ceremonious privacy . . . [by] a group of Aristocrats, life-trained as statesmen or diplomats,"[11] who considered themselves responsible to crowned sovereigns and barely worried about partisan pressures.

---

[11] Churchill, *Aftermath*, p. 120. Cf. Satow, "Peacemaking Old and New," pp. 52–53.

The situation was not so serene a century later, when seasoned party politicians of *petit bourgeois* background—two professors, a journalist, a solicitor—gathered around the conference table. The Big Four were responsible to parliaments, and they never seriously considered insulating themselves from the political parties, pressure groups, mass media, and mass electorates, which were highly agitated over the peace question. To be sure, compared to Metternich, Castlereagh, and Talleyrand, the Big Four were "amateur" diplomats. It does not follow, however, that because they aligned the methods and procedures of diplomacy with the prevailing requirements of party and mass politics they understood less about international affairs than their illustrious predecessors.

Churchill rightly emphasized that the peacemakers of 1918–1919 were orators, mass leaders, and men of action, "each of whom had to produce a triumph for himself and his Party and give satisfaction to national fears and passions well founded or not." But why go on and call them "embarrassed demagogues," as Churchill did?[12] Probably nostalgia for both cabinet diplomacy and status politics accounts for the still widely espoused defamation that these "plenipotentiaries were essentially politicians, old parliamentary hands, and therefore expedient-mongers whose highest qualifications for their own profession were drawbacks which unfitted them for their self-assumed [diplomatic] mission."[13]

Even during the prewar decades the growth of party, mass, and crisis politics had substantially eroded cabinet diplomacy, with politically based foreign policy actors superseding professional diplomats. By 1918–1919 this erosion of the methods, procedures, style, and personnel of the Old Diplomacy was completed. There was no going back, least of all at the opening of a revolutionary era with soaring class and party strife at home and abroad. And yet, the very day the Conference was formally inaugurated the *Temps* called on the Central Powers not to allow party conflicts to disturb international relations; not to use foreign intervention "to upset the internal equilibrium of nations"; and not bring into play party polemics in the peace deliberations. At the same time it inveighed against making partisan use

---

12 Churchill, *Aftermath*, pp. 120–121.
13 Dillon, *Inside Story*, p. 99.

of half-accurate information about these negotiations.[14] *Mirabile dictue.*

With the Armistice the political truce burst wide open in the victor nations, the forces of order and reaction seizing the offensive. In the United States the congressional elections of November 1918 returned a Republican Senate, thereby undermining domestic support for Woodrow Wilson's moderate peace project; in England the coupon election of mid-December 1918 returned a grim House of Commons, resolved to hold Lloyd George to a Carthaginian course; in Italy, in late December, Leonida Bissolati, Italy's foremost Wilsonian, resigned from Orlando's cabinet. Heartened by these developments, on December 29 Clemenceau defiantly proclaimed his skepticism of the Wilsonian program, certain that the war-hardened Chamber of 1914 was determined to have a punitive settlement.

According to Nicolson this upsurge of vindictiveness was a spontaneous prolongation of wartime passions into the post-Armistice period. Irrational hatreds swelled up and consumed "alert but ignorant electorates," which thereafter made it "impossible even for supermen to devise a peace of moderation and righteousness."[15] But was this outburst of revengeful jingoism all that spontaneous? And, if it was, did the governments and their supporters, which had known how to mobilize these hatreds, do anything to revaluate these mass sentiments?

There are numerous indications that the clamor for a punitive peace was stirred up as part of a vast political design. Except for the protofascist new Right the leaders, parties, pressure groups, patriotic leagues, and newspapers that sparked this agitation also favored rigorously conservative or outright reactionary social and economic policies. In fact, the forces of order appear to have taken advantage of the intoxication of victory either to preserve or advance their class interests and status positions under an ideological cover which was a syncretism of jingoist nationalism, baleful anti-Wilsonianism, and rabid anti-Bolshevism. Whoever was not a superpatriot was denounced as a fellow traveler of the Bolsheviks and stood accused not only of disloyalty but also of advocating a sellout peace.

The revolutionary segments of the Socialist and labor movements

---

[14] *Le Temps* (January 18, 1919).
[15] Nicolson, *Peacemaking,* pp. 7, 63–65.

FIGURE 9. Beware the Reefs!—The good ship *Democracy* faces a period of close and careful sailing. From the Brooklyn *Eagle*. (Historical Pictures Service, Chicago)

were not the primary target of the jingoist *cum* anti-Bolshevik campaign. Its aim was to rout and disconcert the very core of the forces of change, to do so now, pre-emptively, before the fast-growing Left had a chance to rally around Wilson and to make political gains from the high cost of living, rising taxes, and the strains of reconversion. In addition to championing a Wilsonian peace, this Left—this non-Communist Left—was battling for the forty-eight hour week, collective bargaining, graduated income taxes, and social welfare measures.

Already in the prewar decade the Left and the Right in Britain, France, and Italy had faced each other with mounting bitterness over these same issues. Compared to then, of course, in 1918–1919 the economic and fiscal crisis was infinitely more acute; the membership and following of the labor movement was vastly greater; the Russian Revolution stood forth both as an invigorating and a frightening example; and the Right was able to claim credit for timely preparedness as well as victory. But notwithstanding these important permutations and mutations the continuities with the prewar situation were all too apparent. Specifically, in the struggle over labor, tax, and welfare issues, the extremists of the Right frightened Conservatives into inflexibility by deliberately exaggerating the revolutionary posture and the foreign policy pacifism of the Left. In turn, this creeping inflexibility played into the hands of the radical Left, which charged the Right with domestic reaction and warmongering. By mid-1914 the moderate leaders of both camps were rapidly becoming hostages to their respective extremists, with the result that the politics of compromise and accommodation became increasingly deadlocked. Witness the threatened strike by the Triple Industrial Alliance and the Ulster crisis in Britain, the impasse over the three-year law in France, and Red Week in Italy.

The war merely sharpened this polarization of politics and labor-management relations, at the expense of the conservative-reformist center. Victory strengthened, hardened, and emboldened the refractory Right; the Russian Revolution had a similar impact on the militant Left. Both extremes left indelible marks on the politics and diplomacy of the victor powers in 1918–1919. Because the jingoist Right had champions or sympathizers in the legislatures, foreign offices, interior ministries, armed services, conservative parties, and editorial offices, its preemptive thrust was felt in a vast range of developments: in America, in the November elections, in congressional obstruction of a Wilsonian peace, in the Red Scare, and in the drive for "normalcy"; in England, in the coupon election, in Parliamentary opposition to the appeasement of Germany and Soviet Russia, and in the government's sham reconstruction program; in France, in the gestation of the *chambre bleu horizon,* in Clemenceau's intransigence toward Germany and Soviet Russia, in the resolute repression of strikes, and in parliament's obstinate refusal to approve nonregressive taxes; and in Italy, in Sidney Sonnino's domination of the peace delegation, in Gabriele d'Annunzio's expedition to Fiume, in the growth of the *Fasci de combattimento,* and in Orlando's failure to check inflation.

Except for frightening established governments and societies and serving as a pretext for the excesses of the avant-garde of anti-Bolshevism, the extreme Left had no leverage outside the labor movement. Its leaders, most of them nationally unknown, concentrated their organizational, propagandist, and conspiratorial activities on the rapidly expanding Socialist parties and trade unions, making special efforts to enlist the new recruits. They fed on each and every grievance, sparked local strikes, participated prominently in mass demonstrations, and worked their propaganda presses overtime. In 1918–1919 these zealots helped generate a mood of impatience among the rank and file, thereby goading their Majoritarian and Independent rivals into a greater sense of urgency about the labor cause. These political and syndicalist militants should not be denied their share of the credit for the enactment of the forty-eight-hour week by the Allied parliaments and for labor movements concerted and partially successful opposition to direct military intervention in Russia.

Without this impatience and activism on the Left Woodrow Wilson's moderating influence would have been completely nullified. As it was, precisely because the moderate forces of movement were so decisively checked even before the start of the Conference, Wilson had only limited leverage. Moreover, he was hesitant to appeal to the Left for help for fear that the militants would seize the initiative for themselves. Wilson was condemned to labor in a political field, both national and international, in which measured reformism, so essential to the achievement of his diplomatic aims, was fatally emasculated.

Wilson's principles and aims, like all such pronunciamentos, were destined to be honored in the breach. The conditions that had prompted their formulation and acceptance in early 1918 had passed into history: there was no longer any need to restrain the Soviet government from signing a separate peace with the Central Powers; with the success of the revolution from above in Berlin the rebellion against the Kaiser and Erich Ludendorff no longer required encouragement; and after the Armistice the Allied Governments could dispense with the support of their own forces of movement. Above all, the Allied cabinets were much less prone to bend to the ideological and diplomatic wishes of the Wilson Administration once victory had drastically reduced their dependence on American military and economic power. Besides, no programmatic guidelines had complicated the labors of the peacemakers of 1814–1815.

US power no longer needed

Even so, the President's Fourteen Points and subsequent pronouncements were not simply shunted aside. By making their two reservations with regard to the freedom of the seas and reparations the Allies conceded that Wilson's prescriptions had crystallized into a public touchstone for the coming peace negotiations; and the pre-Armistice exchanges with Germany even endowed them with a measure of contractual force.[16]

But quite apart from any moral or legal obligation to Germany, until May 1919 the Allied Governments could not afford to disavow Woodrow Wilson publicly. The President's ideology and America's economic bounty were expected to exercise a moderating influence on revolutionary conditions in defeated Europe and on the post-Armistice neurasthenia in the victor nations. Without the still potent spell of Wilsonianism the swing toward Leninism within the Left might well have assumed considerable proportions. Especially the Independents, but also the Majoritarians, trusted in the President to block a punitive peace, thereby thwarting the offensive of the Allied Right, consolidating the reformist regimes in the defeated nations, and giving the lie to Lenin's charge that Wilsonianism was but an insidious bourgeois-capitalist smokescreen.

The frenzied enthusiasm that greeted the President upon his arrival in Europe was not without political and class overtones. While Social-

---

16 Webster, "The Congress of Vienna 1814–1815 and the Conference of Paris 1919," pp. 8–9.

ist, labor, and radical-bourgeois leaders and their followers widely cheered him, their opponents berated them for apotheosizing Wilson for selfish, partisan purposes. On the eve of the Conference the Allied Governments were sufficiently apprehensive about this united front of Wilson and the Left that they purposely obstructed contacts between them. On the other hand, the governments of the defeated nations continued to profess their faith in Wilson until well after they knew that his cause was lost. As for the governments of the successor states, they courted Wilson's favor in their bid for favorable frontiers and economic aid. In sum, throughout most of the Conference the President and his arsenal of spiritual and material resources were considered indispensable by each delegation as well as by the Berne International. Significantly, even Clemenceau was careful not to risk a break with Wilson; and notwithstanding his anti-Wilsonian tirades, Lenin was eager for the President to blunt the military edge of the counterrevolutionary intervention.

At the time of the Congress of Vienna Tsar Alexander I certainly did not play such a pivotal role as did Wilson. Quite apart from the fact that the League of Nations was to serve as an instrument for peaceful change in the international arena while the Holy Alliance was designed to freeze the new status quo at home and abroad, the Tsar had considerably less leverage than Wilson. Whereas Alexander was confined to cooperation with fellow sovereigns and to military means of intervention, Wilson could marshal popular support for the League and dispose of substantial economic and financial resources which were of critical importance to the exhausted nations of Europe.[17]

R. S. Baker quite rightly stressed that the use of the "economic weapon" to achieve diplomatic and political ends "was only in its crude beginnings at Paris," and that the world would get "a fuller taste of it in the future."[18] During the Conference all nations—large and small, old and new—brought their economic resources into play; and the Conference as a whole, supported by the neutrals, enforced a strict blockade against Bolshevik Russia and Hungary.

[17] See Satow, "Peacemaking Old and New," p. 37; and H. W. V. Temperley, "Attempts at International Government in Europe: The Period of the Congress of Vienna (1814–1825) and the Period Since the Treaty of Versailles (1919–1922)," Historical Association, *Leaflet No. 56* (London, 1923), pp. 16–17.
[18] Baker, *World Settlement*, II, p. 349.

But America's use of the economic weapon was particularly note- *US econ power* worthy. She had a vast reservoir of instantly available capital, food, and manufactures, and her delegation had a precocious understanding of economic power as an instrument of control in the international politics of this dawning era of civil war.

The Armistice was not signed as yet when U.S. officials in Europe advised Washington that since America's "economic and financial support would be essential to the Allies in the post-war period" material pressures might be used to force an acceptable interpretation of "our own principles and policies."[19] Wilson himself chose Armistice Day solemnly to declare that it would be America's "fortunate duty to assist by example, by sober, friendly counsel and by *material aid* in the establishment of a just democracy throughout the world";[20] and he may well have had the economic weapon in mind when he told his advisers, during the crossing to Europe, that the U.S. would fight for a new order "agreeably if we can, disagreeably if necessary."[21]

Colonel House shared the view of many U.S. officials and business leaders that the Allies were "vitally interested in what manner we propose to our great strength" in finance, commerce, shipping, raw materials, and food.[22] As for D. H. Miller, he confidently predicted that Wilson's covenant would be accepted without any American concessions because "Europe was bankrupt financially and her Governments were bankrupt morally . . . [and] the mere hint of the withdrawal of America . . . would see the fall of every government in Europe without exception, and a revolution in every country of Europe with one possible exception."[23]

Members of the British Delegation confirmed this diagnosis. According to Keynes, in early 1919 "Europe was in complete dependence on the food supplies of the United States; and financially she was even more absolutely at their mercy." In Nicolson's judgment this economic dependence made the Allies "entirely subservient to

[19] George McFadden, representative of the War Trade Board in Europe, to Robert Lansing, November 9, 1918, cited in *F.R., P.C., 1919*, II, pp. 729–731.
[20] Cited in *F.R., P.C., 1919*, I, p. 1.
[21] Cited in Charles Seymour, *The Intimate Papers of Colonel House*, 4 vols. (Boston: Houghton Mifflin, 1928), IV, p. 282.
[22] House to Lansing, November 23, 1918, cited in *F.R., P.C., 1919*, I, p. 170. See also Patrick Hurley to Wilson, December 12, 1918, cited in *F.R., P.C., 1919*, II, p. 662.
[23] Miller, *My Diary*, III, p. 259.

the dictates of Washington" and gave Wilson an "overwhelming force of compulsion." In retrospect, both Keynes and Nicolson recall that it never occurred to them that, "if need arose, Wilson would hesitate to use" America's economic and financial power, and both attribute this hesitancy to his having been a prophet instead of a man of power.[24]

In actual fact, the American Delegation played a leading role in the formulation and implementation of diplomatically and politically intended economic policies toward Soviet Russia, Bolshevik Hungary, the successor states, and the new regimes in Germany and Austria. But whereas Wilson readily used the economic weapon to strangle Bolshevism, to support fledgling nations, and to stabilize the governments of the defeated nations, he hesitated to exert pressure on the Allies. This hesitation, however, was due to political considerations, both domestic and foreign, rather than to his prophetic disposition. At home influential senators, the patriotic leagues, the jingoist press, and select interest groups mounted a campaign against the use of the economic weapon for a Wilsonian peace of the sort advocated by the European Left. To make matters worse, the three Allied premiers were well informed about this opposition and proposed to foster and harness it for their own purposes. By early December 1918 the London *Spectator* assured its readers that Wilson did not have the "least chance of getting any treaty ratified which was repugnant to the sentiments of the Republican party"; and that since the opinions of that party were "framed in unreserved support of Great Britain and France" the Allies could approach the Conference "with all confidence."[25] Within a month the Boston *Transcript* (independent Republican) hinted that since the Allied statesmen were familiar with the American opposition as well as with the American Constitution they might be "inclined to heed rather the view of the American majority than that of a President whose general policies had been discredited by the popular vote."[26] Meanwhile Senator Henry Cabot Lodge set out to encourage the Allied Carthaginians to join him in standing up to Wilson.[27]

---

[24] John Maynard Keynes, *The Economic Consequences of the Peace* (New York: Harcourt, Brace, 1920), pp. 38–39; and Nicolson, *Peacemaking*, pp. 41–42.
[25] Cited in *The New Republic* (December 14, 1918), p. 176.
[26] Cited in *The Literary Digest* (January 11, 1919), p. 10.
[27] "I am sending you a copy of the speech which I made on Saturday [December 21, 1918, in Congress] which was intended chiefly for the benefit of the Allies." Lodge

As the *Springfield Republican* suggested, in order to "neutralize the influences working against him in his own country" the President would have "to rally sympathetic elements in Great Britain, France and Italy."[28] In fact, the Right on both sides of the Atlantic was apprehensive about the progressive *domestic* implications of a peace of reconciliation, just as the Left was nervous about the conservative domestic consequences of a vindictive settlement.

Radical publicists called attention to this political struggle "not between nations but between parties whose constituency transcended all national boundaries." For the purposes of peacemaking "the progressive wings of the American parties, British labor and liberals, French and Italian and Belgian liberals and socialists were one party; the Lodges and Milners and Carsons and Clemenceaus and their following of imperialists and protectionists constituted the opposing party."[29] To be sure, Radicals were blind to the broad popular support of the Right and crudely divided the political spectrum into two monolithic blocs. But except for these blind spots this characterization of the transnational political confrontation had considerable merit, not least because it acknowledged the inevitability of the politics of intervention. Frederick Jackson Turner quite rightly anticipated that the conservative forces of different nations were on the verge of cooperating internationally, in imitation of their Socialist rivals.[30]

Theoretically the Right indignantly and violently objected to external intervention in the internal affairs of nations. In practice, however, it championed counterrevolutionary intervention in Bolshevik countries and relied on informal transnational contacts elsewhere. Naturally Lenin and Karl Radek disdainfully rejected this principle of the nonintervention in the internal affairs of other nations[31] and proceeded

to Theodore Roosevelt, cited in Roger Burlingame and Alden Stevens, *Victory Without Peace* (New York: Harcourt, Brace, 1944), p. 204. See also Lodge's letter to Henry White on the eve of White's departure for Paris, cited in Allan Nevins, *Henry White* (New York: Harcourt, Brace, 1944), p. 172.

[28] *Springfield Republican,* December 15, 1918, forwarded by Tumulty to Wilson, December 17, 1918, in Wilson Papers, VIII A:3.

[29] *The New Republic* (December 21, 1918), p. 212. By March 21, 1919, in discussing the outburst of Republican opposition to Wilson, the *Daily News* (London) commented that "the lines of division today run not perpendicularly between nations, but horizontally through nations."

[30] Frederick Jackson Turner, "International Political Parties in a Durable League of Nations" (November 1918), in Ray Stannard Baker Papers, Firestone Library, Princeton University.

[31] This principle of nonintervention was the principle which guided legitimist Europe

to devise organizational mechanisms with which to maximize the effectiveness of their predesigned interference abroad. Meanwhile, Wilson searched for political support for the material and ideological intervention for which he was so much better equipped than Lloyd George, Clemenceau, Orlando, and even Lenin.

As noted before, his supporters were in retreat in the United States as well as in Europe. In America *The New Republic, The Nation,* the League of Free Nations Society, the Committee of 48, segments of organized labor, and internationally minded businessmen and financiers were fighting a rear-guard battle against onrushing conservatives, superpatriots, and anti-Communists. Simultaneously in the Allied nations the non-Communist Left and the radical bourgeoisie were in disarray. Perhaps this narrow political base at home and in the Allied countries accounts for Wilson's hesitancy to go over the heads of the Big Three. The hardening of opinion in his own country sensitized him to the hardening of opinion in London, Paris, and Rome. Moreover, quite apart from being careful not to encourage the revolutionary Left, Wilson was worried about weakening governments, including the Polish and Rumanian governments, that carried the brunt of the containment of and the intervention in Russia.

In sum, a frontal attack on the victory-hardened Allies, which Socialists and Radicals on both sides of the Atlantic urged upon the President, was not to be undertaken lightly. The task and responsibility would have been staggering, the risk immense—the more so for a statesman and politician sworn to reason rather than passion, to agreement by consent rather than coercion, to reform rather than revolution. The issue is hardly whether or not Wilson was sincere about his principles and aims; nor is the issue one of the quality of his strategic and tactical skills as diplomatist and politician. Even assuming Wilson scored exceptionally high on all these counts, a prior question must be considered: how pertinent and consequential was Wilson's reformist project in the crisis setting of 1918–1919?

Unlike Clemenceau, the President strained to understand this crisis in its world historical context. Both he and Lloyd George consistently

---

after the Congress of Vienna, while in the struggle for liberation, international Communists all along advocated the energetic intervention in the affairs of the whole world." Karl Radek, *Ein offener Brief an Philipp Scheidemann* (*ca.* November 20, 1918; w.p.), pp. 2–3.

rejected the conspiratorial view of the Russian Revolution, which they saw as a variant of the French Revolution in scale, ecumenical appeal, and duration.

Wilson's concern was less with the importance of the Revolution for Russia than for Europe and the world. He saw the example of the Revolution, embellished by stirring manifestoes, acting upon crisis-torn societies which in the prewar years had been rife with discontent and agitated by revolutionary parties and ideologies. According to Isaiah Bowman, the President told his advisers on the S.S. *George Washington* that the poison of Bolshevism was spreading because it was "a protest against the way in which the world had worked."[32] William Bullitt, who was present on this same occasion, recorded Wilson as saying that the only way he could "explain the susceptibility of the people of Europe to the poison of Bolshevism, was that their Governments had been run for wrong purposes." Wilson then added his prediction that unless the peace were made "on the highest principles of justice it would be swept away by the peoples of the world in less than a generation." In that event he intended "to run away and hide on the Island of Guam or somewhere else remote, for there would follow not mere conflict but cataclysm."[33] A bit later, when pleading with the Big Three for an accommodation with Lenin, he warned that "there was certainly a latent force behind Bolshevism which attracted as much sympathy as its more brutal aspects caused general disgust." Wilson attributed this sympathy to "a feeling of revolt throughout the world against large vested interests which influence the world both in the economic and in the political sphere."[34]

It was precisely because the Russian Revolution was "a menace to others" that Wilson was so reluctant to leave Russia to "settle her own affairs in her own way."[35] With the help and encouragement of his key advisers, notably Herbert Hoover, Wilson spearheaded various Allied efforts to tame the Russian Revolution. In fact, these efforts came to be central to Wilson's overall peacemaking strategy.

[32] Cited in Seymour, *Intimate Papers*, IV, p. 282.
[33] Bullitt's diary notes on the S.S. *George Washington*, entry of December 9, 1918, in Bullitt Papers.
[34] *F.R., P.C., 1919*, III (January 16, 1919, a.m.), p. 583.
[35] In late December Wilson told a British official that "Russia should be left to settle her own affairs in her own way so long as she did not become a menace to others." Notes on interview with Wilson by Frank Worthington, Deputy Chief Censor, dated December 28, 1918, National Archives, Secret File, Document 811.001W/163.

Whereas the Entente Governments tended to advocate either direct or indirect military intervention—with America providing most of the funds, the material, and the food supplies—the American Delegation gave first priority to diplomatic, economic, and ideological intervention. Not that the Wilson Administration backed out of or cut back the armed intervention started in mid-1918. Still, by comparison it was particularly intent on exploring those avenues that might obviate military measures partially or altogether. Of course this nonmartial approach suited Wilson's view of the dynamics of the Russian Revolution, his diplomatic style, and America's foreign policy capabilities.

Rather than denounce the Bolshevik Revolution as either a sinister conspiracy or a vile crime, Wilson saw it as the natural and fitting culmination of lingering popular dissatisfactions with tsarist regime, catalyzed by the strains of war and enthusiasm for the seductive promises of the Bolshevik ideology. Such dissatisfaction and ardor could not be conquered by force of arms, not least because a military onslaught threatened to restore the *ancien régime*. Clemenceau and, to a lesser extent, Lloyd George were not particularly bothered by the prospect of the Whites replacing Lenin, so that the irresolution of their intervention in the Russian Civil War was not a function of political scruples but of overstrained resources and anti-interventionist pressures. Wilson, however, refused to close his eyes to the ideological and political aftergrowth of the destruction of the Soviet regime. The qualified recognition of Alexander Kolchak, which was delayed until late May 1919, mirrored his desperate but unrealistic and self-deceiving attempt to transform the unmistakably counterrevolutionary intervention into a crusade for the democratization of Russia. That even his worst fears were justified was amply demonstrated once the Allied-sponsored overthrow of Béla Kun was followed by a White terror and by anti-Semitic pogroms.

On the intellectual plane the President understood that revolution and counterrevolution inevitably incited and needed each other. In terms of policy, however, he simply could not admit the impossibility of a moderate middle course. Like it or not, America was one of the senior partners in a coalition resolved to contain or destroy the Bolshevik Revolution. To achieve this objective the Allies needed the military services of Finland, Poland, Rumania, and Germany, even at

Paradox : Wilson must allow conserv. elements(Russ. pon) to be built up in order to contain Bolshevism

the price of allowing conservative and reactionary forces in these countries to benefit from this anti-Bolshevik campaign.

It was to avoid paying this distasteful political price that the American delegates wanted to explore the use of nonmilitary methods of intervention. Their aim was to moderate and domesticate rather than destroy the revolutionary regime in Russia. In their judgment the ideological canons of Bolshevism and the lust for power of the Bolshevik leaders were not the primary moving force of the Soviet dictatorship. According to some American officials Lenin's iron rule at home and revolutionary agitation abroad were part of a *levée en masse* by a revolutionary government fighting for its life against internal insurgents and foreign invasion in a country bled white by war. Provided these mainsprings of revolutionary dictatorship were removed or reduced, the Soviet leaders could afford to relax their iron grip and agree to a united front of the Left for the reconstruction, modernization, and reform of Russia. The Allies could contribute to this relaxation of revolutionary discipline and terror not only by stopping their intervention and lifting the blockade but also by providing economic and technical assistance.

The Buckler-Litvinov conversations, the Prinkipo proposal, and the Bullitt Mission were so many efforts in this direction. All alike were opposed and sabotaged by the entire French Delegation, by key members of the American and British delegations, by antiappeasement forces in the Allied parliaments, by all but one of the Russian *émigré* groups in Paris, by the Whites in Russia, and by the governments of most of the new states along Russia's western borders. Some were motivated by power-political considerations and others by age-old national hatreds, but all alike called forth and embodied counterrevolutionary economic, social, and political forces. There was no corresponding reservoir of support for moderation. Wilson knew this; and so did Lenin.

Chances for a negotiated accommodation were never very good. The Big Four, including Wilson, insisted on military conditions that were designed to favor the Whites and their borderland allies and sought to extract deliberating political concessions in exchange for lifting the blockade and providing food. In turn, Lenin was careful not to play any of his spare trumps, notably critical and advanced military positions and control of the railways. Whereas strictly territorial issues might have been compromised, mutual distrust stemming from irreconcilable political, economic, and social persuasions stood in the way of an overall settlement—at a time that both sides still hoped for total victory. Lenin was not about to trust Wilson, whom he rightly suspected of being a prisoner—even if a reluctant prisoner—of the counterrevolution.

With the March–April crisis the Russian question once again became acute. The stand of the Right toward Bolshevism both inside and outside Russia stiffened still further in the face of rising labor unrest in the Allied countries, renewed Spartacist outbreaks in Germany, the establishment of a Soviet outpost in Bavaria, the triumph of Béla Kun in Hungary, and the explosive instability in Vienna. This rigidification was well under way when rumors of the Bullitt Mission incited the die-hards to protest furiously against any dealings with Lenin and to urge stepped-up military measures.

Once again caught between the appeasers and the irreconcilables, Wilson abandoned a direct diplomatic approach in favor of an untried economic formula. The Nansen Plan for a commission of neutrals to feed Russia originated in the American Delegation. At first, in order to broaden its ideological appeal, the letter drafted by Hoover for Fridtjot Nansen's signature was supposed to be countersigned by Karl Hjalmar Branting. But the leader of the Second International preferred to stay in the background. Under the Nansen scheme the Russian Bolsheviks were asked to halt military operations "against our allies" on all fronts and to waive "political recognition or negotiation" in exchange for food and other essential supplies to be provided by a neutral relief agency. Obviously, the arrangements for the distribution in Russia of this "wholly nonpolitical" relief would be decisive, primarily because their political implications were the crux of this proposal.

In fact, political rather than humanitarian purposes were at the heart of the Nansen Plan. This political design was forcefully sketched out by Hoover in a remarkable letter to President Wilson, dated March 28, 1919.[36]

---

[36] The full text of this letter is in the House Papers, 10:37; excerpts are cited in Herbert Hoover, *The Ordeal of Woodrow Wilson* (New York: McGraw-Hill, 1958), pp. 117–119.

As the result of Bolshevik economic conceptions, the people of Russia are dying of hunger and disease at the rate of some hundreds of thousands monthly in a country that formerly supplied food to a large part of the world.

I feel it is my duty to lay before you in just as few words as possible my views as to the American relation to Bolshevism and its manifestations. These views at least have the merit of being an analysis of information and thought gleaned from my own experience and the independent sources which I now have over the whole of Europe, through our widespread relief organization.

It simply cannot be denied that this swinging of the social pendulum from the tyranny of the extreme right to the tyranny of the extreme left is based on a foundation of real social grievance. The tyranny of the reactionaries in Eastern and Central Europe for generations before the war, and the suffering of their common people is but a commonplace to every social student. This situation was thrown into bold relief by the war and the breakdown of those reactionary tyrannies. After fighting actually stopped on the various fronts the famine which followed has further emphasized the gulf between the lower and upper classes. The poor were starved and driven mad in the presence of extravagance and waste.

It is to be noticed that the Bolshevik ascendancy or even their strong attempts so far are confined to areas of former reactionary tyranny. Their courses represent the not unnatural violence of a mass of ignorant humanity, who themselves have learned in grief of tyranny and violence over generations. Our people, who enjoy so great liberty and general comfort, cannot fail to sympathize to some degree with these blind gropings for better social condition. If former revolutions in ignorant masses are any guide, the pendulum will yet swing back to some moderate position when bitter experience has taught the economic and social follies of present obsessions. No greater fortune can come to the world than that these foolish ideas should have an opportunity somewhere of bankrupting themselves.

It is not necessary for any American to debate the utter foolishness of these economic tenets. We must all agree that our processes of production and distribution, the outgrowth of a hundred generations, in the stimulation to individual initiative, the large equality of opportunity and infinite development of mind and body, while not perfect, come about as near perfection as is possible from the mixture of avarice, ambition, altruism, intelligence, ignorance and education, of which the human animal is today composed. The Bolshevik's land of illusion is that he can perfect these human qualities by destroying the basic processes of production and distribution instead of devoting himself to securing a better application of the collective surplus.

Politically, the Bolsheviki most certainly represent a minority in every country where they are in control, and as such they constitute a tyranny that is the negation of democracy, for democracy as I see it must rest on the execution of the will of the majority expressed by free and unterrified suffrage. As a tyranny, the Bolshevik has resorted to terror, bloodshed and murder to a degree long since abandoned even amongst reactionary tyrannies. He has even to a greater degree relied upon criminal instinct to support his doctrines than even autocracy did. By enveloping into his doctrines the cry of the helpless and the downtrodden, he has embraced a large degree of emotionalism and has thereby given an impulse to his propaganda comparable only to the impulse of large spiritual movements. This propaganda, however, in my view will stir other populations only in ratio to their proportions of the suffering and ignorant and criminal. I feel myself, therefore, that the political danger of spread of Bolshevism by propaganda is a direct factor of the social and political development of the population which they attempt to impregnate. Where the gulf between the middle classes and the lower classes is large, and where the lower classes have been kept in ignorance and distress, this propaganda will be fatal and do violence to normal democratic development. For these reasons, I have no fear of it in the United States, and my fears as to other countries would be gauged by the above criterion. It is possible that the Soviet type of government might take hold in some other countries as a primitive form of democracy, but its virulence will be tempered by their previous degree of political subversion.

There remains in my mind one more point to be examined, that is as to whether the Bolshevik centers now stirred by great emotional hopes will not undertake large military crusades in an attempt to impose their doctrines on other defenseless people. This is a point on which my mind is divided with the evidence at hand, and it seems to me that the whole treatment of the problem must revolve on the determination of this one question. If this spirit is inherent in their doctrine, it appears to me that we must disregard all other questions and be prepared to fight, for exactly the same reasons that we entered the European War against Germany. If this is not the case, then it appears to me that from an American point of view we should not involve ourselves in what may be a ten-year military entanglement in Europe. The American people cannot say that we are going to insist that any given population must work out its internal social problems according to our particular conception of democracy. In any event, I have the most serious doubt that outside forces entering upon such an enterprise can do other than infinite harm, for any great wave of emotion must ferment and spread under repression. In the swing of the social pendulum from the extreme left back toward the right, it will find the point of stabilization based on racial instincts that could never be established by outside intervention.

I think we have also to contemplate what would actually happen if we undertook military intervention in, say, a case like Hungary. We should probably be involved in years of police duty, and our first act would probably in the nature of things make us a party to reestablishing the reactionary classes in their economic domination over the lower classes. This is against our fundamental national spirit, and I doubt whether our soldiers under these circumstances could resist infection with Bolshevik ideas. It also requires consideration as to whether or not our people at home, on gradual enlightenment as to the social wrongs of the lower classes in these countries, would stand for our providing power by which such reactionaries held their position, and we would perchance be thrown in to an attempt as governors to work out some social reorganization of these countries. We thus become a mandatory with a vengeance. We become, in fact, one of four mandatories, each with a different political and social outlook, for it would necessarily be a joint Allied undertaking. Furthermore, in our present engagements with France, England and Italy, we become a junior in this partnership of four. It is therefore inevitable that in these matters where our views and principles are at variance with the European Allies we would find ourselves subordinated and even committed to policies against our convictions.

In all these lights, I have the following three suggestions: *Nonrecognition*

First: *We cannot even remotely recognize this murderous tyranny without stimulating actionist radicalism in every country in Europe and without transgressing on every National ideal of our own.*

Hoover aid

Second: *That some Neutral of international reputation for probity and ability should be allowed to create a second Belgian Relief Commission for Russia. He should ask the Northern Neutrals who are especially interested both politically and financially in the restoration of better conditions in Russia, to give to him diplomatic, financial and transportation support; that he should open negotiations with the Allied governments on the ground of desire to enter upon the humane work of saving life, and ask the conditions upon which ships carrying food and other necessaries will be allowed to pass. He should be told that we will raise no obstructions and would even help in his humanitarian task if he gets assurances that the Bolsheviki will cease all militant action across certain defined boundaries and cease their subsidizing of disturbances abroad; under these conditions that he could raise money, ships and food, either from inside or outside Russia; that he must secure an agreement covering equitable distribution, and he might even demand that Germany help pay for this. This plan does not involve any recognition or relationship by the Allies of the Bolshevik murderers now in control any more than England recognized Germany in its deals with the Belgian Relief. It would appear to me that such a proposal would at least test out whether this is a militant force engrossed upon world domination. If such an arrangement could be accomplished it might at least give a period of rest along the frontiers of Europe and would give some hope of stabilization. Time can thus be taken to determine whether or not this whole system is a world danger, and whether the Russian people will not themselves swing back*

to moderation and themselves bankrupt these ideas. This plan, if success-
ful, would save an immensity of helpless human life and would save our
country from further entanglements which today threaten to pull us from
our National ideals.

oppose Red *Third: I feel strongly the time has arrived for you again to reassert your*
spiritual leadership of democracy in the world as opposed to tyrannies
of all kinds. Could you not take an early opportunity to analyze, as only
you can, Bolshevism from its political, economic, humane and its criminal
points of view, and, while yielding its aspirations, sympathetically to show
its utter foolishness as a basis of economic development; show its true
social ends; rap our own reactionaries for their destruction of social bet-
terment and thereby their stimulation of Bolshevism; point, however, to the
steady progress of real democracy in these roads of social betterment.
I believe you would again align the hearts of the suffering for orderly
progress against anarchy, not alone in Russia but in every Allied country.

If the militant features of Bolshevism were drawn in colors with their
true parallel with Prussianism as an attempt at world domination that we
do not stand for, it would check the fears that today haunt all men's minds.

In this letter Hoover brilliantly summarized the key tenets of the
Wilsonian view of the Bolshevik problem: Russian Bolshevism was a
condition to be cured rather than a conspiracy to be destroyed;
there were considerable sources of Bolshevik contagion outside Russia; the spiritual appeals of the Bolshevik ideology were far from
negligible; the reactionary consequences of a military crusade against
Bolshevism could not be ignored; and a military truce combined with
economic aid was most likely to redirect the revolutionary currents
into reformist channels in Russia.

But the letter also struck some novel chords. Above all, Hoover
made an insidious comparison of the "foolishness" of Bolshevik economic doctrines with the unequaled excellence of the American economic system. Moreover, he envisaged the possibility that doctrinally
the Bolsheviks were sworn to export their economic and political system, if need be even by force of arms. Without abandoning the view
that the Bolshevik system was primarily a product of historical conditions Hoover now stressed the doctrinal sources of Soviet conduct.

As a result, while Hoover's policy recommendations dovetailed
with Wilson's drive to give priority to nonmilitary intervention, they
also embodied a new departure. Accordingly, Wilson was urged to
couple his economic intervention with an ideological counteroffen-
sive. Hoover wanted the President to issue a manifesto criticizing the

doctrine, promise, and practice of Bolshevism and setting forth the aims and methods of reformist and democratic capitalism. In other words, just as the recently completed crusade against the Central Powers had required and profited from the Fourteen Points, so this incipient crusade against the rival social-political system required an anti-Bolshevik manifesto.

Even though Wilson successfully insisted on certain political assurances as a precondition for recognizing Kolchak, he never went on to issue a full-blown manifesto proclaiming the objectives of the Big Powers' participation in armed containment and intervention. Perhaps he never did so because he could at best be halfhearted about an operation whose carriers and objectives were too counterrevolutionary for his own liking. The words and principles of a Wilsonian pronouncement would have been blatantly incompatible with the whole thrust of the enterprise, thus making it that much easier for Lenin and his champions to expose the hypocrisy of the democratic-reformist ideology. A declaration like that issued at Pillnitz against the French Revolution would have been more appropriate, but Foch or Churchill, rather than Wilson, would have had to formulate it.

Documents
WILSON AND RUSSIA AT PARIS

The following documents, presented in chronological order, are selected to reveal Wilson's Russian policy at the Paris Peace Conference. Did Wilson's approach to Bolshevism foreshadow later Cold War attitudes in America?

WILSON ON THE PRINKIPO CONFERENCE

Notes of Conversations Held at the Quai d'Orsay in Paris on January 16, 21, and 22, 1919

The following three documents relate specifically to Wilson's role in the genesis of the Allied effort early in 1919 to arrange an all-Russian political conference at Prinkipo Island.

Meeting of January 16, 1919. Mr. Lloyd George referred to the objection that had been raised to permitting Bolshevik delegates to come to Paris. It had been claimed that they would convert France and England to Bolshevism. If England becomes Bolshevist, it will not be because a single Bolshevist representative is permitted to enter England. On the other hand, if a military enterprise were started against the Bolsheviki, that would make England Bolshevist, and there would be a Soviet in London. For his part, Mr. Lloyd George was not afraid of Bolshevism if the facts are known in England and the United States. The same applies to Germany. He was convinced that an educated democracy can be always trusted to turn down Bolshevism.

Under all the circumstances, Mr. Lloyd George saw no better way out than to follow the third alternative. Let the Great Powers impose their conditions and summon these people to Paris to give an account of themselves to the Great Powers, not to the Peace Conference.

M. Pichon suggested that it might be well to ask M. Noulens, the French Ambassador to Russia, who had just returned to France, to appear before the meeting tomorrow morning, and give those present his views on the Russian situation.

From United States Department of State, *Papers Relating to the Foreign Relations of the United States: The Paris Peace Conference of 1919,* 13 vols. (Washington, D.C., 1942–1947), III, pp. 591–593, 647–649, 676–677, 1042–1043; V, pp. 528–530, 560, 735–737; VI, pp. 15, 34–36, 233.

President Wilson stated that he did not see how it was possible to controvert the statement of Mr. Lloyd George. He thought that there was a force behind his discussion which was no doubt in his mind, but which it might be desirable to bring out a little more definitely. He did not believe that there would be sympathy anywhere with the brutal aspect of Bolshevism. If it were not for the fact of the domination of large vested interests in the political and economic world, while it might be true that this evil was in process of discussion and slow reform, it must be admitted, that the general body of men have grown impatient at the failure to bring about the necessary reform. He stated that there were many men who represented large vested interests in the United States who saw the necessity for these reforms and desired something which should be worked out at the Peace Conference, namely, the establishment of some machinery to provide for the opportunity of the individuals greater than the world has ever known. Capital and labor in the United States are not friends. Still they are not enemies in the sense that they are thinking of resorting to physical force to settle their differences. But they are distrustful, each of the other. Society cannot go on on that plane. On the one hand, there is a minority possessing capital and brains; on the other, a majority consisting of the great bodies of workers who are essential to the minority, but do not trust the minority, and feel that the minority will never render them their rights. A way must be found to put trust and cooperation between these two.

President Wilson pointed out that the whole world was disturbed by this question before the Bolsheviki came into power. Seeds need soil, and the Bolsheviki seeds found the soil already prepared for them.

President Wilson stated that he would not be surprised to find that the reason why British and United States troops would not be ready to enter Russia to fight the Bolsheviki was explained by the fact that the troops were not at all sure that if they put down Bolshevism they would not bring about a re-establishment of the ancient order. For example, in making a speech recently, to a well-dressed audience in New York City who were not to be expected to show such feeling, Mr. Wilson had referred casually to Russia, stating that the United States would do its utmost to aid her suppressed people. The audience exhibited the greatest enthusiasm, and this had remained in the

President's mind as an index to where the sympathies of the New World are.

President Wilson believed that those present would be playing against the principle of free spirit of the world if they did not give Russia a chance to find herself along the lines of utter freedom. He concurred with Mr. Lloyd George's view and supported his recommendations that the third line of procedure be adopted.

President Wilson stated that he had also, like Mr. Lloyd George, received a memorandum from his experts which agreed substantially with the information which Mr. Lloyd George had received. There was one point which he thought particularly worthy of notice, and that was the report that the strength of the Bolshevik leaders lay in the argument that if they were not supported by the people of Russia, there would be foreign intervention, and the Bolsheviki were the only thing that stood between the Russians and foreign military control. It might well be that if the Bolsheviki were assured that they were safe from foreign aggression, they might lose support of their own movement.

President Wilson further stated that he understood that the danger of destruction of all hope in the Baltic provinces was immediate, and that it should be made very clear if the British proposal were adopted, that the Bolsheviki would have to withdraw entirely from Lithuania and Poland. If they would agree to this to refrain from reprisals and outrages, he, for his part, would be prepared to receive representatives from as many groups and centers of action, as chose to come, and endeavor to assist them to reach a solution of their problem.

He thought that the British proposal contained the only suggestions that led anywhere. It might lead nowhere. But this could at least be found out. . . .

Meeting of January 21, 1919. M. Clemenceau said they had met together to decide what could be done in Russia under present circumstances.

President Wilson said that in order to have something definite to discuss, he wished to take advantage of a suggestion made by Mr. Lloyd George and to propose a modification of the British proposal. He wished to suggest that the various organized groups in Russia should be asked to send representatives, not to Paris, but to some other place, such as Salonica, convenient of approach, there to meet such representatives as might be appointed by the Allies, in order to see whether they could draw up a program upon which agreement could be reached.

Mr. Lloyd George pointed out that the advantage of this would be that they could be brought straight there from Russia through the Black Sea without passing through other countries.

M. Sonnino said that some of the representatives of the various Governments were already here in Paris, for example, M. Sazonoff. Why should these not be heard?

President Wilson expressed the view that the various parties should not be heard separately. It would be very desirable to get all these representatives in one place, and still better, all in one room, in order to obtain a close comparison of views.

Mr. Balfour said that a further objection to M. Sonnino's plan was that if M. Sazonoff was heard in Paris, it would be difficult to refuse to hear the others in Paris also, and M. Clemenceau objected strongly to having some of these representatives in Paris.

M. Sonnino explained that all the Russian parties had some representatives here, except the Soviets, whom they did not wish to hear.

Mr. Lloyd George remarked that the Bolsheviks were the very people some of them wished to hear.

M. Sonnino continuing, said that they had heard M. Litvinoff's statements that morning. The Allies were now fighting against the Bolsheviks, who were their enemies, and therefore they were not obliged to hear them with the others.

M. Balfour remarked that the essence of President Wilson's proposal was that the parties must all be heard at one and the same time.

Mr. Lloyd George expressed the view that the acceptance of M. Sonnino's proposals would amount to their hearing a string of people, all of whom held the same opinion, and all of whom would strike the same note. But they would not hear the people who at the present moment were actually controlling European Russia. In deference to M. Clemenceau's views, they had put forward this new proposal. He thought it would be quite safe to bring the Bolshevik representatives to Salonica, or perhaps to Lemnos. It was absolutely necessary to endeavor to make peace. The report read by President Wilson that morning went to show that the Bolsheviks were not convinced of the error of their ways, but they apparently realized the folly of their present methods. Therefore they were endeavoring to come to terms.

President Wilson asked to be permitted to urge one aspect of the case. As M. Sonnino had implied, they were all repelled by Bolshevism, and for that reason they had placed armed men in opposition to them. One of the things that was clear in the Russian situation was that by opposing Bolshevism with arms they were in reality serving the cause of Bolshevism. The Allies were making it possible for Bolsheviks to argue that Imperialistic and Capitalistic Governments were endeavoring to exploit the country and to give the land back to the landlords, and so bring about a reaction. If it could be shown that this was not true and that the Allies were prepared to deal with the rulers of Russia, much of the moral forces of this argument would disappear. The allegation that the Allies were against the people and wanted to control their affairs provided the argument which enabled them to raise armies. If, on the other hand, the Allies could swallow their pride and the natural repulsion which they felt for the Bolsheviks, and see the representatives of all organized groups in one place, he thought it would bring about a marked reaction against Bolshevism.

M. Clemenceau said that, in principle, he did not favor conversation with the Bolsheviks; not because they were criminals, but because we would be raising them to our level by saying that they were worthy of entering into conversation with us. The Bolshevik danger was very great at the present moment. Bolshevism was spreading. It had invaded the Baltic Provinces and Poland, and that very morning they had received very bad news regarding its spread to Budapest and Vienna. . . .

Meeting of January 22, 1919. President Wilson read a draft proclamation which he had prepared for the consideration of his colleagues, in accordance with the decision reached at yesterday's meeting.

After a discussion the following text was adopted, to be publicly transmitted to parties invited:

The single object the representatives of the associated Powers have had in mind in their discussions of the course they should pursue with regard to Russia has been to help the Russian people, not to hinder them, or to interfere in any manner with their right to settle their own affairs in their own way. They regard the Russian people as their friends not their enemies, and are willing to help them in any way they are willing to be helped. It is clear to them that the troubles and distresses of the Russian people will steadily increase, hunger and privation of every kind become more and more acute, more and more widespread, and more and more impossible to relieve, unless order is restored, and normal conditions of labor, trade and transportation once more created, and they are seeking some way in which to assist the Russian people to establish order.

They recognize the absolute right of the Russian people to direct their own affairs without dictation or direction of any kind from outside. They do not wish to exploit or make use of Russia in any way. They recognize the revolution without reservation, and will in no way, and in no circumstances, aid or give countenance to any attempt at a counterrevolution. It is not their wish or purpose to favor or assist any one of those organized groups now contending for the leadership and guidance of Russia as against the others. Their sole and sincere purpose is to do what they can to bring Russia peace and an opportunity to find her way out of her present troubles.

The associated Powers are now engaged in the solemn and responsible work of establishing the peace of Europe and of the world, and they are keenly alive to the fact that Europe and the world cannot be at peace if Russia is not. They recognize and accept it as their duty, therefore, to serve Russia in this matter as generously, as unselfishly, as thoughtfully, as ungrudgingly as they would serve every other friend and ally. And they are ready to render this service in the way that is most acceptable to the Russian people.

In this spirit and with this purpose, they have taken the following action: They invite every organized group that is now exercising, or attempting to exercise, political authority or military control anywhere in Siberia, or within the boundaries of European Russia as they stood before the war just concluded (except in Finland) to send representatives, not exceeding three representatives for each group, to the Princes Islands, Sea of Marmara, where they will be met by representatives of the associated Powers, provided, in the meantime, there is a truce of arms amongst the parties invited, and that all armed forces anywhere sent or directed against any people or territory outside the boundaries of European Russia as they stood before the war, or against Finland, or against any people or territory whose autonomous action is in contemplation in the fourteen articles upon which the present negotiations are based, shall be meanwhile withdrawn, and aggressive military action cease. These representatives are invited to confer with the representatives of the Associated Powers in the freest and frankest way, with a view to ascertaining the wishes of all sections of the Russian people, and bringing about, if possible, some understanding and agreement by which Russia may work out her own purposes and happy cooperative relations be established between her people and the other peoples of the world.

A prompt reply to this invitation is requested. Every facility for the *journey of the representatives, including transport across the Black Sea, will be given by the Allies, and all the parties concerned are expected to give the same facilities. The representative[s] will be expected at the place appointed by the 15th February, 1919.*

WILSON ON INTERVENTION IN RUSSIA

Minutes of a Supreme War Council Session Held at the Quai d'Orsay, Paris, February 14, 1919 and of a Meeting Held at President Wilson's House in the Place des Etats-Unis, Paris, May 9, 1919.

The following two documents evidence Wilson's opposition at Paris to any large-scale extension of Allied armed intervention in Russia.

Meeting of February 14, 1919.   President Wilson said that since Mr. Churchill had come over specially to anticipate his departure, he felt that he should express what his personal thoughts on the subject were. Among the many uncertainties connected with Russia, he had a very clear opinion about two points. The first was that the troops of the Allied and Associated Powers were doing no sort of good in Russia. They did not know for whom or for what they were fighting. They were not assisting any promising common effort to establish order throughout Russia. They were assisting local movements, like, for instance, that of the Cossacks, who could not be induced to move outside their own sphere. His conclusion, therefore, was that the Allied and Associated Powers ought to withdraw their troops from all parts of Russian territory.

The second related to Prinkipo. The policy tending to a meeting at Prinkipo had been instituted in order to find out what the people in Russia were thinking and purposing to do. As far as he was concerned, he would be quite content that informal American representatives should meet representatives of the Bolsheviks. In their reply the Bolsheviks offered a number of things which had not been asked for, such as repayment of debts, concessions and territorial compensations. This answer was not only uncalled for, but might be thought insulting. What the Allies had in mind was the establishment of peace in Russia as an element of the world's peace. The first condition of the meeting asked for by the Allies was the cessation of attacks by Russian troops on the communities outside their borders. If the other Russian Governments would not come to Prinkipo to meet the Allies, why should the Allies not imitate Mahomet, and go to them? What we were seeking was not a *rapprochement* with the Bolsheviks, but clear information. The reports received from Russia from various official and unofficial sources were so conflicting that it was impossible to form a coherent picture of the state of the country. Some light on the situation might be obtained by meeting the Russian representatives.

Mr. Churchill said the complete withdrawal of all Allied troops was a logical and clear policy, but its consequence would be the destruction of all non-Bolshevik armies in Russia. These numbered at the present time about 500,000 men and though their quality was not of the best, their numbers were nevertheless increasing. Such a policy would be equivalent to pulling out the linch-pin from the whole machine. There would be no further armed resistance to the Bolsheviks in Russia, and an interminable vista of violence and misery was all that remained for the whole of Russia.

President Wilson pointed out that the existing forces of the Allies could not stop the Bolsheviks, and that not one of the Allies was prepared to reinforce its troops.

M. Sonnino asked whether the Allies might not continue to supply arms to the non-Bolshevik elements?

President Wilson observed that they made very little use of them when they had them.

Mr. Churchill agreed that none of the Allies could send conscript troops to Russia. He thought, however, that volunteers, technical experts, arms, munitions, tanks, aeroplanes, etc. might be furnished.

President Wilson understood the problem was to know what use would be made of these forces and supplies. In some areas they would certainly be assisting reactionaries. Consequently, if the Allies were asked what they were supporting in Russia they would be compelled to reply that they did not know. Conscripts could not be sent and volunteers probably could not be obtained. He himself felt guilty in that the United States had in Russia insufficient forces, but it was not possible to increase them. It was certainly a cruel dilemma. At present our soldiers were being killed in Russia, if they were removed many Russians might lose their lives. But some day or other the

Allied troops would have to be withdrawn; they could not be maintained there for ever and the consequences to the Russians would only be deferred.

Meeting of May 9, 1919.   President Wilson presented a military problem to his colleagues. The United States, he said, as agreed between the Allied and Associated Powers some time back, had been trying to send supplies to the civilian population of Siberia from Vladivostock. By agreement between the Allies and [omission] a Mr. Stevens, who, long ago in the days of the old regime had been in Siberia, had become the head of a somewhat inconvenient Commission to run the railroads of Siberia.[1] The United States had agreed to police the railroads as far west as Irkutsk.[2] The position was that the United States Government did not believe in Kolchak. The British and French military representatives in Siberia, however, were supporting him. Kolchak had become irritated by the presence on the railway of United States soldiers, whom he regarded as neutrals. Moreover, the impression had got abroad among the peasants of Siberia that the United States was the standard of a free Government which they ought to imitate. When they saw the attitude of neutrality taken by the United States soldiers, they thought there must be something wrong with the Government of Kolchak. Further, the Cossacks were out of sympathy with the United States soldiers and he suspected that the Japanese would be glad to have a collision between the Cossacks and American soldiers. As a consequence of this state of affairs the United States Government found itself faced with the two following alternatives:—

1. To take sides with Kolchak and send much stronger forces to Siberia.
2. To withdraw.

If the former alternative were adopted and the United States increased their forces it was certain that the Japanese would increase

---

[1] The agreement was between the Allies and the United States. For the Inter-Allied Railway Agreement and correspondence concerning the American Railway Mission in Russia, headed by John F. Stevens, see *Foreign Relations,* 1918, Russia, vol. III, pp. 183–307; *ibid.,* 1919, Russia, pp. 236–260; *ibid.,* 1923 vol. I, pp. 758–777; *ibid.,* The Lansing Papers, vol. II, pp. 329–331, 334, 336–337, 339–342, 359.
[2] For assignment of sections of the Siberian railways to be guarded by American and Allied troops, see telegram No. 240, April 22, 2 p.m., from the Consul at Vladivostock, *Foreign Relations,* 1919, Russia, p. 555.

theirs still more. The original agreement had been that the Japanese and the United States should send roughly equivalent forces. When the United States sent 9,000 men the Japanese sent 12,000 men. He had not objected to this slight discrepancy, but the numbers of Japanese had subsequently gone up to 70,000, which had afterwards been reduced to a nominal 30,000. This, however, left a great disproportion. If the United States troops continued merely to guard the railway and to maintain, as it were, a neutral position, he was advised that collisions were bound to occur. If United States soldiers were attacked, it could not be expected that they would do nothing. If they were withdrawn, the field would be left to the Japanese and Kolchak, who was supported by the Allies.

He then read a series of telegrams from General Graves commanding the United States forces in Siberia, bearing out the above summary of the position, and pointing out that if the present policy were continued, there would almost certainly be a collision between the United States troops and Russian troops.

Mr. Lloyd George said that this strengthened his view as to the need of arriving at a policy in regard to Russia. Kolchak was advancing Eastward [*westward?*] at a very remarkable rate. He was in a position either to move Northwards and join hands with the forces based on Archangel, or to march on Moscow.

President Wilson said he had always been of opinion that the proper policy of the Allied and Associated Powers was to clear out of Russia and leave it to the Russians to fight it out among themselves.

Mr. Lloyd George asked that before a decision should be taken, the Council should hear M. Tchaikowsky.

President Wilson agreed.

Mr. Lloyd George suggested that President Wilson should send a reply to General Graves asking him to take no action for the moment, as the whole problem was being considered by the Allied and Associated Powers.

President Wilson said the risk of this was that there might be a collision between the United States and Russian troops. He suggested that the Allied and Associated Powers should simultaneously ask Kolchak what his program was.

Mr. Lloyd George suggested he might be asked two definite questions:—

1. Will you allow the peasants to retain the land or do you propose to restore the old seigneurial rights?
2. Are you prepared to revive the Constituent Assembly?

President Wilson in regard to the first point, said that a few days
ago he had asked a very Russophile friend whether the peasants had
really got the land out of all the chaos in Russia. His friend had
replied that they had only got it in a very inequitable way, each man
having seized the land nearest to him. The difficulty would not only
be to distribute the land to the peasants, but to systematize the existing distribution involving in some cases dispossession of individuals
and groups.

(After some further discussion during which Mr. Lloyd George
produced a map showing the great advance that Kolchak's troops
had made, it was agreed that M. Tchaikowsky should be heard on
the following day at noon.)

WILSON ON KOLCHAK

Notes of Meetings Held in President Wilson's House in the Place des Etats-Unis, Paris, May 10, 20, 24, and June 7, 1919

The following four documents show the manner in which Wilson moved,
albeit ambivalently, in the spring of 1919 to join with the other Allied leaders
in seeking a liberal-nationalist solution in Russia through a promise of
limited support for Admiral Kolchak's White Russian forces in Siberia.

Meeting of May 10, 1919. . . . Mr. Lloyd George asked what impression M. Tchaikowsky had made.

President Wilson said that he had not been as definite as he himself would wish. He had received the impression that Kolchak's ad-
visors had inclined to the Right as soon as they had got power. This
very often happened.

Mr. Lloyd George said he got the impression that M. Tchaikowsky
did not quite trust Denekin. He did evidently like Kolchak, though he
himself had got a very clear impression of Kolchak's "entourage."
He did not think public opinion would allow us to abandon Kolchak
even if he should establish a reactionary Government, because the
world would say that the establishment of order was so important. It
would be awkward to be placed in the position of supporting a
Government that we did not believe in.

President Wilson said he thought a fresh view ought to be obtained of Kolchak. He did not like being entirely dependent upon the views of British and French military men.

Mr. Lloyd George pointed out that Colonel John Ward, who commanded the Middlesex Battalion, was a Labour Member of Parliament.

(After some discussion President Wilson undertook to ask an American gentleman named Mr. [Roland S.] Morris [Ambassador to Japan], who was at present at Tokyo, to proceed as rapidly as possible to Omsk in order to gather as much information as he could about Admiral Kolchak's political intentions.

He undertook to instruct him to consult Colonel Ward, and Colonel Johnson, Commanding the 5th Hants. Battalion, as to their view of the political situation.)

President Wilson said that Kolchak's program was all right viewed in the background of M. Tchaikowsky's mind. What, however, did it look like, he asked, viewed in the background of Admiral Kolchak's mind?

Mr. Lloyd George said he felt sure that a soldier was bound to get to the top in Russia. Even if the Bolsheviks ultimately prevailed, it would probably be by military action. . . .

Meeting of May 20, 1919. M. Clemenceau said he did not see how any change could be made in what the Council had tried to do. There was no doubt that the Bolshevists were now going down hill. Dr. Nansen had suggested a humanitarian course, but Lenin was clearly trying to draw it into a political course.

President Wilson said that Lenin's argument was that the price the Allied and Associated Powers were trying to exact for food was that their enemies should beat the Bolshevists by compelling the latter to stop fighting. What was really intended was to stop aggressive fighting by the Bolshevists, because this was inconsistent with food distribution. They were perfectly correct in claiming that the Allies were supporting Kolchak and Denekin, and not putting pressure on them to stop fighting. Lenin's argument was that for him to stop fighting was to sign his death warrant.

M. Clemenceau pointed out that Lenin was not in the hands of the Allies.

President Wilson replied that if supplies were stopped, Kolchak and Denekin would have to stop fighting too.

M. Clemenceau said it was impossible to stop Lenin fighting, and his word could not be trusted.

President Wilson said he did not feel the same chagrin that he had formerly felt at having no policy in regard to Russia. It had been impossible to have a policy hitherto.

Mr. Lloyd George said there had been very little choice. There had been a lunatic revolution which certain persons, in whom little confidence was felt, were trying to squash. The only reason why the Allies had encouraged them was to prevent Germany from getting supplies. They were, however, now entitled to say, having supported us so far "you cannot leave us in the lurch."

President Wilson said that the Americans had only gone to Siberia to get the Czechs out, and then the Czechs had refused to go.

Mr. Lloyd George said that his Government's object had been to reconstitute the Eastern front. They had succeeded in doing this, though somewhat East of the line on which they had hoped to establish it. Nevertheless, the reconstitution of the front did prevent the Germans from getting supplies, with which they might have broken the blockade. The feeling in Great Britain was that it was impossible now to leave these people in the lurch.

President Wilson said that at least pledges could be exacted for further support.

M. Clemenceau fully agreed.

Mr. Lloyd George agreed, and said it could be done in either of two ways:—

1. By a formal dispatch;
2. By summoning the representatives of the various Russian groups now in Paris and putting the conditions to them.

President Wilson preferred the first proposal. The second would be contrary to the idea that had been at the basis of the Prinkipo scheme, namely, that it would not be fair to hear one party without hearing the other. His view was that a formal demand and notice ought to be sent to the various Russian groups. He had himself sent something that was almost equivalent to this, as he felt he was entitled to do.

(After some discussion it was agreed that Mr. Philip Kerr [Secretary to Lloyd George] should be asked to prepare a draft for the consideration of the Council.)

Mr. Kerr was sent for. While awaiting Mr. Kerr President Wilson read extracts from a document which had been alluded to at a discussion on the previous day, signed by M. Kerensky and some of his friends, and which contained a number of proposals, including the following:

i. That the Powers should only help the various Russian groups on certain fundamental conditions for the establishing of Russia on a democratic basis with a constituent assembly, and Governments which declined to agree should not be supported.

ii. That as a Constituent Assembly could clearly not be called at the present time, Regional Assemblies should be elected on a democratic basis for the re-establishment of Local Government.

iii. That a representative mission should be sent by the Great Powers to Russia to give assurance of sympathy and assistance.

iv. That proposals for supplying food were harmful.

These proposals in short, President Wilson continued, were that the Powers should obtain an assurance from each group that it would be united with the other groups to form an all-Russian Government on a constituent basis, and that in the meantime each group should do what it could in its own area.

Mr. Lloyd George was afraid of splitting up Russia.

President Wilson said it was merely proposing to substitute a democratic for an autocratic basis.

(After some further discussion Mr. Kerr entered.)

President Wilson informed Mr. Kerr that the Council desired to make a further effort with Russia along the lines of definite assurance to the several groups as to what they were aiming at. They had been reading a document prepared by certain Russian groups in Paris who, though anti-Bolshevist, were suspicious of reactionary tendencies among the groups fighting the Bolshevists. These suggested that pledges should be demanded from the various groups fighting the Bolshevists to establish a government on a democratic basis. In the meanwhile it was proposed to establish a democratic Government in these Regions by setting up Provincial Central Assemblies. The idea of the Council was to embody these demands in a message to the several Governments, and they hoped Mr. Kerr would prepare a draft for their consideration.

Meeting of May 24, 1919.   The Council had under consideration a draft despatch for Admiral Kolchak prepared by Mr. Philip Kerr at the request of the Principal Allied and Associated Powers. . . .

President Wilson explained to Viscount Chinda that he and his colleagues had felt some misgivings lest Admiral Kolchak might be under reactionary influences which might result in a reversal of the popular revolution in Russia. They also feared a military dictatorship based on reactionary principles, which would not be popular in Russia and might lead to further bloodshed and revolution. This despatch had been prepared for consideration in order to lay down the conditions of support for Admiral Kolchak and the groups working with him at Archangel and in South Russia. Should Admiral Kolchak accept the conditions, he would continue to receive the countenance and support of the Principal Allied and Associated Powers, otherwise he would not. The substance of the document was contained in the six conditions laid down in the last half.

Despatch to Admiral Kolchak.   Paris, 26 May, 1919. The Allied and Associated Powers feel that the time has come when it is necessary for them once more to make clear the policy they propose to pursue in regard to Russia.

It has always been a cardinal axiom of the Allied and Associated Powers to avoid interference in the internal affairs of Russia. Their original intervention was made for the sole purpose of assisting those elements in Russia which wanted to continue the struggle against German autocracy and to free their country from German rule, and in order to rescue the Czechoslovaks from the danger of annihilation at the hands of the Bolshevik forces. Since the signature of the Armistice on November 11th, 1918, they have kept forces in various parts of Russia. Munitions and supplies have been sent to assist those associated with them at a very considerable cost. No sooner, however, did the Peace Conference assemble than they endeavored to bring peace and order to Russia by inviting representatives of all the warring Governments within Russia to meet them in the hope that they might be able to arrange a permanent solution of Russian problems. This proposal and a later offer to relieve the distress among the suffering millions of Russia broke down through the refusal of the Soviet

Government to accept the fundamental condition of suspending hostilities while negotiations or the work of relief was proceeding. Some of the Allied and Associated Governments are now being pressed to withdraw their troops and to incur no further expense in Russia on the ground that continued intervention shows no prospect of producing an early settlement. They are prepared, however, to continue their assistance on the lines laid down below, provided they are satisfied that it will really help the Russian people to liberty, self-government, and peace.

The Allied and Associated Governments now wish to declare formally that the object of the policy is to restore peace within Russia by enabling the Russian people to resume control of their own affairs through the instrumentality of a freely elected Constituent Assembly and to restore peace along its frontiers by arranging for the settlement of disputes in regard to the boundaries of the Russian state and its relations with its neighbors through the peaceful arbitration of the League of Nations.

They are convinced by their experiences of the last twelve months that it is not possible to attain these ends by dealings with the Soviet Government of Moscow. They are therefore disposed to assist the Government of Admiral Kolchak and his Associates with munitions, supplies and food, to establish themselves as the government of all Russia, provided they receive from them definite guarantees that their policy has the same objects in view as that of the Allied and Associated Powers. With this object they would ask Admiral Kolchak and his Associates whether they will agree to the following as the conditions upon which they accept continued assistance from the Allied and Associated Powers.

In the first place, that, as soon as they reach Moscow they will summon a Constituent Assembly elected by a free, secret and democratic franchise as the Supreme Legislature for Russia to which the Government of Russia must be responsible, or if at that time order is not sufficiently restored they will summon the Constituent Assembly elected in 1917 to sit until such time as new elections are possible.

Secondly, that throughout the areas which they at present control they will permit free elections in the normal course for all local and legally constituted assemblies such as municipalities, Zemstvos, etc.

Thirdly, that they will countenance no attempt to revive the special privileges of any class or order in Russia. The Allied and Associated Powers have noted with satisfaction the solemn declaration made by Admiral Kolchak and his associates that they have no intention of restoring the former land system. They feel that the principles to be followed in the solution of this and other internal questions must be left to the free decision of the Russian Constituent Assembly; but they wish to be assured that those whom they are prepared to assist stand for the civil and religious liberty of all Russian citizens and will make no attempt to reintroduce the regime which the revolution has destroyed.

Fourthly, that the independence of Finland and Poland be recognized, and that in the event of the frontiers and other relations between Russia and these countries not being settled by agreement, they will be referred to the arbitration of the League of Nations.

Fifthly, that if a solution of the relations between Esthonia, Latvia Lithuania and the Caucasian and Transcaspian territories and Russia is not speedily reached by agreement the settlement will be made in consultation and cooperation with the League of Nations, and that until such settlement is made the Government of Russia agrees to recognize these territories as autonomous and to confirm the relations which may exist between their *de facto* Governments and the Allied and Associated Governments.

Sixthly, that as soon as a Government for Russia has been constituted on a democratic basis, Russia should join the League of Nations and cooperate with the other members in the limitation of armaments and of military organization throughout the world.

Finally, that they abide by the declaration made by Admiral Kolchak on November 27th, 1918, in regard to Russia's national debts.

The Allied and Associated Powers will be glad to learn as soon as possible whether the Government of Admiral Kolchak and his associates are prepared to accept these conditions, and also whether in the event of acceptance they will undertake to form a single Government and army command as soon as the military situation makes it possible. *G. Clemenceau; D. Lloyd George; V. E. Orlando; Woodrow Wilson; Saionji.*

Meeting of June 7, 1919. President Wilson reported the receipt of a telegram from the American Representative at Omsk, dated 31st May, enclosing a copy of a very satisfactory proclamation which Admiral

Kolchak was about to issue. The telegram reported that the question of recognition kept the people in Siberia in a state of expectancy, and, he hoped that, if Kolchak was not recognized, the United States would not get the blame. The gist of the proclamation was somewhat as follows. The efforts of Kolchak's army are steadily drawing to an end. He proclaimed ceaseless war not with the Russian people but with the Bolshevists. Those people who had been forced to serve the Bolshevists had committed no crime and had nothing to fear, and a full pardon and amnesty would be granted them. Kolchak had only accepted office in order to restore order and liberty in Russia. As his army advanced, he would enforce law and restore local governments. His office was a heavy burden to him and he would not support it for a day longer than the interests of the country demanded. After crushing the Bolshevists, he would first carry out a general election for the Constituent Assembly and a commission of his Government was now working out a law. This general election would be carried out on the basis of universal suffrage. After the establishment of a representative Government, he would hand over all his powers to it. For the moment, he had signed a law giving the produce of the fields to the peasants, leaving to the large landowners only a just share. Russia could only be strong when the peasants owned the land. Similarly, workmen must be secured the same safeguards as in the countries of Western Europe and a commission of his Government was preparing data in regard to this. The day of victory was approaching. President Wilson considered this a very good proclamation.

Mr. Lloyd George said that it was very important, as soon as Kolchak's reply was received, to publish the original telegram of the Allies and the reply.

M. Clemenceau said that the whole of the telegram from Kolchak would be available by the evening.

V WILSON'S CONCEPTIONS OF A LIBERAL WORLD ORDER ASSESSED

Walter Lippmann
MIRAGES OF WILSON'S FOREIGN POLICY

Walter Lippmann is perhaps America's most accomplished twentieth-century journalist. As a young man he worked on Wilson's staff at Paris where he came eventually to share the left-liberal disdain for the President's work at the Peace Conference. The present selection, written almost twenty-five years after Paris during World War II, is also critical of Wilson, but more from the perspective of realism than from the perspective of Lippmann's earlier disillusioned idealism.

When the prejudice against alliances encountered the desire to abolish war, the result was the Wilsonian conception of collective security. As Wilson saw it, the cause of the First World War was the system of alliances which had divided Europe into the Triple Alliance and the Triple Entente, and in his mind it was necessary to liquidate alliances in order to organize peace through the League of Nations. Articles 23, 24, 25 were written into the Covenant by President Wilson in order to liquidate old alliances and prevent the formation of new ones. Thus collective security was to be the remedy and the substitute for alliances.

There was a negligible minority at the time who did not share this, the Wilsonian view, but held that a system of collective security could not be maintained unless within it there existed an alliance of strong and dependable powers. They held that a nucleus of leading states, allied for the defense of their vital interests, was needed in order to enforce peace through a system of collective security.

Wilson, however, not only shared the traditional prejudices against alliances but was deeply influenced also by the idea that the nations could be brought together by consent, as the thirteen American colonies had been brought together first in a confederation and then in a federal union. This analogy has long been cherished by Americans as affording the hope that it might become a model for the rest of the world.

Yet it is, I submit, a profoundly misleading analogy. For the thirteen colonies had been planted and had matured under one sovereign power, that of the English crown. They had fought the War of Independence under the government of a Continental Congress which resolved to draw up Articles of Confederation even before the Battle of Bunker Hill, which adopted the Articles in 1777, and saw them ratified and in force before Cornwallis surrendered at Yorktown. The former colonies remained a confederation after the war was over, and when they adopted the present Constitution they were, as they themselves insisted, forming "a more perfect union."

They were not forming an altogether unprecedented union; they were perpetuating and perfecting a union which had always existed since the plantation of the British colonies. The fact that none of the Spanish or French colonies joined the union is fairly conclusive evidence that even in North America—three thousand miles from Europe —political unions do not become comprehensive by voluntary consent.

If the historic experience of Britain, France, Russia, Germany, and Italy is a guide, it tells us that the large states have grown up around the nucleus of a strong principality—England, the Ile de France, Muscovy, Piedmont, Prussia. By conquest, by royal marriages, by providing protection to weaker principalities, by the gravitation of the smaller to the bigger, the large national unions were gradually pulled together.

President Wilson's conception of collective security did not take into account this historic pattern. He held that there should be a union of fifty juridically equal but otherwise unequal states, and not the evolution of a union from a nucleus of firmly allied strong states. Refusing to regard alliances as the effective means by which collective security could be made to operate, Wilson forbade the founders of the League of Nations to perfect their alliance which had been tested in the fires of war. He did, to be sure, reluctantly agree to the French demand for a special guarantee in return for France's giving up the Rhine frontier. But he regarded this as a compromise of his principles and readily abandoned it.

Wilson identified collective security with antipathy to alliances, rather than with the constructive development of alliances. The influence of this idea played a great part in dividing the Americans from the British and the French, and the British from the French. For the French saw from the first, being closer to the realities of Europe, that the League could enforce the peace only if the League were led by a strong combination of powers resolved to enforce the peace. The French, therefore, sought allies in Europe, all the more urgently as they saw their alliance with Britain dissolving. This alienated the British, who believed in the Wilsonian League, and pushed them toward encouraging the German revolt against the settlement.

Then, as time went on, the League became impotent because the nuclear alliance of Britain, France, and America had been dissolved. Above all, the League was impotent to prevent our present enemies from forming their Tripartite Pact. Twenty years after the League was founded, the great military alliance of Germany, Italy, and Japan had been formed. But the generalized, abstract system of collective security had fallen to pieces.

It will be said that the Wilsonian ideal could have been realized if the Senate had not refused to ratify the Treaty of Versailles. Perhaps so. But if it had been realized, the League would, I submit, have succeeded, because American participation would in practice have been tantamount to a working nuclear alliance—in Monroe's phrase to "a concert by agreement"—with Great Britain primarily, and with France indirectly. This alliance has had to be reconstructed in order to conduct the present war. If it had existed after 1919, and had been perfected, it might have prevented the present war. Certainly it would at least have prevented Britain and America from disarming one another in the presence of Japan and Germany. And if the war had come nevertheless, we should not have been brought so perilously near to disaster.

The American opponents of the League saw truly that if the League was actually going to enforce peace, then it must imply the equivalent of an Anglo-American alliance. If the League did not imply that, then the generalized commitments of the Covenant were too broad and too unpredictable to be intelligible. Thus Wilson was placed in a dilemma: if the League was a practical instrument, it contained an alliance, and all good and true men including Wilson were opposed to any idea of an alliance; if in fact the League outlawed alliances, and still sought to enforce peace, then it was an unlimited commitment supported by no clear means of fulfilling it. Thus the League was attacked both as a concealed alliance in the realm of power politics and as a utopian pipe dream.

The dilemma was presented because Wilson was trying to establish collective security without forming an alliance. He wanted the omelet. He rejected the idea of cooking the eggs. The people agreeing that an alliance was abhorrent, proceeded by intuitive common sense to the conviction that without an alliance, the League was unworkable and unpredictably dangerous.

Thus in the debacle of Wilson's proposals we see the culminating effect of the American misunderstanding of alliances. Wilson as well as the men who opposed him had carried over into the twentieth century the illusion fostered in the nineteenth century—that the United States had never had allies and that the purest American tradition was opposed to alliances. The concert with Britain, which Monroe, Jefferson, and Madison had established in 1823, had been the foundation of American foreign relations for seventy-five years. But though it existed in fact, it had never been avowed as a policy.

George Frost Kennan
AMERICAN DIPLOMACY

Kennan had spent a number of years as a career diplomat when in 1950 he wrote the book from which this excerpt is taken. He had been Director of the Policy Planning Staff in the State Department, author of an influential article expounding the containment policy for dealing with Russia, and was about to be appointed Ambassador to Russia himself in 1952. Kennan's intent in American Diplomacy *was to assess the entire twentieth-century diplomatic tradition and the place in that tradition of such central figures as Wilson. How does Kennan's view of Wilson relate to Lippmann's?*

. . . A democracy is peace-loving. It does not like to go to war. It is slow to rise to provocation. When it has once been provoked to the point where it must grasp the sword, it does not easily forgive its adversary for having produced this situation. The fact of the provocation then becomes itself the issue. Democracy fights in anger—it

Reprinted by permission of the publisher, from George F. Kennan, *American Diplomacy, 1900-1950*, Mentor ed. (Chicago: University of Chicago Press, 1951), pp. 59-62. Copyright © 1951 by the University of Chicago Press.

fights for the very reason that it was forced to go to war. It fights to punish the power that was rash enough and hostile enough to provoke it—to teach that power a lesson it will not forget, to prevent the thing from happening again. Such a war must be carried to the bitter end.

This is true enough, and if nations could afford to operate in the moral climate of individual ethics, it would be understandable and acceptable. But I sometimes wonder whether in this respect a democracy is not uncomfortably similar to one of those prehistoric monsters with a body as long as this room and a brain the size of a pin: he lies there in his comfortable primeval mud and pays little attention to his environment; he is slow to wrath—in fact, you practically have to whack his tail off to make him aware that his interests are being disturbed; but, once he grasps this, he lays about him with such blind determination that he not only destroys his adversary but largely wrecks his native habitat. You wonder whether it would not have been wiser for him to have taken a little more interest in what was going on at an earlier date and to have seen whether he could not have prevented some of these situations from arising instead of proceeding from an undiscriminating indifference to a holy wrath equally undiscriminating.

In any case, once we were at war, it did not appear to us that our greatest danger might still lie precisely in too long a continuation of the war, in the destruction of Europe's equilibrium, and in the sapping of the vital energies of the European peoples. It did not appear to us then that the greatest interest we had in the war was still that it should be brought to an end as soon as possible on a basis involving a minimum maladjustment and as much stability as possible for the future. Prior to our entry into the war, many people had thought that way. As late as January 1917, Wilson was still arguing against total victory. A "peace forced upon the loser, a victor's terms imposed upon the vanquished," he said, "would be accepted in humiliation, under duress, at an intolerable sacrifice, and would leave a sting, a resentment, a bitter memory upon which terms of peace would rest . . . as upon quicksand."[1] But, once we were in the war, these ideas were swept away by the powerful currents of war

[1] Address to the Senate, January 22, 1917.

psychology. We were then as strong as anybody else in our determination that the war should be fought to the finish of a total victory.

Considerations of the power balance argued against total victory. Perhaps it was for this very reason that people in this country rejected them so emphatically and sought more sweeping and grandiose objectives, for the accomplishment of which total victory could plausibly be represented as absolutely essential.[2] In any case, a line of thought grew up, under Wilson's leadership, which provided both rationale and objective for our part in fighting the war to a bitter end. Germany was militaristic and antidemocratic. The Allies were fighting to make the world safe for democracy. Prussian militarism had to be destroyed to make way for the sort of peace we wanted. This peace would not be based on the old balance of power. Who, as Wilson said, could guarantee equilibrium under such a system? It would be based this time on a "community of power," on "an organized common peace," on a League of Nations which would mobilize the conscience and power of mankind against aggression. Autocratic government would be done away with. Peoples would themselves choose the sovereignty under which they wished to reside. Poland would achieve her independence, as would likewise the restless peoples of the Austro-Hungarian Empire. There would be open diplomacy this time; peoples, not governments, would run things. Armaments would be reduced by mutual agreement. The peace would be just and secure.

In the name of such principles you could fight a war to the end. A future so brilliant would surely wash away the follies and brutalities of the war, redress its injuries, heal the wounds it had left. This theory gave us justification both for continuing the war to its bitter and terrible end—to the end described by that young German soldier in the military hospital—and at the same time for refusing to preoccupy ourselves with the practical problems and maladjustments to which the course of hostilities was leading. Under the protecting shadow of this theory, the guns continued their terrible work for a final year and a half after our entry. Under the shadow of this theory

---

[2] This was not true of Wilson—at least in the beginning of 1917. His mind was able to entertain simultaneously thoughts of peace without victory and expansive concepts of a future world order which explicitly rejected the balance of power.

Wilson went to Versailles unprepared to face the sordid but all-important details of the day of reckoning. Under this theory he suffered his tragic and historic failure. Under this theory things advanced with a deadly logic and precision to a peace which was indeed "forced upon the loser, a victor's terms imposed upon the vanquished, accepted in humiliation, under duress"—a peace that did indeed leave a sting, a resentment, a bitter memory, and upon which its own terms came later to rest "as upon quicksand."

And the tragedy of this outcome was not substantially mitigated by the fact that we were not signatories to the Treaty of Versailles and kept ourselves aloof from its punitive provisions. The damage had been done. The equilibrium of Europe had been shattered. Austria-Hungary was gone. There was nothing effective to take its place. Germany, smarting from the sting of defeat and plunged into profound social unrest by the breakup of her traditional institutions, was left nevertheless as the only great united state in central Europe. Russia was no longer there, as a possible reliable ally, to help France contain German power. From the Russian plain there leered a single hostile eye, skeptical of Europe's values, rejoicing at all Europe's misfortunes, ready to collaborate solely for the final destruction of her spirit and her pride. Between Russia and Germany were only the pathetic new states of eastern and central Europe, lacking in domestic stability and the traditions of statesmanship—their peoples bewildered, uncertain, vacillating between brashness and timidity in the exercise of the unaccustomed responsibilities of independence. And to the other side of Germany were France and England, reeling themselves, from the vicissitudes of the war, wounded far more deeply than they themselves realized, the plume of their manhood gone, their world positions shaken.

Truly, this was a peace which had the tragedies of the future written into it as by the devil's own hand. It was a peace, as the French historian Bainville said, which was too mild for the hardships it contained. And this was the sort of peace you got when you allowed war hysteria and impractical idealism to lie down together in your mind, like the lion and the lamb; when you indulged yourself in the colossal conceit of thinking that you could suddenly make international life over into what you believed to be your own image; when you dismissed the past with contempt, rejected the relevance of the past to the future, and refused to occupy yourself with the real problems that a study of the past would suggest.

Arthur S. Link

WILSON AND THE LIBERAL PEACE PROGRAM

Arthur S. Link is professor of history at Princeton University, chief editor of the Woodrow Wilson Papers, and Wilson's leading biographer. The following selection is taken from Link's Wilson the Diplomatist, *the printed version of the Albert Shaw Lectures delivered by Link at Johns Hopkins University. In these lectures Link undertook a general defense of Wilson's peace program.*

Did Wilson fail at Paris? This is a question that has been asked and answered a thousand times by statesmen and scholars since the Versailles Treaty was signed in 1919. It will be asked so long as men remember Woodrow Wilson and the world's first major effort to solve the problem of recurring wars. The answer that one gives depends not only upon the circumstances and mood prevailing at the time it is given, but as well upon the view that one takes of history and of the potentialities and limitations of human endeavor. That is to say, it makes a great deal of difference whether one judges Wilson's work by certain absolute so-called moral standards, or whether one views what he did remembering the obstacles that he faced, the pressures under which he labored, the things that were possible and impossible to achieve at the time, and what would have happened had he not been present at the conference.

I should perhaps begin my own assessment by saying that the Versailles Treaty, measured by the standards that Wilson had enunciated from 1916 to 1919, obviously failed to fulfill entirely the liberal peace program. It was not, as Wilson had demanded in his Peace

Reprinted by permission of the publisher, from Arthur S. Link, *Wilson the Diplomatist* (Baltimore: Johns Hopkins Press, 1957), pp. 120–125, 155–6.

without Victory speech and implicitly promised in the Fourteen Points, a peace among equals. It was, rather, as the Germans contended then and later, a *diktat* imposed by victors upon a beaten foe. It shouldered Germany with a reparations liability that was both economically difficult to satisfy and politically a source of future international conflict.[1] It satisfied the victors' demands for a division of the enemy's colonies and territories. In several important instances it violated the principle of self-determination. Finally, it was filled with pin pricks, like the provision for the trial of the former German Emperor, that served no purpose except to humiliate the German people. It does not, therefore, require much argument to prove that Wilson failed to win the settlement that he had demanded and that the Allies had promised in the Pre-Armistice Agreement.

To condemn Wilson because he failed in part is, however, to miss the entire moral of the story of Versailles. That moral is a simple one: the Paris peace settlement reveals more clearly than any other episode of the twentieth century the tension between the ideal and the real in history and the truth of the proposition that failure inheres in all human striving. It does not make much sense merely to list Wilson's failures. We can see their meaning only when we understand *why* he failed as he did.

Wilson failed at Paris not because he did not fight with all his mind and strength for the whole of the liberal peace program. Never before in his career had he fought more tenaciously or pleaded more

---

[1] John Maynard Keynes, in his famous *Economic Consequences of the Peace* (New York, 1920), conclusively proved the utter economic absurdity of the reparations settlement (the Carthaginian peace) to the whole postwar generation of scholars in England and America. It is no longer possible to be quite so dogmatic, for Étienne Mantoux, in *The Carthaginian Peace, or The Economic Consequences of Mr. Keynes,* has proved that Keynes was egregiously wrong in his statistical methods and has demonstrated that German resources were in fact fully adequate to satisfy the reparations requirements of the Versailles Treaty. This position is supported by many economists and by Professor Samuel F. Bemis in his *Diplomatic History of the United States* (New York, 1955 ed.). They point out that Hitler spent vastly more money on rearmament than the German nation would have paid in reparations during the 1930's.

These arguments, actually, are unanswerable, but in a larger sense they are also irrelevant. The question is not whether it was possible for the Germans to continue reparations payments over a long period, but whether they were willing to do so; whether the British and French would attempt to coerce the Germans for a long period if the Germans were not willing to continue voluntary payments; and whether the monetary returns were worth all the international ill will that they provoked. To ask the question this way is, it seems to me, to answer it.

eloquently. Nor did he fail because, as John Maynard Keynes and Harold Nicholson have portrayed him in their unkind caricatures, he was incompetent, uninformed, and "bamboozled" by men of superior wit and learning.[2] Indeed, after reading the records of the deliberations at Paris one cannot escape the feeling that Wilson was the best informed and on the whole the wisest man among the Big Four.

Wilson failed as he did because his handicaps and the obstacles against which he fought made failure inevitable. In the first place, he had lost most of his strategic advantages by the time that the peace conference opened. German military power, upon which he had relied as a balance against Allied ambitions, was now totally gone. Wilson had no power of coercion over Britain and France, for they were no longer dependent upon American manpower and resources for survival. His only recourse, withdrawal from the conference, would have been utterly fatal to his program. It would have meant inevitably a Carthaginian peace imposed by the French, as the British alone could never have prevented the French from carrying out their plans to destroy Germany. In these circumstances, therefore, compromise was not merely a necessity, but a compelling necessity to avert (from Wilson's point of view) a far worse alternative.

In contrast to the strength of the French were Wilson's other weaknesses. His claim to the right to speak in the name of the American people had been seriously weakened by the election of a Republican Congress in November 1918, and was denied during the peace conference itself by Republican leaders like Senator Henry Cabot Lodge. In addition, there was the failure of Colonel House, upon whom Wilson had relied as his strong right arm, to support liberal peace ideals during that period of the conference when House was still the President's spokesman. House was so eager for harmony that he was willing to yield almost any demand and on several crucial occasions seriously undercut and compromised the President.

Another of Wilson's obstacles, namely, the character of his antagonists at Paris, has often been overlooked. Clemenceau, Lloyd George, Orlando, Baron Sonnino, and the Japanese delegates were all tough and resourceful negotiators, masters of the game of diplo-

---

[2] Keynes in his *Economic Consequences of the Peace,* cited in the previous footnote, and Nicholson in *Peacemaking 1919, Being Reminiscences of the Paris Peace Conference* (Boston and New York, 1933).

macy, quick to seize every advantage that the less experienced American offered.

To overcome such opposition Wilson had at his command the threat of withdrawal, the promise of American support for the right kind of settlement and of leadership in the League of Nations, and the fact that he did speak for liberal groups not only in his own country, but throughout the world as well. These were sources of considerable strength, to be sure, but they were not enough to enable Wilson to impose his own settlement.

In spite of it all Wilson did succeed in winning a settlement that honored more of the Fourteen Points—not to mention the additional thirteen points—than it violated and in large measure vindicated his liberal ideals. There was the restoration of Belgium, the return of Alsace-Lorraine to France, and the creation of an independent Poland with access to the sea. There was the satisfaction of the claims of the Central European and Balkan peoples to self-determination. There was the at least momentary destruction of German military power. Most important, there was the fact that the Paris settlement provided machinery for its own revision through the League of Nations and the hope that the passing of time and American leadership in the League would help to heal the world's wounds and build a future free from fear.

As it turned out, many of Wilson's expectations were fulfilled even though the American people refused to play the part assigned to them. For example, the reparations problem was finally solved in the 1920s in a way not dissimilar from the method that Wilson had proposed. Germany was admitted to the League in 1926, and that organization ceased to be a mere league of victors. Effective naval disarmament was accomplished in 1921 and 1930. Even the great and hitherto elusive goal of land disarmament and the recognition of Germany's right to military equality was being seriously sought by international action in the early 1930s. In brief, the Paris settlement, in spite of its imperfections, did create a new international order that functioned well, relatively speaking. And it failed, not because it was imperfect, but because it was not defended when challenges arose in the 1930s.

Thus I conclude by suggesting that for Woodrow Wilson the Paris Peace Conference was more a time of heroic striving and impressive achievement than of failure. By fighting against odds that would have caused weaker men to surrender, he was able to prevent the Carthaginian kind of peace that we have seen to our regret in our own time; and he was able to create the machinery for the gradual attainment of the kind of settlement that he would have liked to impose at once. The Paris settlement, therefore, was not inevitably a "lost peace." It could have been, rather, the foundation of a viable and secure world order and therefore a lasting memorial to its chief architect, if only the victors had maintained the will to enforce what Wilson signed.

*   *   *

. . . The truth is that the American people were not prepared in 1920 to assume the world leadership that Wilson offered them, and that the powers of the world were not yet ready to enforce the worldwide, universal system of collective security that the President had created.

Collective security failed in the portentous tests of the 1930s, not because the League's machinery was defective but because the people of the world, not merely the American people alone, were unwilling to confront aggressors with the threat of war. As a result a second and more terrible world conflict came, as Wilson prophesied it would, and at its end the United States helped to build a new and different league of nations and took the kind of international leadership that Wilson had called for. But events of the past decade have not fully justified Wilson's confidence in international organization; the only really promising systems of collective security, the regional ones like NATO, have been of a kind that Wilson fervently denounced; and only the future can reveal whether his dream of a universal system can ever be made a reality.[3]

And so it was Wilson the prophet, demanding greater commitment, sacrifice, and idealism than the people could give, who was defeated in 1920. It is also Wilson the prophet who survives in history, in the hopes and aspirations of mankind and in whatever ideals of international service that the American people still cherish. One thing is certain, now that men have the power to sear virtually the entire face of the earth: The prophet of 1919 was right in his larger vision; the

[3] For a provocative reply in the negative, see Robert E. Osgood, "Woodrow Wilson, Collective Security, and the Lessons of History," *Confluence* 5 (Winter 1957): 341–354.

challenge that he raised then is today no less real and no less urgent than it was in his own time.

William Appleman Williams
THE RISING TIDE OF REVOLUTION

William Appleman Williams is professor of history at Oregon State University and is the author of many important books in American history. While at the University of Wisconsin in the 1950s and 1960s Williams inspired the "Wisconsin School" of revisionist historiography critical of the American diplomatic tradition from a radical perspective. The following selection is from Williams' most influential book, The Tragedy of American Diplomacy, *and it conveys the essential revisionist perspective on Wilson.*

. . . Colonial societies began to realize that America's anticolonialism neither implied nor offered freedom from extensive and intensive foreign influence. Whatever the evidence that Wilson ever entertained any idea of actually trying to limit such absentee authority to its absolute minimum of voluntary respect and emulation, and such data is neither extensive nor convincing, it is clear that he never developed or pushed such a program.

At best, Wilson's actions were in keeping with the principles of a moralistic and paternalistic open-door imperialism. At worst, he intervened with force in the affairs of other nations. America's verbal support for the principle of self-determination became in practice the reordering of national boundaries in Europe on the basis of ethnic and linguistic criteria. Though it had considerable relevance for Western Europe, this principle and practice of nationality had less meaning in Eastern Europe—and still less throughout the rest of the world. But it was not even applied to many areas. Japan was treated as an inferior, for example, and the colonial empires were hardly touched. They were most certainly not broken up into independent states ac-

Reprinted by permission of The World Publishing Company from *The Tragedy of American Diplomacy* by William Appleman Williams, pp. 94-102. Copyright © 1959, 1962 by William Appleman Williams.

cording to the principle of self-determination. And even though some improvements did result from the mandate system where it was applied, that approach was characterized by minimum changes in the existing pattern of colonialism.

Taken seriously, a commitment to the principle of self-determination means a policy of standing aside for peoples to make their own choices, economic as well as political and cultural. It is based on a willingness to live and let live—a broad tolerance for other peoples' preferences and a willingness, if the opportunity is offered, to help them achieve their own goals in their own fashion. It is the philosophy of an integrated personality, and it might be defined as the foreign policy of a mature society.[1] Though it avowed this principle, the actions of America in the realm of foreign affairs did not follow this pattern. Hence it was not surprising, as Wilson's actions became apparent, that many peoples of the world felt misled by Wilson's slogans about self-determination. It was one thing to shape one's own culture, but quite another to be pushed aside while others haggled over ethnic statistics and then drew lines on a map.

As suggested by many of his actions in Mexico, and by his call for war without quarter until Germany erected a government that "we can trust," Wilson's liberal practice was not in keeping with his liberal principles. This became even more apparent as he began to reveal his ideals about a League of Nations. That program amounted to a direct and almost literal application of the principles of America's domestic liberalism to the world at large. The League of Nations became the state, and its function was to maintain order and enforce the rules of the game at the international level. Given such security, the national pursuit of self-interest would, according to the doctrine of a harmony of interests, produce peace and prosperity throughout the world.

Beyond that point, however, the attempt to formulate an international system on the principles of such liberalism encountered a difficult issue. It was simple to say that the League corresponded to the state, but it was not at all easy to specify the power structure of

[1] It could of course be maintained with considerable power that the philosophy of self-determination actually leads, if followed rigorously, to pacifism, and to anarchism practiced within small communities. Both Wilson and the Bolsheviks declined to pursue the logic that far.

the international state. The logical answer defined it as a Parliament of Man, but that did not answer the question; it only asked it in a different way. It was still necessary to specify such mundane but vital things as the nature of the franchise and the institutional structure of the government. Wilson answered such questions by combining his concept of America's supremacy with the political theory of classical liberalism. Every nation could vote, but nothing could be done without the prior existence of a concert of power (or harmony of interests) among the big nations. That was as weighted a franchise as ever proposed under the name of liberalism, particularly since Wilson assumed that America (in association with Great Britain) would lead the concert of major powers.

Considered on its own merits, the idea of a concert of power among the strongest nations had much to recommend it on the grounds that it assigned responsibility to those with the ability to make basic decisions. But when judged against the rhetoric and principles of classical liberalism it was quite clearly a contradiction in terms. For by the key tenet of liberalism, namely the existence of a harmony of interests, it was possible to produce the general welfare only under conditions of free competition. Yet by establishing an oligopoly of power, and formalizing it in an unconditional guarantee of "the territorial integrity and existing political independence" of the nations admitted to the League (on criteria prescribed by the oligopoly itself), Wilson's proposal destroyed the possibility of free competition. And it was precisely on this point that the League of Nations was attacked by some American liberals themselves, as well as by radicals and conservatives in the United States and throughout the world.

Both at home and abroad, the radicals made the most fundamental criticism because they also challenged all of Wilson's definitions of liberal democracy. Their assault was supported, particularly in the early years of the revolutionary upsurge throughout the world, by a heretical movement within liberalism itself which strengthened the radicals by weakening Wilson's position. Left-wing liberalism developed from the same philosophy of natural law which classical liberalism cited as the sanction for its own program. But while they accepted the doctrine of a natural harmony of interests, the heretical liberals went on to raise the question as to why the existing society did not correspond to the ideal society. In reply, they argued that certain institutions, particularly that of private property in its large, concentrated, and consolidated forms, prevented the natural harmony from emerging from the free interplay of individuals pursuing their self-interest. That analysis led the heretics to the conclusion that it was necessary to make structural changes in the existing society before the workings of natural law could produce the general welfare. In sharp contrast, Wilson (and the conservatives) would support nothing more than a "slow process of reform" in which they saw no need, and most certainly had no intention, of shaking the foundations of the status quo. Hence the heretics proposed many measures, particularly in economic, social, and international matters, which approximated some of those advanced by the radicals. But the heretic liberals were drastic reformers, not revolutionaries. This was a vital distinction, for in time it led the heretics to oppose the radicals as vigorously as did the classical liberals or even the conservatives.

For their part, the radicals started from a fundamentally different premise. They denied the existence—save perhaps in some mythical past—of a natural harmony of interests. They held that conflict was the essence of life and that it would never end short of death. Yet they also argued that each broad conflict within society was resolved on a higher level and thus produced a better life in the new society. And, in some of their most free-wheeling arguments and prophecies, they asserted that later conflicts would be nonviolent and would concern ideas and broad cultural issues. Men would dispute the best means of becoming more human, not the distribution of wealth and power. In its own way, therefore, the radical theory promised a society not too different from the one prophesied by the heretical liberals on the quite different basis of a harmony of interests inherent in natural law. But the radicals not only thought it necessary to go further in changing society, they also accepted revolution as a justifiable and honorable method.

In economic matters, for example, they denied the validity of the liberals' market economy. They judged it neither fair nor truly efficient. They advocated instead the idea of planned production for use and welfare. To accomplish this, they proposed that the government should take title to resources and direct the production of goods and services for all the society on an equitable basis. Such economic decisions would not only facilitate development in other areas of life, they would also become the stuff of politics, and in that fashion politics, and in that fashion politics would once again become relevant and meaningful to each citizen. This mode of production and distribution would not only make work itself meaningful to the individual and the group, but would end the struggle for raw existence and hence free men for personal and cultural development.

Radicals made no discrimination as to which men would enjoy such fruits of the revolution, except that they excluded those who fought to retain their privileges of the past. They handled the question of religion in two ways. In the broadest sense they secularized it, converting it into a faith in the ability of man to realize his full potential in this world. More immediately, either they attacked it as a façade for privilege and power or interpreted its idealism as support for their program. As for color or ethnic origins, they denied the validity of such criteria as the basis of any decision, an attitude that enabled them to avoid Wilson's contradiction between self-determination and nationality and the exclusiveness of his Protestant Christianity and Anglo-Saxonism. In this way, radicals appealed to all men across all existing—or proposed—boundaries.

Their approach to self-determination gave the radicals a double-edged weapon against colonialism and the less overt forms of imperial expansion such as the Open Door Policy. For by asserting the right of self-determination, they identified themselves with anticolonialism, which was the lowest common denominator of nationalism, yet also aligned themselves with the more developed and specific expressions of nationalism. Thus they offered leadership to those who wished to end formal colonialism, as well as to others who sought to assert their full sovereignty against spheres of influence and similar restrictions established under the Open Door Policy.

In the broadest sense, therefore, the radicals offered the peoples of the world an explanation of their existing hardships, a program to end such difficulties and build a better world, and leadership in that common effort. This radical assault on classical liberalism and conservatism was a direct challenge to Wilson and to the United States. And through the Communist victory of November 1917, in Russia, all those separate revolutions—in economics, politics, social values, and international affairs—seemed to become institutionalized in a nation of tremendous potential.

Though obviously of great importance to an understanding of American diplomacy in the twentieth century, the Bolshevik Revolution and the subsequent rise of the Soviet Union as a thermonuclear power can nevertheless be overemphasized to the point of creating serious errors of analysis and interpretation. Indeed, that very preoccupation (and the warped perspective that it created) does a great deal to explain many otherwise perplexing actions by American leaders. It helps tremendously, for example, to account for the near-panic manifested by otherwise perceptive, intelligent, and sober men when Castro sustained his power in Cuba. And in a broader sense, it offers considerable insight into the way that American leaders persistently interpreted political and social unrest throughout the world as a consequence of the Bolshevik Revolution, and also into the way that they steadily expanded the nation's commitments beyond a rational calculation (even by the axioms of their expansionist *Weltanschauung*) of the country's resources.

This myopic and self-defeating preoccupation with the Bolshevik Revolution existed long before the Soviet Union orbited a man in space. Fundamentally, and from the outset, American leaders were for many, many years more afraid of the implicit and indirect challenge of the revolution than they were of the actual power of the Soviet Union. Communist Russia never posed a direct and significant danger to the vital national interests of the United States, let alone to its existence as a state, until—at the earliest—the period between 1949 and 1952. Up to that time, at any rate, it had neither the power nor the freedom of maneuver at home to initiate such action.

It is essential to remember, in this connection, that American leaders expected Hitler to conquer Russia in six weeks; and that they were not only well informed about the serious and extensive damage suffered by the Soviet Union during World War II, but expected to benefit from that relative and absolute weakness of Russia. From 1917 to 1950, the United States had, *and knew it had*, a preponderance of power as compared to the Soviet Union. It is very probable, moreover, that the United States sustained that position for at least five more years. All the talk after 1955 about the balance shifting to Russia has to be interpreted in the light of the avowed American objective of restoring the situation as of 1939 or 1941. An inability to do that short of war does not mean that the balance has actually shifted.

It means only that the epoch of Western superiority has ended in a stand-off. What happens in the future has yet to be determined. No analysis or interpretation of American-Soviet relations can be taken seriously unless it is based on a recognition and acknowledgment of those elementary truths.[2]

It thus seems clear that the great majority of American leaders were—like President Wilson—concerned so deeply with the Bolshevik Revolution because at bottom they were so uneasy about what Wilson called the "general feeling of revolt" against the existing order, and about the increasing intensity of that dissatisfaction. From this it follows that the Bolshevik Revolution was only the symbol of all the revolutions that grew out of that discontent. And that is perhaps the crucial insight into the tragedy of American diplomacy.

Those other specific and general revolutions would have continued and come to their climaxes even if the Bolsheviks had never seized power in Russia. They were revolutions that had been fed and sustained by the policies of the West itself for more than a century. American policy was fundamentally no more than a sophisticated version of those same policies.

The underlying nature of the tragedy is defined by the confrontation between those two elements, not just or primarily by the conflict between the United States and the Soviet Union. The tragedy was of course dramatized, and unquestionably made more intense, by the way that American leaders reduced all such revolutions to the Bolshevik Revolution. Indeed, their behavior could be offered as a textbook example of the reductionist fallacy. Or, to use a metaphor from daily life, they blinded themselves at the outset of their search for an answer to the "general feeling of revolt" that disturbed them so much.

It is vital to realize, therefore, that the radical and revolutionary impact was not limited—even between 1917 and 1921—to events in Russia. On the European scene, communists came to power in Hungary and showed strength in Germany;[3] and the heretical liberals attacked the status quo in England and other countries. The Arab

---

[2] . . . It was the collapse of the illusions encouraged by the awareness of this power that led ultimately to the emotional intensity of American feeling against Russia.

[3] The reader should remember that the army of the Soviet Union had nothing to do with this communist revolution in Hungary at the end of World War I. As will be seen, it was the West, under the leadership of President Wilson and Herbert Hoover, which intervened to overturn the earlier communist revolution.

Revolution in the Middle East, while it was predominantly anticolo-
nial and nationalistic and was led by liberals and conservatives,
nevertheless represented the international elements of the broad
radical movement. A similar pattern emerged in the Far East. Chinese
revolutionaries, some of whom did look to Russia for advice and
leadership, asserted their rapport with the radical challenge—on
domestic as well as international issues. And Japanese conservatives
(and liberals), who asserted their nationalistic and ethnic equality
with the West, pre-empted certain radical policies as weapons for
their own purposes. All of these developments, considered individ-
ually and en masse, posed serious problems for American leadership
at the end of World War I.

Confronted directly by the opposition overseas, Wilson faced still
other difficulties. His original hope to establish a concert of power
with Great Britain and France was weakened by their initial opposition to certain of his proposals. The revolutionary ferment in Europe,
Asia, and the Middle East only intensified the determination of the
imperial powers to retain and strengthen their existing empires. A
similar reaction occurred in America, and Wilson's coalition for the
crusade to make the world safe for democracy disintegrated into a
great internal struggle over what policy would enable America to
assert its power most effectively in dealing with Japanese and European competitors and the wave of revolutions engulfing the world.

Wilson's personal dilemma symbolized the broader difficulties
faced by classical liberalism. According to the basic principles of
natural law, he should have accepted the revolutions as competing
units which would contribute their share to a broader and deeper
harmony of interests. But his expansionist philosophy of history, his
Calvinism, and his nationalism—which also were integral parts of his
liberalism—prompted him to oppose the revolutions as barricades on
America's road to domestic well-being and world leadership. The
tragedy was defined by his attempt to resolve the dilemma by preserving and extending democracy through a policy of open-door expansion.

His approach satisfied neither his own followers nor the foreigners
who looked to America (and to Wilson in particular) for a creative
alternative to the revolutionaries. Instead, it left the battleground to
the conservatives and the radicals. By attempting to achieve security

through the traditional policy of the open door, America's conservatives emphasized the weakest aspects of Wilson's own program. And the liberals, having failed to offer a positive and effective alternative of their own, had in the end no place to go but into a bipartisan alignment with the conservatives.

Suggestions for Additional Reading

The primary source for further study of Wilson's role at the Paris Peace Conference is United States Department of State, *Papers Relating to the Foreign Relations of the United States: The Paris Peace Conference, 1919,* 13 vols. (Washington D.C. 1942–1947). The following two edited collections of documents and papers provide both primary materials and analyses essentially sympathetic to Wilson: Ray Stannard Baker, *Woodrow Wilson and World Settlement,* 3 vols. (Garden City, N.Y., 1922–1923); and Charles Seymour, ed., *The Intimate Papers of Colonel House,* 4 vols. (Boston, 1926–1928).

The memoir literature on the Paris Peace Conference in general and the American role in particular is vast. On the European side see especially Georges Clemenceau, *Grandeur and Misery of Victory* (New York, 1930); Winston Churchill, *The Aftermath, 1918–1928* (New York, 1929); David Lloyd George, *The Truth about the Peace Treaties* (London, 1938); John Maynard Keynes, *The Economic Consequences of the Peace* (New York, 1920); Harold Nicolson, *Peacemaking, 1919* (Boston, 1931); and André Tardieu, *The Truth about the Treaty* (Indianapolis, 1921). On the American side, see especially Bernard M. Baruch, *The Making of the Reparation and Economic Sections of the Treaty* (New York, 1920); Stephen Bonsal, *Unfinished Business* (Garden City, N.Y., 1944); Herbert Hoover, *The Ordeal of Woodrow Wilson* (New York, 1958); Edward M. House and Charles Seymour, eds., *What Really Happened at Paris: The Story of the Paris Peace Conference, 1918–1919* (New York, 1921); Robert Lansing, *The Peace Negotiations: A Personal Narrative,* and *The Big Four and Others of the Peace Conference* (Boston, 1921); Frederick Palmer, *Bliss, Peacemaker: The Life and Letters of Tasker Howard Bliss* (New York, 1934); and James T. Shotwell, *At the Paris Peace Conference* (New York, 1937).

For a secondary account critical of Wilson's role at Paris see Thomas A. Bailey, *Woodrow Wilson and the Lost Peace* (New York, 1944). For general secondary accounts more sympathetic to Wilson's policies at Paris see Paul Birdsall, *Versailles Twenty Years After* (New York, 1941); N. Gordon Levin, Jr., *Woodrow Wilson and World Politics* (New York, 1968); Arthur S. Link, *Wilson the Diplomatist* (Baltimore, 1957); and Daniel M. Smith, *The Great Departure: The United States and World War I, 1914–1920* (New York, 1965). For background on Wilsonian foreign policy prior to the Paris Peace Conference see Edward H. Buehrig, *Woodrow Wilson and the Balance of Power* (Bloomington, 1955); William Diamond, *The Economic Thought of Woodrow Wilson* (Baltimore, 1943); Alexander L. George and Juliette George, *Woodrow Wilson and Colonel House: A Personality Study* (New York, 1956); George F. Kennan, *Soviet American Relations, 1971–1920: Russia Leaves the War* (Princeton, 1956); Kennan, *Soviet-American Relations, 1917–1920: The Decision to Intervene* (Princeton, 1958); Arthur S. Link, *Wilson: The New Freedom* (Princeton, 1956); Link, *Wilson: The Struggle for Neutrality, 1914–1915* (Princeton, 1960); Link, *Wilson: Confusions and Crises, 1915–1916* (Princeton, 1964); Link, *Wilson: Campaigns for Progressivism and Peace, 1916–1917* (Princeton, 1965); Victor S. Mamatey, *The United States and East Central Europe, 1914–1918* (Princeton, 1957); Laurence W. Martin, *Peace Without Victory: Woodrow Wilson and the British Liberals* (New Haven, 1958); Ernest R. May, *The World War and American Isolation* (Cambridge, 1959); Arno J. Mayer, *The Political Origins of the New Diplomacy, 1917–1918* (New Haven, 1959); Harley Notter, *The Origins of the Foreign Policy of Woodrow Wilson* (Baltimore, 1937); Daniel M. Smith, *Robert Lansing and American Neutrality* (Berkeley, 1958); William Appleman Williams, *Russian-American Relations, 1781–1947* (New York, 1952).

For further studies of the Paris Peace Conference and Wilson's role there see Mitchell P. Briggs, *George D. Herron and the European Settlement* (Stanford, 1932); Roy Watson Curry, *Woodrow Wilson and Far-Eastern Policy, 1913–1921* (New Haven, 1957); Russell H. Fifield, *Woodrow Wilson and the Far East: The Diplomacy of the Shantung Question* (New York, 1952); Lawrence E. Gelfand, *The Inquiry: American Preparations for Peace, 1917–1919* (New Haven, 1963); Louis L. Gerson, *Woodrow Wilson and the Rebirth of Poland* (New Haven, 1953); F.S. Marston, *The Peace Conference of 1919: Organization and Procedure* (New York, 1944); Allan Nevins, *Henry White: Thirty Years of American Diplomacy* (New York, 1930); George B. Noble, *Policies and Opinions at Paris, 1919: Wilsonian Diplomacy, the Versailles Peace, and French Public Opinion* (New York, 1935); Charles Seymour, "The Paris Education of Woodrow Wilson," *Virginia Quarterly Review* 32 (Autumn 1956): 578–593; Seth P. Tillman, *Anglo-American Relations at the Paris Peace Conference of 1919* (Princeton, 1961);

David F. Trask, *General Tasker Howard Bliss and the "Sessions of the World," 1919* (Philadelphia, 1966); and Richard L. Watson, Jr., "Woodrow Wilson and his Interpreters, 1947–1957," *Mississippi Valley Historical Review* 44 (September 1957): 207–236.

More specialized regional and national studies of the Peace Conference include George L. Beer, *African Questions at the Paris Peace Conference*, ed. Louis H. Gray (New York, 1923); Philip M. Burnett, *Reparation at the Paris Peace Conference, from the Standpoint of the American Delegation,* 2 vols. (New York, 1940); René Albrecht-Carrie, *Italy at the Paris Peace Conference* (New York, 1938); Burton F. Beers, *Vain Endeavor: Robert Lansing's Attempt to End the American-Japanese Rivalry* (Durham, N.C., 1962); Francis Deak, *Hungary at the Paris Peace Conference* (New York, 1942); Benjamin Gerig, *The Open Door and the Mandates System* (London, 1930); Harry N. Howard, *The Partition of Turkey: A Diplomatic History, 1913–1923* (Norman, 1931); Ivo J. Lederer, ed., *The Versailles Settlement: Was It Foredoomed to Failure?* (Boston, 1960); Lederer, *Yugoslavia at the Paris Peace Conference* (New Haven, 1963); Sherman D. Spector, *Rumania at the Paris Peace Conference* (New York, 1962).

For further studies of the German question at Paris see Joseph A. Berlau, *The German Social Democratic Party* (New York, 1949); George G. Bruntz, *Allied Propaganda and the Collapse of the German Empire in 1918* (Stanford, 1938); Rudolf Coper, *Failure of a Revolution, Germany, 1918–1919* (Cambridge, England 1955); Harold J. Gordon, Jr., *The Reichswehr and the German Republic, 1919–1926* (Princeton, 1957); W. M. Jordan, *Great Britain, France, and the German Problem, 1918–1939* (New York, 1943); Alma Luckau, *The German Delegation at the Paris Peace Conference* (New York, 1941); Étienne Mantoux, *The Carthaginian Peace* (Pittsburgh, 1965); Harold I. Nelson, *Land and Power: British and Allied Policy on Germany's Frontiers, 1916–1919* (London, 1963); Harry R. Rudin, *Armistice, 1918* (New Haven, 1944); Frank M. Russell, *The Saar, Battleground and Pawn* (Stanford, 1951); Louis A.R. Yates, *The United States and French Security, 1917–1921* (New York, 1957).

For further studies of the question of Bolshevism at the Peace Conference see Beatrice Farnsworth, *William C. Bullitt and the Soviet Union* (Bloomington, 1967); George F. Kennan, *Russia and the West under Lenin and Stalin* (Boston, 1960); Christopher Lasch, *The Ameri-*

can *Liberals and the Russian Revolution* (New York, 1962); Alfred D. Low, *The Soviet Hungarian Republic and the Paris Peace Conference* (Philadelphia, 1963); Arno J. Mayer, *Politics and Diplomacy of Peacemaking: Containment and Counterrevolution at Versailles, 1918–1919* (New York, 1967); John M. Thompson, *Russia, Bolshevism and the Versailles Peace* (Princeton, 1966); Pauline Tompkins, *American-Russian Relations in the Far East* (New York, 1949); and Betty M. Unterberger, *America's Siberian Expedition, 1918–1920* (Durham, N.C., 1956).

For Wilson's place in the American diplomatic tradition, see George F. Kennan, *American Diplomacy, 1900–1950* (New York, 1950); Arthur S. Link, *Wilson the Diplomatist* (Baltimore, 1957); N. Gordon Levin, Jr., *Woodrow Wilson and World Politics* (New York, 1968); Walter Lippmann, *U.S. Foreign Policy: Shield of the Republic* (Boston, 1943); Robert E. Osgood, *Ideals and Self-Interest in America's Foreign Relations* (Chicago, 1953); and William Appleman Williams, *The Tragedy of American Diplomacy* (New York, 1962).

1 2 3 4 5 6 7 8 9 10